# THE LAZINE~ ... · ...

# THE LAZINESS MYTH

Narratives of Work and the Good
Life in South Africa

## Christine Jeske

ILR PRESS

AN IMPRINT OF CORNELL UNIVERSITY PRESS   ITHACA AND LONDON

First published 2020 by Cornell University Press


Library of Congress Cataloging-in-Publication Data

Names: Jeske, Christine, author.
Title: The laziness myth : narratives of work and the good life in South Africa / Christine Jeske.
Description: Ithaca [New York] : ILR Press, an imprint of Cornell University Press, 2020. | Includes bibliographical references and index.
Identifiers: LCCN 2020012060 (print) | LCCN 2020012061 (ebook) | ISBN 9781501752506 (hardcover) | ISBN 9781501752513 (paperback) | ISBN 9781501752537 (pdf) | ISBN 9781501752520 (epub)
Subjects: LCSH: Work ethic—South Africa. | Laziness—South Africa. | Work—South Africa—Psychological aspects. | Blacks—Employment—South Africa. | Unemployment—Social aspects—South Africa. | Unemployed—South Africa—Attitudes. | Well-being—South Africa. | Quality of life—South Africa. | Happiness—South Africa.
Classification: LCC HD4905.3.S6 J47 2020 (print) | LCC HD4905.3.S6 (ebook) | DDC 306.3/6130968—dc23
LC record available at https://lccn.loc.gov/2020012060
LC ebook record available at https://lccn.loc.gov/2020012061

# Contents

# Acknowledgments

I will never forget the moment early in my fieldwork when Mtoko suddenly shouted down the street, "I'm going to be in a book! In America!" Mtoko, this is for you. Like too many black lives, Mtoko's ended too soon. It has not gone unnoticed. I am grateful beyond words for each person described in this book, named and unnamed. In sharing your stories, your time, and your experiences, you teach me and others how to think and also how to live.

I am also deeply grateful for the generosity of the many others who walked with me on the journey of this book. First, to those who welcomed my family to South Africa and taught us to love their country: Barbara and John David Borgman, Vanessa and Rouen Bruni, Geoff and Sarah-Beth Gould, Sam and Sarah Groves, Sabelo Hadebe, Penny and John Jardine, Lungile Mayaba, Betsy and Eugene Meyers, Thathu and Lineo Mokoena, Sofi Ntshalintshali, Paul and Sue Ross, and Caryn and Richard Shacklock. In America, my church offered hugs, prayers, and Thursday dinners that held me together through graduate school and beyond. South African colleagues offered early and continued conversations that convinced me to pursue this line of research. They include Patrick Bond, Daniela Casale, Philani Dlamini, Dorrit Posel, Imraan Valodia, and especially Hylton White. Frances Benson, my editor, saw something valuable in this research years ago and advocated for this book throughout the publishing process. I was fortunate to receive funding for the research and writing of this book from an Aldeen Grant, a John Stott Faculty Research Grant, a Scott Kloeck-Jenson Research Fellowship, two Foreign Language and Area Studies Fellowships, and a Hawkinson Foundation for Peace and Justice Award. I am also grateful to *Economic Anthropology* and the American Anthropological Association for permission to reprint portions of the article "People Refusing to Be Wealth: What Happens When South African Workers Are Denied Access to 'Belonging In.'" The many people who generously shared feedback on this manuscript include Hannah Dawson, Jeremy Foltz, Sarah Hamersma, Larry Nesper, Karen Rignall, Zhou Yongming, and my research assistants, Joe Saperstein and Anna Cole. I would not have achieved proficiency in isiZulu without the instruction of Bongani Mbatha, whose isiZulu lessons also included many insightful conversations that steered the direction of this research. Rachael Goodman and Christina Cappy have shaped this manuscript and my own life immeasurably as we laughed, cried, cursed, and celebrated together through researching, writing, and other trials of academic life. Claire Wendland deserves special thanks for her incredible ability to see to the heart of a topic, articulate my own thoughts sometimes better than I can, copyedit meticulously, and give practical advice and friendship through every step of a PhD program and beyond. My parents taught me never to stop learning, to make teaching an adventure, and to respond to every risk in life with faith. And finally, thank you to my hilarious, encouraging, flexible, and fun children who go happily wherever we take you; and my husband, who sees me not only as I am but also as I should be, who discussed every bit of this work, and who is the best life partner a person could ever have. This is a story of people seeking the good life, and I will remember our years in South Africa as a time when we found the good life, not only in the stories I heard others tell, but also in the life we experienced. Thank you to all those who made that possible.

# Author's Note

Many of the names of people and businesses in this book are pseudonyms. Some identifying details have been altered to protect identities. In the interest of confidentiality, I have also intentionally used generic terms such as "employer," "company," or "food industry" to designate individuals and businesses, especially when similar comments and events occurred in more than one instance.

# THE LAZINESS MYTH

# "WE WANT TO LIVE A GOOD LIFE"

Bullet, a South African man now in his late twenties, graduated from one of the top public high schools in his province. Upon graduation, he accepted a partial scholarship to enter a prelaw degree program at the University of Witwatersrand, one of the most prestigious universities in the country. One year later, Bullet walked out of the university, never to return. He had not had a job for years when I met him in 2014. And he said he was doing exactly what he was made to do.

This is a book about the ways people seek a good life. Specifically, it's about how their various ways of seeking a good life do—or don't—intersect with work. It's a book that will help you understand some of the global political and economic trends that make it rare for people like Bullet to find the good life through a paid job, and how people like Bullet go on finding the good life anyway. Ultimately, it's a book meant for generating new ways of thinking about work and the good life so that more people can find lives that they consider good.

Bullet grew up in Mpophomeni, a location or township where many black South Africans were forcibly relocated in the mid-twentieth century under apartheid, the government-imposed system of racial discrimination.[1] Like most of the black South Africans in his province of KwaZulu-Natal, he was ethnically Zulu and spoke isiZulu with his family and township friends. Unlike most of his peers in the township, though, he attended a school that had once been reserved only for white South Africans descended mainly from English and Dutch settlers. Since 1994 when the country held its first elections including citizens of all racial backgrounds, changes in the constitution made this school available to anyone. The only catch was that they had to pay the annual school fees of about 10,000

1

rand (written R10,000, about $1,000 in US dollars). His family had pooled thousands of rand each year from his father's job as a truck driver and other sources to pay the school fees and transportation money for him to attend school in the predominantly white town of Howick. Mpophomeni and Howick are spaced about fifteen kilometers apart, in KwaZulu-Natal Province of South Africa. His parents were proud when their son graduated from Howick High School and headed to law school, seeing this as a clear step toward the good life. Bullet, however, grew up hearing conflicting messages about what made life good.

"I never went to bed and just had this beautiful dream of going to court," he told me. "Maybe I shouldn't have dropped out, but just, it seemed, it seemed so unnatural to me. You know? 'Cause I come from a location, I don't feel comfortable in that environment. I never did."

I met Bullet through one of his friends, a young man named Cat who I first talked with at a computer training center for unemployed youth. Cat decided to tell me what he did in a typical day, but as he started listing his daily progression from sleep, to smoking weed, to watching television, to smoking more, he seemed to get discouraged. "Smoke it with the homies, that's all we do seriously in the location," he shrugged. "You'd be surprised. You think I'm lying. Shit. We don't really do much." Then suddenly he interrupted his train of thought. "Oh! There's a friend, I have a friend—I have hip hop, I mean, there's a hip hop crew actually. My friend Bullet, we sit in his studio and make some tracks. 'Cause he has a studio, like plenty of equipment. Small things. Two speakers, like general things. We sit there and make some tracks."

Cat took me to meet Bullet, and we talked for a couple of hours. In the months ahead, I often ran into Bullet around the township and came back to his home to ask more questions. He impressed me as one of the most astute social scientists I had ever met, despite never thinking of himself as such. He had keen insights about the culture he lived in, plus a cutting sense of humor and blatant honesty that tended to make his friends exclaim their agreement by laughing, cursing, or both.

The first time Cat brought me to Bullet's house, an album that Bullet and his hip hop crew had produced was playing on a computer on a desk along one wall. Bullet's three-year-old nephew poked his head in the doorway and mouthed along with the lyrics for a while, imitating rapping hand motions. We sat on half-broken office chairs and benches tucked between microphones and speakers in Bullet's recording studio in a room behind his parents' house. I asked Bullet what it meant to live a good life, and he and Cat started talking about what young men in the township had grown up wanting.

Bullet said one way to see what young people wanted was by what they liked in movies. "We all respect a lawyer who has a beautiful car in the movie." He shrugged and puckered his lips in a gesture of mild interest. "But you see a gangster with a beautiful car, and we like 'Oh! That's it! That's what I wanna be! I don't wanna be the lawyer in the movie. I wanna be the gangster in the movie.' You know, 'cause the lawyer don't get nothing, he don't get the girls in the movie. He don't get the guns. All he gets to do is sit and read."

By this point Cat was laughing so hard he nearly tipped off his wobbly chair.

"I don't want that," Bullet went on. "I want an exciting life. We all know an exciting life is short. We all get that, you know. But we don't care. 'Cause you know, a long life is not very exciting. Nobody wants to be fifty. Fifty for what?"

Cat cut in with a remark about becoming like the old man we'd seen slow-walking with a limp past Bullet's house earlier.

"It's not happy in the location," Bullet went on. "You can't be happy at fifty. It's very rare. Unless you a survivor of the bad, you've just done all your bad and you were not caught for some reason and you're not in jail. I know a couple of old guys who have come up just the wrong way, you know. They've sold the drugs, they did whatever they had to do, dug up a few dead bodies to save money, you know. And they still alive today. But now they good, they living a good life. You see what I'm saying?"

Bullet often talked in hyperbole, but when he alluded to people digging up dead bodies, Cat shook his head soberly. Stories circulated in the township of desperate people harvesting body parts for ceremonies meant to bring good luck, and it wasn't clear whether Bullet was referring to these literally or metaphorically.[2] Stories of witchcraft mingled in the popular imagination with awareness that everyone from drug dealers to mothers faced the question of what life was worth when resources were too few to go around. In South Africa, as in much of the world, "black deaths are produced as normative"—that is, social circumstances make black deaths commonplace, even as society ignores the causes and effects for those surviving "in the wake" of death.[3] Life expectancy in South Africa at the time of this interview was the lowest in the world, at just under fifty years.[4]

"It's either you gonna be a gangster and die, or be a gangster and maybe survive in the end," he shrugged again, pausing with a cynical expression. Throughout our conversations, Bullet seemed to be describing some life he wanted but couldn't quite identify, some option between becoming the lawyer nobody wants to be, the gangster getting his friends hooked on drugs, or the next black man who dies young of AIDS, knife wounds, or a drug overdose. Bullet often shifted between talking about the township as if he were part of it, and distancing himself from it through critique. His upbringing, riding every day from Howick to Mpophomeni, gave him both an insider's and an outsider's perspective of the township and the white middle-class world. He saw himself as very much a part of a complex social system, a product of it, and sometimes losing to it.

Bullet had often been told he had potential, but when it came to finding a job, he kept getting turned down. He had worked just after high school for a trucking company with his dad, but in the years I knew him he mentioned only once that he was pursuing a job. He volunteered at a radio station for a couple of weeks before leaving when it became clear that they were not hiring. In his assessment, black managers, hearing his ability to speak English and seeing his high grades, saw him as a threat to their own positions. In government jobs, he said, people only wanted to hire those who supported their political party. And white managers expected black employees to stay in lower-tier jobs. He guessed they looked at him and thought, "You got that kind of education, you ask too many questions." Bullet saw himself in a system that had no good options. "There's no way out of it, the way they've made it for us."

Often, conversations with young people in South Africa unfolded something like the conversation I had with a group of youths sitting around outside a rural home. They talked for a while about the worst jobs they had ever had—digging holes, fighting fires in the hot sun, and being a "kitchen girl." One young man turned to me and tried to explain what made these jobs so bad. "Our parents were not educated, so they would take what job they can get." These youth have been called the Born Free generation, born around or after 1994, when the racial segregation system called apartheid (meaning separateness) ended. Under apartheid, each South African was categorized into one of four racial groups—black, colored (mixed race), Indian, or white. Through a long series of laws passed from the eighteenth century through to the latter half of the nineteenth century, the South African government sanctioned destroying black people's homes and relocating them to neighborhoods, townships, and rural areas designated according to race. Black people were denied the right to set foot in white-only areas unless they were carrying personal identification with proof of employment. They were forbidden from higher-skilled jobs and paid less than whites in equivalent jobs. Any marriage across the government-designated racial categories was illegal, and public spaces and institutions including hospitals, parks, schools, and universities were segregated by race.[5]

Unlike their parents, Born Free youth grew up hearing that they could be anything and do anything. When they encountered the same discrimination and dead ends that their parents had, they experienced a new kind of discouragement. "Why did I go to school and waste twelve years of my life to work in a garden for seventy or eighty rand a day?" In the ten-to-one rand-to-dollar exchange rate at the time, he was talking about seven or eight dollars a day, which was beneath the official farm minimum wage but still not uncommon. With a tone of sarcasm and mockery, he repeated the accusation every person there had heard spoken about Zulu young people: "We are a little bit lazy." He went on to explain where that assumption comes from. Usually, they could find no work at all, or when they did, they got bossed around until "you feel like punching someone." That's the way work is, he said, but "we want to live a good life."

Bullet and many of his peers didn't expect to like work. "Everybody who has a normal job, they don't like it," Bullet said. His older sister had what he called "a good job" as a nurse, but even she usually came home with stories of disappointment. "Nobody likes working, you know. But the gangsters love working. They love it. They can't wait to go to work. They can't wait to sell you the drugs."

The picture Bullet saw of formal work included prejudice, jealousy, and disrespect. The alternatives he saw outside formal work included crime, boredom, addictions, and violent death. That's where music came in.

"That's why we're doing hip hop," Bullet said in our first conversation, after we'd talked for a long time about the problems he'd witnessed in the township. "The only way to reach people is music." Music was what Bullet turned to when he realized he didn't want to stay in law school. He found a sound-recording school where he took enough classes to learn the basics of recording. For years he had been scribbling down hip hop lyrics between classes, during lunch breaks, and riding along on his dad's trucking job. Now he began spending most of his waking hours on it.

I asked if he loved what he did now, making music. "I love it, but it's frustrating," he said. "Very frustrating. Because we all need to make money somehow, and it's very hard making money with a weird qualification like sound engineering in a place like this."

Cat had told me about the kind of hip hop he and Bullet worked on. He called it "conscious" music and "underground hip hop." Cat said they dared to write lyrics about township life that were more honest and more focused on change than commercial music. Commercial music, he said, talked only about sex, money, and fashion. Radio stations bought commercial music, but never conscious music. Cat said conscious music told about real life in the township. "They're talking history. That's why I want you to listen," he had insisted, promising to take me to Bullet's place. "I want you to listen to this hip hop."

When he took me to meet Bullet, one of Bullet's CDs, *Blaque Conversation*, was playing in the background. I caught bits of the lyrics.

> We need building blocks, better schools, and more black faces in the
>     science labs . . .
> Fighting for my own home town . . .
> Y'all don't know me. Life is hard . . .
> Come together to fight this evil that's come among us . . .
> Time for us to rise, to be who we thought we'd never be . . .

> I hate this life but don't wanna die . . .
> Maybe if we had better lives we wouldn't take each other's lives . . .
> Change the mentality—only then will we have the better life . . .

Bullet chose that name for himself as an artist, and he asked me to use the name Bullet when I wrote about him. As he explained why he chose the name, he revealed a piece of how he and many other South Africans thought about work. "The 'bullet' is the black man who is no longer willing to turn the other cheek; he's had enough. He says it's time to fight back—I'm not gonna allow you to keep treating me like this anymore. I didn't choose to be treated this way, but I am choosing to say this is enough." That, Bullet said, was the kind of person he wanted to create in his hip hop. "When you listen to my music, it's about, 'Dog, don't just lie down and play dead!'"

In prioritizing choices that often do not lead to formal work, unemployed black South Africans like Bullet are shaping their own places in societies that have often treated them little better than dogs. They are, with Bullet, refusing to play dead.

## Where Work Is Not Working

Bullet grew up in a social world where, as his lyrics said, "life is hard." In 2014–15 when I began research, only about two in five working-age adults were counted as employed.[6] The official number of those classified as unemployed, 22 percent of the population and rising, counts only people who have spent time actively searching for work in the past week.[7] That number left out people in the position Bullet was in, neither actively seeking work nor employed. They were counted instead as "not economically active" or "discouraged work seekers."[8] Fifteen million South Africans—42 percent of the working-age population—fit Bullet's category of non-job-seekers, a number nearly equal to the number of South Africans who did have jobs.

These statistics have described South Africa for so long that unemployment has become "the new normal."[9] For comparison, the highest unemployment rate recorded in the United States, measured at the height of the Great Depression, was 22 percent. South Africa has sustained roughly the same unemployment rate for over twenty years, never dropping below 20 percent since reliable employment surveys began around 1994. Unemployment rates for young people in their late teens and twenties have typically been even 20 to 25 percentage points higher. In an opinion poll in the early 2000s, the overwhelming majority of South Africans cited unemployment as the most significant problem facing their nation.[10]

South Africa's employment landscape in the latter decades of the twentieth century has been described as undergoing a "seismic mutation" whereby unemployment became a condition in which "most people, most of the time will, for the foreseeable future, live."[11] When people talk about unemployment, though, they are often scratching the surface of deeper issues. Asking the question of what causes unemployment can lead us to questions about how inequalities are made and maintained, and how people decide who deserves to have a good life.

When good work is hard to find, politically polarized discourses of scapegoating abound. In South Africa, as in other settings where unemployment rises, some people blame corporations for pushing the balance of wealth from waged workers to top CEOs. Others point to a shortage of skills training amid a postindustrial shift toward service sector jobs. Others blame unregulated globalization and the international race to the bottom in wage competition. Some say we need more trade protection, some say less. Some call the government an inflated welfare state, dishing out handouts as disincentives to work; some say that without social supports people lack resources to apply for jobs. The ways people assign blame trace an increasingly divisive, racialized, and politicized public discourse on employment.

Popular answers to these questions often blame the unemployed themselves, narrating stories of individuals failing to muster the personal inclination for hard work. Bullet's life path fits at the heart of questions that people ask when they see others who are unemployed: Why are they not working? Are they somehow choosing not to work? Is there something morally wrong with them? Bullet had grown familiar with these messages from people around him. "It's like they see the wrong, but they don't see why," he said. "They'll say, 'You're so young, you got so many opportunities in life.' OK, show me one! It's so easy to say we have a chance. Everybody's talking about, 'Oh man, the youth now just have so many opportunities, the doors are just wide open for you.' I'm like, 'These doors are so limited.'"

## The Stories We Tell Ourselves

At the point in the story where Bullet dropped out of law school, many readers probably wanted an answer to the question, *Why?* If jobs are so hard to find, why would someone with a scholarship and good grades on track to a good job drop out of school? Bullet also mentioned having a job for a while at the trucking company where his dad worked, so why wasn't he still in that job? Did he quit? Isn't some job better than no job at all?

At the heart of these questions is a more important question: What kind of life did Bullet and his peers want? People everywhere tell stories about how to attain better lives, and those narratives help humans make sense of the world around them.[12] As some anthropologists have explained, "Narratives shape action just as actions shape stories told about them."[13] In other words, people figure out how to live based on the narratives they believe, even as they come to believe those narratives because of the cultural, historical, and social setting in which they live. Stories are more than a way of entertaining ourselves; they are a reflection of the circumstances that surround us. We use them to give purpose to past events, make decisions in the present, and form expectations about the future. We see the world through plot structures that involve predicting what appears likely to happen and prescribing what should rightly happen. They can be therapeutic, helping people deal with difficult circumstances even when they cannot change those circumstances. And narratives can serve as moral tales for reinforcing beliefs about what should happen, perhaps especially when it does not happen. At their worst, these narratives can entrap us as actors in nightmarish realities. At their best, they are the foundations for resilience, motivation, and hope when people encounter difficulties. They offer the moral and aspirational compass by which people aim their lives.

For example, in September 2011 after thousands of people died in the terrorist attacks on the World Trade Center, many Americans responded by telling stories of overcoming hardship to attain new successes. John McAdams calls this "the redemptive self narrative." He finds examples of it running through commonly told American stories ranging from escaped-slave accounts to biographies of Ben Franklin and Oprah Winfrey.[14] But that is not the only narrative that shapes life in America, or elsewhere in the world.

As I began comparing people's narratives of the good life, I noticed that they bring together at least four elements: (1) end goals, (2) messages about what is effective for attaining these goals, (3) normative messages about what makes a particular goal and path moral or immoral, and (4) a social and cultural setting. In the redemptive self narrative, the goal is not simply happiness but transformation. The effective means of attaining that transformation includes suffering and hardship, and these are also central to moralities of how good people seek a good life. In the example of the redemptive self narrative, one could trace the social origins of that schema across the complicated history of the United States, from European colonists taking land from American Indians, to an Enlightenment-inspired founding government distinguishing its national identity from Europe, to immigration policies, and far more.

In this book you'll read about a wide range of narratives. One narrative, described in chapter 3, shows that a certain kind of relationship is both an effective moral means to the good life and an element of the end goal of that good life. Another narrative, mentioned in chapter 4, names suffering as an expected aspect of the route to the good life, much as the redemptive self narrative does, but with significantly different ideas about who causes that suffering for whom, and what people's end goals can and should be. You'll read about some narratives that focus on the importance of individual agency to make certain choices, whereas others show the route as steered mainly by the influence of other people, luck, fate, or spiritual forces. All these narratives come to make sense in a specific socioeconomic setting. They offer guidance through moral questions like whether certain ends justify certain means, and what loyalties, obligations, sacred rites, and fair practices matter in a given situation.

As people envision various ways to attain a good life, their ideas about work come into play. To understand how people make choices about work, we can start by considering how work fits together with people's narratives about the good life. We could envision some simple Venn diagrams. For some people, work and the good life might fit together something like figure 1.1.

In this picture, employment scarcely overlaps with the good life at all. In this way of thinking of the world, jobs are likely to be painful and disappointing in various ways—much about work detracts from what makes life good. People expect to have little chance of finding jobs that improve their lives. Jobs may be a necessary part of life, but not the part that makes life good. There are certainly ways to achieve the good life, but probably not through work.

In contrast, other narratives look more like figure 1.2.

Here, the good life fits almost entirely inside employment. Someone who sees the world in this way will assume that there is almost no way to have a good life without employment. This person's focus is on having a good job, and the assumption is that by having a good job, the good life will follow. They will believe that good, moral, effective, happy people work. These two diagrams represent two extremes in a spectrum—there could be any amount of overlap between the good life and employment, and any number of reasons why a person sees the two overlapping in the ways they do.

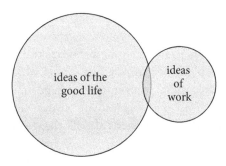

**FIGURE 1.1**

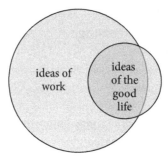

**FIGURE 1.2**

To add a further complication, people have various ideas of what the word "work" means. The differing ways that people imagine what constitutes work will necessarily shape how they envision work interacting with the good life. For example, does work have to be done in exchange for pay or economic benefits? Or does it include activities like making a friend or caring for an elderly relative, which are often unpaid, but may have economic benefits and certainly have social benefits? Many such socially productive and economically productive but unpaid activities have in much of the world historically been done by women. Often activities that are gendered as women's work are considered to be less valuable. Activities such as caring for one's own children, preparing food for one's family, or traveling to purchase goods bring the same (or arguably greater) value to a household as paying for daycare, going to a restaurant, or paying a grocery delivery service. Many scholars have argued that such activities are work, and yet power dynamics reinforce popular ideas that work includes only activities exchanged for money.[15]

In another popular usage of the word, work is anything disagreeable that someone is required to do—the opposite of leisure, which a person chooses to do. For example, a person might say, "That job is so fun, I don't even feel like it's work" or "Walking up that hill is hard work." Such a definition places work nearly always outside of what makes life good, casting doubt on whether enjoyable paid employment is still work. Meanings of the word "work" are culturally constructed—that is, they come about through particular combinations of historical circumstances, place, and human interactions, which are always in flux. Perhaps the only reliable way to explain work, as Pope John Paul II put it in an encyclical letter, is that work is simply "activity . . . that can and must be recognized as work."[16] The fact that definitions of work change through human interactions means that definitions of work are also an important site of power and resistance. As feminists have discovered, defining domestic activities conducted by women as work is an important means of recognizing not just the value of

women's activities but of women themselves. Rather than choose my own definition of work, I point to the ways in which people contest and push back against
various uses of words like "work," "hard work," and "worker."

The word "work" also interacts problematically with some other similar words:
"labor" and "employment." Historically, among scholars, the word "labor" has
been used to emphasize the ways that people employed by others—"laborers"—
become part of a market economic system. As chapter 5 will show, South Africans
sometimes used the word "laborer" to voice their refusal to participate in that
system in certain ways. The word "employment" narrows the idea of work down
to a specific subset—situations in which people have an "employer," whether
oneself or someone else. Even this definition of employment leaves room for
disagreement, though. In the year 2000, South Africa began issuing a new survey,
the South African Labour Force Survey, to measure employment rates. Unlike a
previous survey, it gave specific prompts to count even one hour per week spent
gardening or fishing as work. Unsurprisingly, employment rates after the survey
appeared to be higher (by as many as two million new jobs). This was politically
convenient for then-president Jacob Zuma.[17] As a practical representation of how
people understood their experiences, however, such a definition of employment
raised concerns. Most South Africans I met did not see household activities in the
same category as paid employment. Nor did they tend to follow government definitions of "unemployed" or "not economically active." A person without work
was just that, no matter how many applications they dropped off, and "searching
for work" could also include uncounted activities like asking a pastor or shaman
for prayer. These disagreements over definitions have real effects. For example,
a person dismissed from a job could claim government compensation for up to
thirty-four weeks but must first register as an "unemployed job seeker," differentiating themselves from the "economically inactive." The words people use to
describe what they do—whether it be work, labor, or employment—play a key
role in how people envision and seek to attain the good life.

The point is this: not everyone thinks about the interplay between work and
the good life in the same way. And therein lies a lot of tension.

## A Dominant Narrative of Work and the Good Life

Throughout our lives, we learn more than one narrative of work and the good
life. We draw on various narratives strategically at different times or even simultaneously, even when they logically conflict. Not all narratives have equal power,
though. Some keep certain people in power and others out of power. In the next
chapter, we'll see how narratives that reinforce power inequalities can become

so deeply threaded through culture that people accept those schemas without question. These dominant narratives often leave blind spots, preventing people from accurately explaining events and drowning out narratives from marginalized voices.

The dominant narrative about work and the good life that many people in the world grow up hearing is most like the second Venn diagram. It goes something like this: Good people work hard. They overcome obstacles in life to pursue education and training so they can get good jobs. Because they work hard in those jobs, good things come to them. Working hard is key to living a life that is morally good, and working hard also leads to attaining a life that is materially good. Hard work and the good life go hand in hand.

The point in the story where Bullet dropped out of law school causes many listeners to stop and ask *why* precisely because that's the point where his own life's drama stopped fitting this dominant tale of hard work and the good life. For Bullet, that narrative wasn't working. He grew up seeing the differences in how society rewarded the hard work of people in Mpophomeni township versus white middle-class people in Howick. He tried law school, and he realized it did not fit with what he had learned about the good life growing up in the township. Neither did the hard-work narrative make sense when he left law school. He spent hours perfecting every detail of music tracks, and actively networked with people in the area who might hire him and his friends for performances. But that hard work didn't seem to count as hard work, or at least it didn't generate much financial benefit.

This hard-work narrative has a dangerous power when it goes unexamined. If hard work is the key to the good life, then it may follow that anyone who seems not to be attaining the good life must not be working hard. In the terms I heard used over and over again in South Africa, they must be lazy. Apply that in broad brushstrokes to groups of people who seem more often to be poor or unemployed, and people conclude that there must be something culturally, racially, or historically wrong with certain groups of people that has made them end up especially lazy. The hard-work narrative can easily slide into blaming a societal problem on traits of some supposedly homogeneous "other" group, rather than on wider systems of causes.

The situation described in this book is one in which hard work is not working. The myth that promises success as a reward for hard work, conversely blaming poverty on a lack of hard work, does not accurately describe how people get from poverty to wealth. No amount of hard work was going to get most unemployed South Africans a job if there simply were not enough jobs for the three million plus people actively seeking employment. At the same time, not working is hard work. People like Bullet engage in the socially productive work of seeking a good life outside the often-disappointing world of employment. As Bullet mentors other men, helps neighbors and family with gardening and other sometimes-paid jobs, and speaks purpose into the lives of people around him through music, he conducts work that has been rendered invisible and valueless by the narrative that treats him as not working, and thereby lazy. In this book you will not meet lazy people. Instead, you will find people who, like yourself, work to envision, seek, and at times attain the good life, even in settings marked by inequality and unemployment.

Societies and individuals often hit crises when old familiar narratives no longer make sense in new circumstances. When high unemployment rates plague an entire nation for decades, a crisis of narratives takes place on a societal scale. As marginalized groups of people are relegated to work experiences that are often dehumanizing, purposeless, and devoid of opportunities for promotion, the hard-work account of reality fails to make sense. And when people look around and see some groups of people getting rewarded for their hard work and others not, the story unravels further. Black people in South Africa and in much of the world have been systematically denied the rewards of work for centuries, while being simultaneously culturally constructed as inherently poor workers. In this book you will meet employers, employees, and unemployed people who are all frustrated in various ways by social systems that systematically exclude black people from the good life, and hear the narratives that uphold those systems but fail to explain reality.

When a narrative does not work to make sense of circumstances, resilient people find alternatives. My research sought to describe some of these alternative narratives that are deeply rooted in black, Zulu, and working-class identities. Throughout history, people who have built new social systems have done so by also building new narratives, often by amplifying alternative narratives that already exist among marginalized people in a society.[18] Anyone interested in imagining new possibilities for a more humanizing and more equitable world will do well to pay attention to the perspectives offered in these narratives.

## Envisioning the Good Life

This study began as I started noticing how jarring it was for people to interact when they had differing narratives of work and the good life. I had spent about four years living in South Africa, during which I worked as a codirector of a small pilot microfinance organization. The organization was designed to empower young people in rural areas to start businesses by offering business training and small loans. After two years, the organization had failed to recruit enough clients to be sustainable. As we made the difficult decision to close, what surprised me most was not so much that the organization was not economically viable, but that people kept telling me business development could never work in rural South Africa.[19] "Zulu people don't run businesses," I kept hearing. Sometimes people said outright, "Zulu people are lazy. It's part of their culture." I heard this most often from white South Africans who employed Zulu people, but also from Zulu South Africans themselves. Clearly, I thought, there must be something more going on beneath the surface of these complaints. I began to notice that accusations about lazy groups of people were not unique to South Africa. Similar statements had been made throughout the colonial history of the African continent and toward lower-class people everywhere. It seemed as though some groups of people were making certain choices about work given the options they had, and other people were interpreting those behaviors as lazy. Narratives about what work had to do with a good life were clashing, and blaming poverty on a lack of hard work did not offer an accurate explanation of what was happening in people's lives. I wanted to know, was the hard-work narrative drowning out other valuable narratives of how to achieve a good life?

So, about five years after the microfinance organization closed, I returned to South Africa to study the high unemployment plaguing the country, but also to understand something broader. I called that something "the good life" originally because I heard black South Africans using that phrase. Greek philosophers a millennia ago and countless scholars since have also debated over its meaning.[20] As the anthropologist Sherry Ortner writes, "Every culture, of course, embodies some vision of success, of the good life, but the cultural variation occurs in how success is defined, and given that, what are considered the best ways of achieving it."[21] As I began experimenting with what it would mean to investigate such cultural variations in South Africa, I came to appreciate the ambiguity in the word "good." In both English and Zulu, people use the same word (good or *hle*) to refer to a wide range of positive qualities. Something described as good can be aesthetically pleasing like a good bowl of soup, materially valuable like good pay, or morally right like a good deed. Often things, acts, and situations we deem good are all of these simultaneously. Using the term "good life" allowed people to describe lives they wished for without having to disentangle the intertwining reasons they desired such lives.

Anthropological research is usually based on a sort of carefully applied "hanging out," geared toward meeting people within the complexity of their real-life situations rather than bringing them into artificial lab situations or limiting them to multiple-choice options on surveys. Having already lived in South Africa for about four years, I did the bulk of the research for this book from 2014 to 2015, plus return visits in 2017 and 2019 and social media connections in the intervening years. From 2014 to 2015, I rented a home with my husband and two children on a farm near Howick and Mpophomeni. I spent most days visiting workplaces, job-readiness trainings, and the homes of unemployed people like Bullet. I interviewed thirty-two people who claimed to have no form of work-related income and twenty-one who generated at least some income through self-employment.[22] Over time, I selected ten of those people—five females and five males from a range of ages—to visit on a regular basis. I also spent a good amount of time in the neighborhood where most of Howick's informal businesses operated. I asked a set of brief questions at each business and also used the survey as a starting point for many longer conversations held between sales of vegetables, nightgowns, flip-flops, and wallets. Reading newspapers and watching television also helped me understand the ways people thought about employment and the good life. I read the local, regional, and national newspapers, taking notes on the articles and discussing news stories with acquaintances. I took notes on over twenty hours of television, spread over several weeks, focusing on shows produced in South Africa including music videos, sitcoms, soap operas, news, and reality television.

At each of seven businesses in the area—a chicken farm, forestry company, food processing plant, shoe factory, health clinic, clothing store, and petrol station—I spent one to five days meeting with employers and employees and also learning by getting involved. I weighed chickens, pried open the heavy tools for planting tree saplings, and loaded yogurt tubs into crates. I also met with employers and/or employees at eighteen other businesses. These included five in the manufacturing industry, four in retail, three in agriculture, and six in service occupations (including health, security, beauty, and hospitality). I anonymize and avoid sharing certain details of the businesses I worked with to avoid negative repercussions for the businesses involved. All the formal-sector employers and managers I met with were white except for three black business owners, four black middle-level managers, and two Indian middle-level managers. Because black business owners and managers were rarer in Mpophomeni and Howick than in urban areas, I sought out and interviewed some black managers in other urban areas. My intention in focusing on an area where managers were nearly all white and low-wage laborers were nearly all black was not to normalize this as the expectable "way things are and will always be." Instead, by placing in front of readers the present reality of this racialized employment system, they have the opportunity to see how it has been created through human-made systems of racism that are stalwart but not impervious.[23]

The central area of Howick remains divided into neighborhoods locally understood as black, Indian, colored (mixed race), and white. Middle-class homeowners from a variety of ethnic backgrounds have moved into at least some formerly white neighborhoods, but no whites live in black townships. White colonists in South Africa created a system that relegated people into four distinct racial categories: black, Indian, colored, and white (made up mainly of people of English and Dutch descent, the latter called Afrikaners). As with all racial categories, the boundaries of these groups were artificially created and ranked hierarchically to give greater privileges to whites. The government attempted to place people in such categories using standards as arbitrary as whether a comb would stay in a person's hair. Since 1994 with the first racially inclusive election, much of the apartheid legal structure has been systematically dismantled, and yet these racial categories continue to be significant in everyday interactions and are very real in their consequences.

The Howick area had a history of violent conflicts over labor, politics, and at times the intersection of the two. One of the area's main employers since the foundation of the town of Howick had been the South African Rubber Manufacturing Company Limited (abbreviated SARMCOL, now owned by Dunlop). In 1985 company management responded to a worker strike by firing over a thousand workers. Soon after, four union-member workers were abducted and three killed by vigilantes hired by the company. As in much of South Africa in the years leading up to the 1994 election, violence broke out around Mpophomeni between members of the two predominantly black political parties: the Inkatha Freedom Party (IFP) and the African National Congress (ANC). The vigilantes hired by SARMCOL to deter union members had been reported to be members of the IFP, one of the many ways in which white employers played members of one party off another in strike-breaking tactics, fueling the political violence. Dozens of people died in the Mpophomeni area in the political conflict.[24] In the decades that followed, union members at the company, now owned by Dunlop Rubber, continued holding frequent strikes and negotiations for better treatment. As recently as 2012, rumors spread saying fourteen striking workers were killed by a private security force hired by the company.

Howick and Mpophomeni together had a population of about twenty thousand, and people there viewed this medium-sized metropolitan area with both pride and disappointment. Migrants from more rural areas came to Howick for the variety of employment options there. An informal settlement called Shiyabazali (meaning "We leave our parents behind"), conspicuously located above the town's waterfall tourist site, houses many of the lowest-income job seekers arriving in the area from elsewhere in South Africa and across Africa. People also left Howick and Mpophomeni for larger metropolitan areas like the provincial capital of Pietermaritzburg thirty minutes away and the city of Durban two hours away. Indeed, people sometimes spoke of big cities like Durban and Johannesburg as symbols of the good life. The Zulu word for Johannesburg is eGoli, "the city of gold"; people sometimes describe it as "the city where you never go hungry" or "the place where your teeth wear out before the meat runs out." In many ways, Howick and Mpophomeni's middle place between more or fewer employment opportunities was analogous to the wider picture of South Africa—a country many Africans aspired to enter, and also a place from which many South Africans dreamed of emigrating. Unemployment in the municipality, at 23.9 percent in 2015, was nearly equal to the national average.[25] Searching through records in the Howick public library, I came across the strategic growth plan of the municipality surrounding Howick and Mpophomeni. The top two of their seven strategic goals—"job creation" and "human resource development"—named the issues I came to learn about: unemployment and the unemployed people often deemed responsible for it.[26]

## Getting People Talking About the Good Life

People in South Africa thought a lot about employment, and whether I was walking down the street in the informal business district or setting up interviews with business managers, people were incredibly generous, sharing their time, thoughts, and many cups of tea. Literally my first conversation when I set foot back in the country in 2014 was about unemployment. The man who stamped my passport asked why I had come to the country, and when I told him I was researching unemployment, he perked up and said, "I could sure tell you a lot about that."

One of the ways I got people talking about the good life was to use a drawing exercise. I would ask people to draw a star somewhere on a piece of paper to represent the good life, whatever that meant to them. Next I would ask them to draw a dot on the paper to represent a time when they were not living the good life. I then asked them to draw anything they wanted, suggesting they might want to use lines, arrows, or symbols, to show how a person could move from a not-good life to the good life. I compiled these drawings and made some of my own to try to represent what I heard people saying (see figure 1.3). Later in the year, I began showing these notecards to people after they tried drawing one. I would ask people to talk about which drawings they liked and which they didn't. One of the benefits of this approach was that people did not know who had created the other drawings, so they felt free to criticize. People often expressed strong opinions about drawings that they associated with immoral or ineffective approaches to the good life, saying they knew other people who were taking that sort of path. The drawings also allowed people to define the good life in various ways. For example, one put the star on a timeline in the past to show the moment she became a Christian; another said he preferred to avoid jealousy by staying in a middle place not too close to the star.

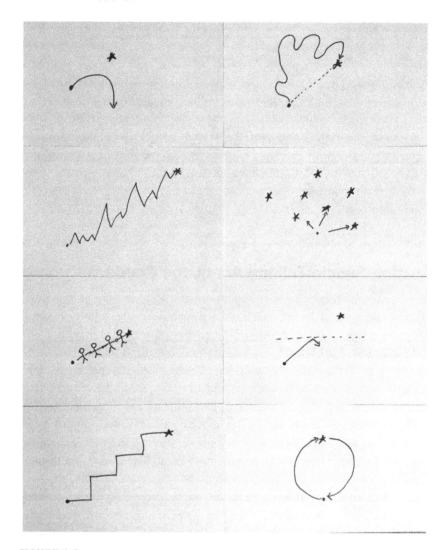

**FIGURE 1.3**

Bullet's drawing appears in figure 1.4.

When he finished, Bullet explained the drawing. He said the dot represented him as a baby, and he placed it "on the same level" as the star because "I already knew who I was when I was born. But you know, I had to find it, who I was, but basically I'm looking for the same person." The point where the line took a sharp downward turn was when Bullet started attending the multiracial primary school in Howick. The line moved away from the good life, Bullet said, because he was moving away from who he was born to be. "I was told, 'No, homey. That's

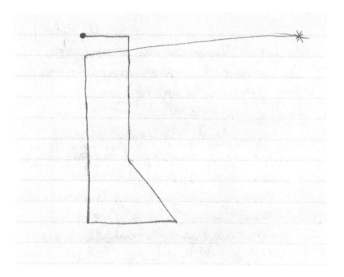

**FIGURE 1.4**

not who you are.'" Bullet said in high school he "started looking for myself," and the line took a slight diagonal bend toward the right. But then the line moved horizontally back to the left, "in the complete wrong direction." That was Bullet's year in university. Only when he dropped out of law school and began training as a musician and sound engineer did his line move upward and eventually take a turn in the direction of the star. "For me the star is *who I am*, not *what I have*," Bullet said, emphasizing each word. "I wasn't looking for a way forward, per se," he said "I was looking for myself." As if reassuring himself of the narrative shape of his life, he said "it's gonna take a long time," but "the way up is not about money." His path to the good life didn't depend on having an income or a job. "When I found me, I don't think anyone could take that away from me," he said. "Man, I'm chasing after that star 'til the day I die."

Bullet's drawing revealed many ideas we'll come back to in subsequent chapters. His goals had to do with identity and right relationships with people around him, not with a particular job. When he talked about the good life, he talked about limited employment opportunities, but also about ways that even someone without a job could attain a good life. Before we move ahead to what's to come in this book, though, let's consider a question some readers may be asking. Why read this book?

This is a book for people who may know very little about South Africa or anthropology, as well as people who may know very much about one or both of those topics. Every author faces innumerable questions in writing for particular audiences. What evidence will lead readers to new ideas, without leaving some readers drowning in oceans of data and other readers bored? In the words of Hal Herzog, "I am convinced that scientists have an obligation to communicate with the public," but to accomplish this, "the trick is to inform readers about the latest results in a way that is interesting, but at the same time respect the complexity of the issues and be honest about what we know and what we don't."[27]

One way a book can become interesting to readers is for readers to feel they have something in common with the situations they read about. As human beings, we are fascinated by ourselves. But learning only about ourselves—or the aspects of other people that seem most similar to ourselves—leaves our perspectives dangerously skewed. Readers may want topics that feel familiar, but they also need topics that are unfamiliar.

Historically, people in the West have not viewed Africa as fitting within what counts as familiar. As Achille Mbembe points out, Africa has nearly always been portrayed and imagined by westerners in ways that make it utterly useless other than as an object of experimentation. Africa is pictured as less-than-human, of a past era, irrational, and unintelligible. Africa has been "the supreme receptacle of the West's obsession with . . . 'absence,' 'lack,' and 'non-being' . . . in short, of nothingness."[28] As such, Africans have been seen as subjects for books about the novelties of history, exotic places, or what went wrong, but not as sources of knowledge for a humanity that includes global audiences.

As an anthropologist, I see my work as connecting the familiar with the unfamiliar and identifying the shared humanity of "us." Anthropology is one of the most widely misunderstood disciplines. (No, I don't study bones, stone tools, apes, or dinosaurs,[29] and yes, students majoring in anthropology do go on to find satisfying jobs.)[30] Anthropology, put simply, is the study of humans. Anthropologists aim to show the complexity of human cultures by giving in-depth, detailed descriptions and analysis. They study people at any time in history and anywhere on the planet. Their research shows both what is unique to a particular group of people, and also what is relatable across many peoples, times, and places. In other words, anthropology reveals both *singularity* and *universality* in human individuals and cultures.

What this means for readers of this book is that at times you will find yourself relating to what you read, and at times you will not. Like a camera with zoom and wide-angle lenses, at times the book zooms in on singularities of individuals and groups that may be quite distinct from some readers, and at times the lens will widen out to seek commonalities and overarching theories that apply across larger groups or all of humanity. Both are crucial, as is recognizing the difference between the two.

For example, Mexican American readers may relate to black Zulu South Africans in that they also navigate exclusion from high-status work and stereotyping according to a supposed propensity for work.[31] However, it's important to recognize differences in various forms of racism and marginalization. As Black-Crit theorists have emphasized, blackness has been constructed, demonized, and dehumanized in ways that create a spectrum from whiteness to blackness.[32] Thus, Latinx workers face discrimination that is different from what black workers face, in that they are socially constructed as seemingly slightly more white, and correspondingly better workers, while still being denied full inclusion and value in society. Taking this a step further, antiblackness in the United States has some, but not everything, in common with antiblackness as it has played out historically in South Africa. Nor will the experience of a black South African reader who is ethnically Sotho and living in Johannesburg have everything in common with an ethnically Zulu South African described in this book. As Kimberlé Crenshaw has shown, there are many dimensions of difference, including race, gender, ethnicity, sexuality, and class.[33] As these differences intersect, being of a marginalized group according to more than one social marker can amplify the effects of marginalization. In this book, I describe human beings of many dimensions and treat readers as diverse individuals who may relate to few, some, or many of these qualities.

Clifford Geertz and other anthropologists have also emphasized that ethnography (writing about culture) is always a process of interpretation.[34] Much as a translator can never communicate precise meanings across languages because connotations and contexts of words can never perfectly match from one language to the next, ethnography is a process of imperfect translation. Research participants, ethnographers, and individual readers will all bring their own perspectives to this book, relating to some things more than others, remembering some things more than others, and attaching different meanings to the text—both to this text and the text of human lives.

When I talk about this book in the United States (where I grew up), I often hear the question, "Does that happen in the United States, too?" If "that" refers to unemployment, or to narratives that blame the effects of racism on the supposed laziness of black and other marginalized people, the answer is "absolutely yes." In her widely read book *Nickel and Dimed*, Barbara Ehrenreich summarizes what she learned as an immersive journalist trying out minimum-wage jobs as a waitress, housekeeper, and caregiver. "I grew up hearing over and over, to the point of tedium, that 'hard work' was the secret of success. . . . No one ever said that you could work hard—harder even than you ever thought possible—and still find yourself sinking ever deeper into poverty and debt."[35] In the United States as in South Africa, the hard-work narrative is infused with antiblack prejudice. One study found that 30 percent of white Americans view black Americans as lazier than whites.[36] Another found that 65 percent of white Americans believed that racial inequalities would disappear if black people would "try harder."[37] White Americans are more likely to blame income disparities between black and white Americans on "lack of personal motivation" than the effects of prejudice and discrimination.[38] Imani Perry, a black scholar, recounts that racialized narratives in the United States have labeled black people as "damaged and morally deficient," "lazy or criminal."[39] With a cautious hope, she suggests that more ethnographies of racial narratives must be written because even these prejudiced racial narratives "have the potential to be changed."[40]

There is also a global trend, not just in South Africa, toward work being increasingly unsatisfying, part-time, and temporary. As the world experiences seismic shifts in the kinds, qualities, and quantities of jobs available, people around the world can relate to Bullet's statement, "Everybody who has a normal job, they don't like it." As in South Africa, people in the United States and elsewhere in low-wage jobs find themselves devalued and dehumanized. As the sociologist Katherine Newman wrote of inner-city fast-food restaurant workers in the United States, "Thousands upon thousands of minority teens, young adults, and even middle-aged adults line up for jobs that will subject them, at least potentially, to a kind of character assassination."[41] The pace of change in the skills demanded in the market has accelerated in recent decades, as fewer jobs involve physically manufacturing a product, and "workers, instead of acquiring a skill for life, can now look forward to at least one if not multiple bouts of de-skilling and re-skilling in a lifetime."[42] For black and brown people, the challenges of finding work are not new, but shifts in job availability are compounded by the long-term effects of discrimination and segregation. For the last forty years, a gap has steadily widened between jobs that do and jobs that do not offer job security, sufficient compensation, autonomy, and satisfactory hours.[43] In 2020, as I completed this book, unemployment in the United States went from record lows to record highs.[44] Even when jobs abounded, though, the likelihood of job satisfaction had been dropping.[45] In the first decade of the twenty-first century, the percentage of college graduates who ended up in part-time, temporary, or under-skilled jobs rose by ten percentage points.[46] Rural and blue-collar whites in the United States have been among the most staunch advocates of a hard-work narrative, but as blue-collar jobs move overseas and real incomes in farming, mining, forestry, and other rural jobs decline, these groups have also increasingly found that the promise of success following hard work fails to explain their real-world conditions.[47] Globally, more women are participating in the workforce, and while this reflects gains in the opportunities available to women, it also reflects the reality that family economic survival often requires two wage earners. For half a century real wages have stayed stable while costs of living have risen. Meanwhile, women still earn lower average wages in the same jobs as men and are more likely than men to give up job seeking without finding work.[48] For men, the combination of scarce employment options and individualized blame for unemployment contributes to what has been called a crisis of masculinity.[49] In the United States and much of the world, voters across the political spectrum look for candidates who promise an improvement in their precarious prospects and rewards for work. Political parties diagnose the causes and solutions to the problem differently, but voters' concerns are the same: they were told that hard work would get them a good life, they try to work hard, but the good life does not happen like they were told.

One of the best ways to solve a problem—like, say, improving the lives of people facing disappointing unemployment options—is to look at the issue from a new perspective.[50] Research has shown that people who learn about situations that apparently differ from their own exhibit increased creativity and problem-solving capacity. Because people in dominant groups are disproportionately represented in scholarship, literature, and the media, some readers will have more exposure than others to situations and people that seem unfamiliar. Robin DiAngelo has called attention to how white people, because society affords them ways to avoid interactions with people of color, can become increasingly "fragile" in their ability to interact with difference. Reading primarily about familiar people is a privilege, but paradoxically, it is a privilege that also harms those who have it.[51]

Ultimately, reading about unfamiliar people and situations offers readers avenues to grow in what Isabel Wilkerson, a black historian, has called "radical empathy." By empathy, she does not mean having to imagine oneself in someone else's place in order to regard that person as human or valuable. Nor does she mean using that person's experience as a tool for one's own emotional or intellectual edification.[52] In contrast to these shallower forms of empathy that tend to be "dismissive of another person's truth" and "a barrier to understanding," Wilkerson calls for what she terms "radical empathy." In her words, this "means putting in the work to learn and to listen with a heart wide open, to understand another's experience well enough to know how they are feeling it, not as we imagine we would feel."[53]

By coming to understand the specific experiences of other people and by identifying commonalities across humankind, this book offers readers opportunities to discover, in the words of Luis Alberto Urrea, the author of several books about life along the Mexican-American border: "There is no them, there is only us."[54]

## An Overview of What's Ahead

In the next chapter, we'll take a look at the dominant narrative I call the laziness myth, exploring the origins and effects of a narrative that tells employers and employees alike that laziness is to blame for unemployment and poverty. In the second chapter, we'll look at employment from the perspective of employers, reading about both their attempts to improve the lives of workers, and their frustrations that workers don't seem to behave as they want. Turning from the perspectives of more dominant voices in society, the next three chapters (chapters 3–5) reveal narratives of underemployed and low-waged Zulu people. While these narratives are not neatly divided between racial, age, gender, or other groups in society, I describe some common patterns in how people navigate between narratives to make meaning within their own choices and constraints. Chapter 3 explores a narrative that people associate strongly with a Zulu identity, but which also resonates beyond South Africa, a moral schema demanding that the good life requires respect for all people. Chapter 4 introduces a narrative of "hustling" that motivates young people to perform their future hopes and never give up, despite full awareness of the disproportionate challenges they face in society. In chapter 5, we investigate how people make meaning of their lives in low-wage, low-status jobs, often by distancing themselves and the good life from work by calling themselves "just laborers." Chapter 6 offers a deeper look into the lives of four individuals who said they were currently living the good life: an engineer in a high-status job, an artist forging new relationships through his church and community, a low-wage worker in an unusual shoe factory, and a recently unemployed woman starting a small business. These contrasting examples demonstrate aspects of the narratives described in other chapters and also complicate connections often drawn between income and well-being. The message of chapter 6 and the concluding chapter resonates throughout the book: even within an unequal society and high unemployment, people find ways to achieve what they consider to be sufficiently good lives. Attempts to help people achieve a good life must begin by understanding the ways they define it.

Throughout the book, we will engage in a process of recognizing both subordinate and dominant narratives. This process of looking at competing narratives of a good life accomplishes two things I consider worth doing in a book. First, it helps us to dismantle class, racial, ethnic, and gendered prejudices. Whether in South Africa or elsewhere, this book trains us to notice the damage done—often unknowingly—through the dominant ways of thinking and acting that uphold and grow out of the structures we live in. Second, it demonstrates how to challenge problematic dominant narratives by uncovering counternarratives that already exist in a society. We will hear stories of real people navigating economic challenges with agency, trying many different approaches to seek good lives. By looking at the complexity in various people's ideas of the good life, we see people in their own context not as inherently immoral, irrational, or somehow lesser, but as people using the narratives that have proven convincing in their context. At times, hearing people's stories can help us understand why people "seeking an alternative to their social marginalization" can "become the actual agents administering their own destruction and their communities' suffering."[55] Other times, we find the sparks of creative possibilities for social change.

# Spill It

On Friday mornings, I often went to the Mpophomeni library to sit in on a nonprofit organization's job-readiness training program. Later, on Friday afternoons, I came back to the same library meeting room for a group dealing with unemployment in a very different way. Bullet and a couple of dozen other young people would show up at the library, not to check out books or use the library computers, but to take turns sharing original music, spoken-word poetry, and prose writing.

One Friday when Bullet's turn came, he stood at the end of the long tables lined with young people. Behind him through tall windows, cows strolled past on their way home to a nearby kraal sheltering most of the cattle in the village. He began, holding his hand before his mouth like a mock microphone and slowly settling into a rhythm with his words and body, piecing together phrases in a spontaneous freestyle performance.

> OK, let me find a good rap
> that I can lay flat on this desk
> like a platform
> trying to grip my own thoughts
> of income, police, lyrical that I speak . . .
> And I feel it in my soul
> this is where I'm at,
> this is what it's supposed to be
> and I never will fall back
> like laying in a casket 'cause
> when I die, my soul's unique . . .
> so why act like I don't got it,
> when you know I got it
> spill it.
> Because whenever I spill it
> this is beyond the grave
> this is immortal technique.

In contexts as diverse as rapping in a library, manufacturing leather shoes, weed-whacking neighbors' yards, inventing new fashions, and sharing water taps with neighbors, the people described in this book have discovered diverse pathways for seeking the good life. In the pages ahead, we'll let them spill.

# "THEY DON'T WANT TO WORK"

## The Laziness Myth

"My mom stayed home while we were growing up, and my dad has never, ever worked in his life." Jabu, the woman sitting on the couch across from me, was telling me about her childhood. "And they were able to put us through the best school in this area. So I really respect my dad for that."

Little buzzers went off in my head. How could their family have found the money for tuition when her parents were not working? Jabu, like Bullet, was one of only a handful of people from Mpophomeni in their late twenties who had attended Howick schools. How had they paid the roughly $1,000 in tuition fees per year charged at the formerly all-white school? Plus they would have needed either a vehicle, a good friend with a vehicle, or money for taxis (mini-buses) to get to the school, which had no free busing option.[1] Jabu had told me earlier that her mom had not worked either while she was growing up, so how did two nonworking parents find that kind of money?

Besides, Jabu had gone so far as to tell me she respected her dad for not working. What was that about? She seemed to have just confirmed the stereotypes that people had been telling me about since my early days in South Africa working with the microfinance organization. I had often heard blanket statements accusing Zulu people of being lazy and aspiring not to work. I found these accusations troubling, and I came looking for deeper explanations. But here was this confident, well-educated young woman seeming to exemplify the laziness narrative people kept talking about: she was actually telling me that she *respected* her dad for not working. I made a mental note to go back through my recording and make sure I had understood her correctly. In the moment, I nodded, and she went on talking. Here's the transcript of what she said next.

> My dad is a taxi owner, but his business only started becoming something just after we had left school. And it was a matter of people would come bring their cars in because my dad is a good mechanic and he would do their cars and get paid and that's how we lived. From the day I was born, I remember there was a time at home when my mom was like, "Okay, now things are really tough." We've got a garden, there by the garage and my dad's got three guys working for him. I remember when they started their garden. I remember there was one day, I think I was eight or nine, and there was going to be a market day [as a fundraiser at the school] and my dad came with potatoes from the garden to sell. You know how we felt embarrassed? We were like, "Dad why don't you bake something at least!" And my dad was like, "This is who I am." We left that market day with all those potatoes gone. All of them gone. He even had orders from other guys, saying, "You know what? We love your potatoes. We want your potatoes." So it's like little things that you don't notice growing up. You don't know how hard your parents are working. Up until you actually stay at home with them. My dad's a real hard worker.

As I listened through the recording later, I marveled at what had happened in the space of this paragraph. She went from telling me that her dad had never worked to telling me—with a tone of real pride—that her dad was "a real hard worker." Along the way, she had mentioned activities that seemed to me to qualify as work. He raised and sold vegetables with three employees, and he fixed people's cars as a mechanic. Later in the conversation, she offhandedly mentioned other ways her dad made money—transporting other kids to school for a fee, and eventually buying multiple minibuses and hiring drivers to run taxi routes. It seemed he had hired multiple employees and run at least four separate businesses. Why, then, did she start describing her father as having "never, ever worked in his life"? And why did she say that she respected him for it?

When Jabu said that her dad had never worked, she was drawing on a piece of a narrative that has been told about black people for centuries. It is a narrative that has always had definite uses. It has kept certain people in positions of power while oppressing others—benefiting some people at the expense of others.

In the same sentence, though, Jabu was revealing one way in which she and others resist this narrative, refusing to conform to the moralities it expects and maintaining dignity within the dehumanizing systems it upholds. As Jabu talked through what she saw of her dad's life, she was describing a reality that gets hidden by the dominant narrative: her dad was not staying at home avoiding work because he or people who resembled him are lazy; he was refusing certain indignities endemic to white spaces, and sculpting a life of respect in his own community. But as Jabu herself noticed, "up until you stay at home" with someone paying attention to their life, it's hard to see past the narrative that says they're just not working.

## Narratives with Power

In the previous chapter, I introduced the dilemma Bullet faced in choosing between pursuing a law degree or producing music. To some, it might seem that making the most of his educational opportunities would be the right path to the good life, but for Bullet something about that path didn't seem right. Was becoming a lawyer his dream, or somebody else's? Would working hard to become a lawyer really pay off for him, or would the prejudices he had experienced in predominantly white spaces elsewhere play out again in law school or a career? His life decisions put him at odds with the narrative that many South Africans believed should and would lead to the good life.

Notice in that previous sentence I just used the phrases *the* narrative and *the* good life. That's the way many people have learned to see it—as if there were no good reason anyone would use any other narrative. This was *the* narrative, the one and only, applicable for any person in any situation. To make choices that didn't fit the narrative would be wrong, irrational, or inconceivable.

Scholars use a word to describe a narrative like that: hegemony.[2] Hegemony is a way of seeing the world that has become so pervasive that people have a difficult time even seeing it as one of any number of possibilities—it becomes *the only* possibility. Hegemony is a set of ideas that are invisible and unnoticed, ideas so taken for granted that people do not bother to question them, like the idea that flowers and trees grow upward toward the sun. In everyday conversation, up is toward the sky, down is toward the earth, and there is no reason to spend much time thinking about why we think this way.

Many of our habitual ways of thinking about the world are built on unquestioned assumptions like the location of up, down, earth, and sky. These assumptions, while not fully accurate, are widely held because they offer certain conveniences. We do not have to bother to explain what we mean by "up" and we do not have to consider whether we are correct. We simply use a word and move on. And much of the time, assumptions like these probably have little influence over who gains power and resources in a society. What sets hegemony apart from any other assumption is that hegemonic assumptions are not neutral in their results across society. They produce winners and losers. Hegemonic narratives are ways of understanding the world that have become so prevalent that people do not consider questioning them, and the fact that they linger beyond refute confers advantages to some people over others. Hegemonic ideas are the silent, unexamined messages telling us who gets to be up and who gets pushed down.

One of the most influential thinkers when it comes to hegemony was Antonio Gramsci, an Italian who did much of his writing in the 1920s and 1930s while starving in a prison on charges of organizing resistance to the Italian Fascist regime. Gramsci noticed that people in dominant political and economic groups, like the political leaders in his own country, did not maintain dominance through force alone. Instead, they perpetuated ways of thinking that became so normal that subordinate people accepted their own subordination, often without protest, no longer even considering that life could be otherwise. Gramsci wrote that "the great masses of the population" offer "spontaneous consent . . . to the general direction imposed on social life by the dominant fundamental group."[3] This spontaneous consent comes about because powerful people in society gradually create and promote whole systems of symbols, values, beliefs, and sentiments that are woven through the very fabric of culture. These ideas spread and reproduce in all the ways culture spreads—workplaces, state-run institutions, religious groups, schools, arts, media, parenting, and everyday conversations. Over time, these ideas come to be equated with common sense, rationality, morality, and reality. The most insidious aspect of this way of reinforcing power inequalities is that people in subservient groups come to not just accept their subordination but to actually play a part in reinforcing their inferiority by embracing and spreading hegemonic views to others.[4]

The antidote to the venomous power of hegemony, then, is to question it. Hegemonies are broken when people talk about possibilities for making life otherwise. By definition, hegemonies do not accurately describe the shape of the world and human existence. There is a hopefulness inherent in that very inconsistency between hegemony and reality. As the anthropologist Marco Di Nunzio wrote, "Authoritarian regimes can be successful in enforcing compliance, but have been less so in making their ideas of society, order, and progress coincide with the desires of the general population."[5] While hegemony, by definition, is that which is not being contested, it *can be* contested and nearly inevitably *will be*. Jean and John Comaroff, who have written at length on hegemony in South Africa, write: "Hegemony is . . . always threatened by the vitality that remains in the forms of life it thwarts."[6] Hegemony is never absolute or stable. One could envision hegemony as the end of a spectrum that compares the ease with which an idea can be contested in society. Hegemonic narratives have the power to shape society because they are invisible and uncontested.[7] As they become increasingly visible and contested, they move along the spectrum toward something else: openly debatable ideas.

Across history, ideas about race have moved in and out of hegemony. During the height of the slave trade, the idea that African people could be rightfully sold as slaves while people from Europe could not was, in some circles, a scarcely debatable idea. While slavery continues today in various forms, a neutral stance on slavery is no longer hegemonic. Why? Because most people question it, if not abhor it. Someone who states that "black people make better slaves," will likely get questioned, if not fired from a job or punched. Slavery was always contested and resisted in various ways, but the more that resistance gathered influence, the further the ideas upholding slavery moved away from hegemony, making the whole social and economic structure of slavery harder to uphold. Through lifetimes of intentional efforts, people dragged the idea of racially determined chattel slavery away from the hegemony end of the spectrum, building the conceptual and support base for resistance. There is no set moment when an idea escapes hegemony. Over time, ideas can swing away from hegemony and back. An idea that is hegemonic among one group of people might become questioned in another group.

With questioning, new space for resistance opens up. Other racist and antiblack ideas, as well as plenty of other oppressive ideas, remain deeply entrenched, but the struggle against racism and antiblackness will always involve challenging hegemonic ideas. Taking ideas from invisible to debatable takes no small effort. The change often involves a great wave of scholars, protestors, media, education, and everyday efforts of ordinary people talking about a topic. To give more recent examples, social media has offered a valuable tool for unveiling hegemonic ideas, as in the #BlackLivesMatter and #MeToo movements that questioned the racial inequalities in police violence and the prevalent silence surrounding sexual assault.

Throughout the history of anthropology and sociology, much theoretical debate has considered the question, How does society change? Does change happen primarily through changing *social structures*, like the economic, governmental, and institutional systems that seem in many ways to steer the course of our lives? Or does change happen primarily through changing *culture*—the ideas, habits, beliefs, language, and spirituality that seems in other ways to guide our lives? Since the late 1970s, a number of theorists who were eventually dubbed "practice theorists" (including Sherry Ortner, Philippe Bourdieu, and Anthony Giddens, among others), articulated a position that says social change happens when *both* structures and culture interact with individual human agency. The contestation of hegemonic narratives is one form of cultural change, and it goes hand in hand with structural change—neither produces lasting results without the other. Taking an idea out of hegemonic invisibility does not mean that changes in structures will necessarily occur. People will not necessarily agree about the changes that should happen, and resources will not necessarily be distributed any more evenly. But people who begin to talk about a hegemonic idea are changing society. They invent hashtags, they make protest signs, they make documentaries, they write the issue into college courses, and they create think tanks and lobbying groups. Movements such as the #MeToo and American civil rights movements entailed structural change that went hand in hand with cultural change, and it would be impossible to disentangle the two.

In more recent vocabulary, hegemony is a matter of how "woke" the general population is about a given issue. The contesting of hegemony is the domain of much political activism and creative energies. As Jean and John Comaroff eloquently write, movements to awaken consciousness are "the realm from which emanate the poetics of history, the innovative impulses . . . the poetic imagination, the creative, the innovative."[8] The very acts of writing, speaking, and thinking, then, can play a part in moving ideas away from hegemony, and thereby a role in changing society. That writing and thinking includes books like the one you are now reading. My writing and your reading are not just informative processes of gathering descriptions; they are, in the Comaroffs' words, "the most critical domain."[9] When you read and learn about a narrative which has been hegemonic, you become not just an observer of an inert story. You become an actor in the process of resistance, innovation, and creativity that moves the narratives that move societies.

## A Hegemonic Narrative: The Laziness Myth

When Jabu stated that her dad had never worked a day in his life, she described him in a way that fit the events of his life into a narrative that lingers mostly in the realm of hegemony. This narrative practically jumped out at me when I started tabulating the words that I had heard repeated in conversations in South Africa, and yet it took me four years of living in South Africa before I put a name to it and started writing about it as a cohesive narrative.[10]

I call this hegemonic narrative the laziness myth.[11] South Africans very often used the word "laziness" with a sort of apologetic hesitancy, as if they wished they knew some other way to talk about what they believed, which was, perhaps, an inkling of questioning the myth. Yet, use the word people do, for all its accusatory ugliness. I found no other more frequently used emic word (that is, a word used by South Africans themselves, not just external scholars) to name the central idea of this narrative. I heard the word "laziness" again and again, by people of all racial, ethnic, class, age, and gender groups, nearly always to express the reasons why certain kinds of people—men, youth, Zulu people, and particularly black people—were not achieving something assumed to be the good life. Over lunch in a restaurant, one white woman who ran a small business explained that she had stopped hiring Zulu people because they "don't last a week, because they say it's too little money for too much work." At this point, a white man near our table leaned over and stated with a sympathetic nod a single word, "laziness." Another time, a white woman told me to expect to find many lazy people in my research. She attempted to distinguish our white selves from young black people by saying, "If you or I were unemployed we would find something to do." Another white woman who led work ethics trainings for Zulu employees complained, "They don't want to work; they don't even want to learn to work." A white Christian development program leader said that in his program, "the lazy ones drop out, peel away," but they press on to train people anyway because "the whole Bible is about hard work."

A dominant narrative drowns out others—it rolls off the tongue before thinking. It makes telling another story difficult, time-consuming, and thought-demanding. Countering it puts a person at risk of being discredited or dismissed. Through generations of being called lazy, many Zulu people have come to join white people in describing their own ethnic group as lazy and blame their own lower socioeconomic status on laziness. Even the Zulu king Goodwill Zwelithini stated in 2015 that the liberation of his people was being damaged because too many Zulu people were "not obeying the law, are thieves, child rapists, and too lazy to plough the fields."[12] When I asked one Zulu man what was unique about Zulu people, his first word was "laziness." In another conversation, a Zulu graduate student, a man who had himself cleaned toilets to pay for his college education, said of his generation, "We are a pack that is very lazy." He said most of his peers "just want an easy job that pays well." He paused, bowing his head with a sigh that seemed to express disappointment in his peers. "We work when we have to." Like Jabu, though, as he talked more about his own experience and the working lives of his parents, he voiced how inaccurate that word was. His mom had worked in a textile factory sweatshop for R150 ($15) a week, and his dad was laid off when a milling company downsized. He had seen his dad among the men who stood on certain street corners every weekday hoping to be selected for day labor jobs at five or ten dollars a day. "They are looking, and how dare you call them lazy." He spat out the words, not just as a correction of what he had said earlier, but as if in rebuttal to all the people he had ever heard calling Zulu people lazy.

I use the word "myth" to distinguish it from the other narratives covered in this book in a couple of ways. A myth is not just any widely told story, it's a story that powerfully shapes moralities and group identity. A myth tells something about who belongs in a group, who is in or out, who is good or bad. Nearly every time people talked about laziness, they did so in ways that distinguished themselves from those "others" who were lazy—people of some other racial, ethnic, gender, generational, or personality type who were considered different for their laziness, and thereby undeserving of the same good benefits. Further, scholars of race have pointed out ways that myths believed and taught by white people were used to maintain white colonial power.[13] Likewise, this myth is a tool of the powerful, a means of morally justifying a system that benefits some to the detriment of others. Scholars have often used the word "myth" regardless of whether the story is rooted in historical fact, whereas in popular usage, it generally means a story whose accuracy is questionable.[14] I use the word "myth" in the latter sense here to mean a story of questioned factual accuracy that reinforces group identities including power inequalities.

In brief, the laziness narrative says that lazy tendencies are the most important factor inhibiting certain people from achieving the good life, thereby determining the socioeconomic hierarchies across society. To break that down further, the narrative says (1) hard work is the determinant of success, (2) laziness is the reason people don't work hard, (3) certain categories of people are inherently lazier than others, and (4) social inequalities can best be righted by eradicating laziness. In what follows, I explain each of these components of the narrative, and then offer evidence that this hegemonic narrative not only harms certain people, but also fails to accurately describe people's lived realities.

## The Laziness Narrative in Conversation

One afternoon I pulled up my motorcycle beside Nobuhle, a young woman I had visited several times. When I asked what was new, she told me with a shrug that she had found a job, then quit after just one day. I asked why, and she explained that on the first day of work she learned that the employer would not give her a contract. He would pay wages only in cash, without paperwork, and she would earn thirty rand per day—about three dollars, a quarter of the minimum wage for most industries. She stayed one day, long enough to confirm from other workers that this was indeed the pay agreement. She came back only once, to collect her thirty rand, barely enough to cover the taxi fare it had taken to get to and from the job twice. The job was at a prominent Howick business, one I had frequented myself. From what I had overheard in another conversation, one of the managers at the business was a well-regarded member of a local church. About a week later, I worked up the courage to walk into the business and ask to speak to the owner about my research.

That's how I met Willem, the white man near retirement age who owned the business. Willem welcomed me immediately with a cup of tea and a seat in his office. When I told him I was interested in learning about South Africans' ideas about unemployment, he was more than eager to keep talking, and I scarcely had to prompt him with questions. A couple of other managers, also white, stopped in during the conversation and contributed their thoughts. Together they described what were, in their opinion, the reasons Zulu people so often seemed to stay at home unemployed, misbehave at work to the point of getting fired, and fail in their own business ventures.

"Entrepreneurship is in our blood, our genes, the marrow of our bones," Willem said, speaking of his own Dutch Afrikaner heritage. "Why must we be blamed for that?" He went on to list ethnic groups that he considered to be inherently good at certain kinds of work. "Who makes the best cars in the world? The Germans. . . . Who grows the best vegetables? The Portuguese. The white engineer is just better. Finished. End of story."

All of this came out as a counterpoint to what he saw was missing in black people, not just in South Africa, but worldwide. "In Atlanta, where there are lots of blacks, you have the same problems," he said. His main arguments were that black people were biologically disinclined to become entrepreneurs or successful leaders in the workplace, that education should be harsher to train people for the working world, and that black union leaders and government officials set the worst examples of the thieving, cheating, and laziness tendencies common among Zulu people.

As evidence, Willem pointed to the postapartheid economy. "Look at the scoreboard. This economy should have been the best in the world. The economy was better in apartheid! . . . People all say 'Everything is apartheid's fault.' But that's wrong." He followed this train of evidence to argue that white people once ran a thriving economy in South Africa, even under severe global economic sanctions. The economy since 1994, he said, has seen slower growth because black people do not run governments as well. (In fact, the five-year average of the economic growth rate in South Africa grew steadily from 1993 until the 2008 global financial crisis, but in his perspective, things had only gotten worse.)[15]

Most irritating to him was black people's seeming disregard for the ways white people's hard work and strong work ethics had supposedly improved the country. "So now we get blamed for being successful," he said. "If you are successful in Europe, it's an achievement. Here it's a sin. Here you're a bloody bastard. If you have white skin, that is." He envisioned himself as a hardworking contributor to South African society, struggling to keep society running amid an epidemic of laziness among black workers, unemployed people, union members, and government officials.

Willem voiced ideas that lay beneath the surface politely unspoken in many other conversations and interactions I'd had. For most South Africans, as among most Americans, overt racism was considered socially unacceptable. Conversations about race were usually limited to politically correct statements that suppressed certain ideas that actually guided individuals and society. People tempered their conversations, apologizing for words like laziness or even racial slurs, even as they went on to use such words. At one point in the conversation Willem claimed outright, "I'm not racist. This isn't racist. It's truth. It's history." He followed this up with a point of tokenism, saying, "There are rich black guys who understand business doesn't just happen, but these are the exception."

Making a disclaiming statement like "I'm not racist" is much like bragging, "I'm the most humble person." The very fact that a person makes the statement proves that the speaker has it wrong. Being racist or not racist is not a binary that can be proven true or false about a person once and for all. Racism is a way of seeing the world and a set of systems that are so ingrained in society as to be impossible to expunge from any individual. Antiblackness is a particular form of racism directed toward black people, who, in the system of racism across much of the Western world, are treated as lowest in a hierarchy of arbitrarily delineated and ranked groups. Antiblackness is embedded in the fabric of society both in durable structures like the racial segregation of neighborhoods, and in the very thoughts and habits that subtly reinforce white privilege, like the fear that ripples through many people's minds when walking in predominantly black neighborhoods.

The laziness myth may be easy to spot in the overtly racist dogma of exploitative employers like Willem, but overt racism is by no means the only way the laziness narrative spreads. Like a mythical creature that multiplies when injured or threatened, the laziness narrative thrives when racism is least obvious in society. When people come to believe that racism is ending, they expect the effects of racism to also disappear. Whether in South Africa after the nation's first free election of 1994, or in the United States after the Emancipation Proclamation, the 1964 Civil Rights Act, or the election of Barack Obama, victories over institutionalized racism can be interpreted as evidence that racism has ended. In reality, the cultural, structural, and institutionalized aspects of racism have yet to be fully eliminated anywhere, and the effects of past injustices continue to play out for generations. When people see the ongoing effects of racism, such as disparities in wealth, criminal convictions, educational attainment, or unemployment, they look for explanations. As Michael Dumas has explained, when the official and dominant teaching is to avoid racist behavior, people incorrectly assume that racism is over. They then interpret the racial disparities in life outcomes as "a result of cultural deficits within the Black. The slave, always suspected of being lazy and shiftless, now must bear primary responsibility for not making it in a society, which—officially, anyway—thrives on multiracial harmony and civic participation."[16] When people discard racial discrimination as a possible cause for inequalities, they often turn to explanations based on dominant Western ideals of individualism and freedom: black and brown individuals must be freely choosing to be lazy.

## Laziness Myth Part 1: Hard Work Determines Who Should Achieve the Good Life

On the surface, the laziness myth appears to be founded on the value of hard work, and in much of the world, that value is taken for granted. Why shouldn't a person who works hard at something receive whatever benefits come from that work? Rewarding hard work is often central in people's ideas of fairness.[17] Studies show that in situations where there is a clear connection between hard work and reward, people work harder.[18] So it would seem that the more society can reward hard work, the more people will work hard, and the greater will be the output and rewards for all. This idea that hard work should be exchangeable for rewards of equal value is a foundational assumption of capitalist labor markets: people offer their own labor for sale, and the more labor they are willing to sell, the more they receive wealth and resources in return.

But life is not that simple. First, the rewards society offers for labor are by no means proportional to the difficulty of the work that goes into that labor. The pay for farm laborers handpicking vegetables is likely to be less than the pay of the accountant who sits at a computer evaluating the profitability of those vegetables. The pay for factory workers loading crates and boxes into shipping trucks is likely to be less than that of the manager who tallies how many crates went into each truck. The pay for a parent who stays home caring for children is typically nothing at all. All of these jobs demand uniquely suited skills acquired through years of training or experience. All require some amount of mental and physical strain, so in some sense they can all be counted as hard work. One could make a case that, to some extent, which job is harder will depend on the preferences and skills of the worker, but most people would agree that jobs like manual farm labor, heavy lifting, and child care are hard, if not harder than average. Yet these are among the lowest paying jobs. Societies tend to reward mental strain at a higher rate than physical strain. Jobs associated with home and femininity tend also to be valued less than jobs associated with working outside the home and masculinity.[19] The rewards offered for hard work are highly situational and shaped by social norms influenced by gender, status, and class.

Further, a social system that allocated resources entirely according to an individual's labor would be nearly impossible to implement. In theory, the society would be relatively equal, since everyone would have only so many hours in a day to work. But how would children, the elderly, and those physically unable to work survive? Every society finds ways to distribute some resources in ways other than according to labor, whether through government-based systems like social security, market-based systems like disability insurance, or family-based systems like grandparents caring for grandchildren. Many goods are distributed publicly based on being a citizen or merely being human, such as police protection or access to roads. Inheritance is an example of distributing wealth based on kinship or relationship rather than work. Nor do profits on investments generally correspond to labor input. Cultures have a wide range of ideas about how to morally allocate resources—what James Ferguson calls "politics of distribution"—and work is only one of many ways in which humans determine who deserves resources.[20]

Yet many people have argued in one way or another that resources *should* be allocated purely according to labor contribution, without seeing all the implications. This argument intertwines with a set of ideological beliefs and policies called neoliberalism, which proposes that the market, when unimpeded by government or other interference, can best allocate resources by allowing individuals to exercise free choice and personal initiative.[21] Neoliberalism was widely influential in global political and economic policies from the 1980s to the 1990s, but the ideas of neoliberalism continue to shape policies and arouse fierce debates today. One aspect of neoliberalism especially relevant to unemployment is a belief that the more societies remove systems that allocate resources in ways other than markets—such as taxes, trade protections, welfare, and publicly owned companies—the more people will seek out their own entrepreneurial paths to success and receive pay and profit in reward.

To unemployed and underemployed people, the neoliberal advice is to keep on believing that the economy will bounce back, the future will be good, and success comes to all who try hard enough.[22] As studies in many neoliberal situations across the globe have shown, low-waged and unemployed laborers in such settings often experience pressure to blame themselves for their circumstances. In groups ranging from unemployed youth in East Germany, to clothing factory workers in Turkey, to unemployed formerly highly paid Californians in the tech industry, anthropologists have documented experiences of low-waged and unemployed workers surrounded by neoliberal messages saying that their economic hardships are caused by their supposed lack of initiative.[23] Workers tend to repeat the narrative among themselves, coming to believe that they must just try harder, market their skills better, search a little wider, and surely they will succeed. They often suppress awareness that there could be other causes for their unemployment: recessions, global competition, investment bubbles bursting, or national-level political and economic collapse. At other times, people come to recognize the disconnect between their supposed personal failure and the reality of limited opportunities. The frustration breaks through in protests, major election swings, and other expressions of discontent and resistance—though because of the invisible, unquestionable nature of hegemonic narratives, people sometimes find it hard to pinpoint exactly what it is they are resisting.

To admit that individual effort does not determine people's success is a politically dangerous admission for those in power. The reality is that humans allocate resources in all sorts of ways—inheritances, welfare, and gift exchanges, as well as through privileges that depend on factors such as class, ethnicity, race, gender, family history, and chance. As people ignore all those other dimensions of distribution, the narrative takes on a defensiveness driven by fear. Will just a few remaining overburdened hard workers be left trying to pull the economic weight for legions of lethargic freeloaders swinging in hammocks, collecting welfare, and begging on the street? And worse yet, will those people become angry about all the ways they've been disenfranchised and discriminated against? From the perspective of those in power, the world can seem less frightening if everyone keeps up the ruse that work equals success.

## Laziness Myth Part 2: People Who Don't Work Hard Are Lazy

Laziness, then, is the feared opposite of hard work in the hegemonic laziness myth. To be lazy is to impede the flow of productive labor. In South Africa, lazy people are imagined as those who miss work, quit work, complain about work, stay at home not seeking work, don't volunteer, don't start businesses, or don't try to get promoted at work. Body language such as frowning, slouching, moving slowly, or lowering eyes is imagined as evidence of laziness. Other methods of attaining resources—theft, corruption, gifts from family members, or welfare—are imagined as the immoral alternatives people use to support their laziness habits. Further, lazy people are imagined as present-oriented in immoral ways—wasting money for immediate gratification on alcohol, fancy clothes, or junk food rather than saving. Among employers and employment-readiness trainers these behaviors came up often as the supposed causes of poverty, stagnated careers, and unemployment.

As I explain further in the next chapter, many employers were concerned about the supposed immoral behavior of employees. Employers wanted hard workers with what they called a "good work ethic." The phrase "hard worker" was the most common phrase employers used when telling me what they thought of as an ideal worker. Such workers would come to work on time every day and convey a willing attitude toward work through body language like erect posture, eye contact, and smiling. These expectations overlooked myriad other possible reasons for behaviors that seemed like laziness. Take, for example, the fact that people often arrived late for work because they spent hours waiting for and riding unreliable taxis. Or the fact that people often chose not to smile when they did not feel valued at work, or that Zulu children were often taught by parents that direct eye contact is disrespectful. Or consider that people often exhausted all their job searching options and found nothing. Starting a small business without generations of business contacts and significant financial start-up capital was nearly impossible, especially in a setting where black businesses were regularly shunned by nonblack customers and suppliers. Or consider how difficult it is to accumulate savings when a person's paycheck does not even cover necessities like food, electricity, and transportation. Consider also that banks routinely discriminated against black people in lending, and that the cost of higher education was unattainable for many families. There are countless factors creating behaviors that seem like laziness. The laziness narrative, though, acknowledges only one explanation: people do not want to work.

## Laziness Myth Part 3: Certain Groups of People Are Especially Lazy

The narrative blaming poverty on laziness becomes even more potent when it labels certain groups—specifically black, brown, and other groups that have been marginalized and subjected to structural violence—as *the* lazy people. When beliefs prevail that already socially subjugated people are inherently lazier than others, ever more limited opportunities are extended to those people. They in turn fall further into poverty, which society takes as further evidence of their laziness.

Patterns exist across the world of depriving groups of people of resources and simultaneously blaming the outcomes on their supposed laziness. As societies construct meanings surrounding ethnic and racial groups, often groups have been ranked against each other according to supposed worker abilities. Paradoxically, both the stereotypes of lazy and hardworking have been used against subordinate groups to justify poor working conditions. A look around the world reveals supposedly entrepreneurial Egyptians, nimble and docile Chinese factory women, tech-savvy Indians, untrainable but cheap Mexican textile workers, and indulgent Moroccans versus spendthrift Yemenites in Israel.[24] In the United States—in addition to African Americans—American Indians, Puerto Ricans, and Somali Bantus, to name just a few, have all at times been stereotyped as lazy.[25] Often these prejudices come and go as one group is compared with another, as when Lummi Indians went from being treated by employers as desirable workers to losing their jobs when Chinese laborers arrived who were willing to work longer hours for less pay.[26] For groups stamped as hardworking rather than lazy, the classification can also operate as an excuse for the broader society to ignore unjust treatment and the structures that caused their low status and desperation. Ruth Gomberg-Muñoz documents how Mexican American immigrants in the United States have made strategic use of the "hard worker" image but have also been restricted by the label.[27]

In the part of South Africa where I lived, the stereotype of laziness was applied in layers across intersecting characteristics of people. Black people were seen as lazier than whites. South African black people were seen as lazier than other black immigrants, and ethnically Zulu South Africans were described as lazier than other black South African ethnic groups. (In different times and places, though, other ethnic groups have been singled out by whites as more or less lazy.) Among Zulu South Africans, men, and most specifically young men, were seen as the laziest, riskiest, and most undesirable of all employees.

Since the seventeenth and eighteenth centuries, white colonialists have constructed ideas of blackness that tied blackness to laziness. White people imagined black people as lacking the natural inclination to work, making them inferior and also in need of white indoctrination through forced labor. In 1735 one of the first white people to attempt to scientifically delineate characteristics of racial groups, Carolus Linnaeus, characterized the African variety of *Homo sapiens* as "crafty, indolent, negligent," and "governed by caprice." Justifications for slavery were built on the argument that slavery could make black and brown people more civilized and moral people by teaching them to value work.[28] Capturing human beings, shipping them across the ocean in torturous conditions, selling them as property, and conscripting them and their offspring into forced labor of course did nothing to inspire a willingness to throw oneself into one's labors. Nor did it inspire white slave owners to treat slaves as worthy of advanced education and promotion. In the post–Civil War era, former slaves in America were believed to be a little better at work than people in Africa for having been tamed by the experience of slavery, but there was still a presumed risk that they would go back to their lazy ways. In the historian Andrew Zimmerman's words, "The Negro" was considered "a servile, hard-working, and inexpensive laborer; at the same time, the 'Negro' was a rebellious, lazy, and excessively demanding threat to the political and economic order."[29] A cycle of disenfranchisement and justification through the laziness narrative rolled on through history and continues to shape societies today.

In Africa, the comparative industriousness of various groups of Africans was a pressing concern for early colonists looking for cheap and productive laborers. When in the early 1800s William Burchell traveled to South Africa to study native peoples, he made notes on the comparative work ethics of various tribes. At one point he seemed pleasantly surprised to find considerable industriousness among a tribal group of Sotho-Tswana people. He wrote that the Bachapins (now spelled Batlhaping) "are active, and, when occasion may require, never shrink from the fatigue of a long journey. They are far from being slothful, although they have in fact, allotted several of the more laborious duties to the women: but they have retained for themselves all those which are the most active. A man's merit is estimated principally by his *industry*."[30]

Zulu people, in contrast, were often judged by early colonists as unindustrious, warlike, and hard to employ. Those perceptions arose in part through the timing of the first colonial encounters with Zulu people, who lived hundreds of miles inland. By the time the colonists had spread eastward, much of Southern Africa was experiencing a catastrophic drought and famine, followed by what is remembered as *Mfecane,* the time of suffering. Meanwhile, the powerful leader Shaka Zulu was consolidating power across African tribal groups using intimidating warfare. He conscripted fifteen to twenty years of service from every able-bodied young man and waged wars that displaced people across a path of three hundred to eight hundred kilometers on the southeast side of South Africa. The internal warfare between Africans intertwined with land seizures and warfare of white settlers at the time of their arrival. Colonists came to envision Zulu people as either warring, idle, or starving, needing either pacification, training, or help through low-wage labor. The justification was fueled by rising international demand and prices for labor-intensive mining and agricultural products from South Africa. When Zulu people turned out not to be so easy to compel into continuous labor, colonists reached the conclusion that they must be inherently lazy.[31]

In other social and economic conditions, however, Zulu workers were compared favorably to other worker groups. Alan Cobley describes the conditions around the turn of the twentieth century in the mines of Witwatersrand (near Johannesburg), where hundreds of Central African immigrants were imported for the harshest underground mine work.[32] As the immigrants suffered eye infections, influenza, and mining accidents, many refused to continue working and were imprisoned for breaking their contracts, even though the contract never stipulated that they would work underground. White employers interpreted their behavior as being "undoubtedly lazy as a class."[33] Colonial mine owners at the time socially constructed a hierarchy of their preferred workers, in which Zulu people fell somewhere in the middle.[34] Much like today, the prescription for solving this supposed laziness was labor. "This indolence, the product of countless ages, cannot be eradicated except by indefinitely sustained necessity of action," one colonial official wrote.[35]

The historian Keletso Atkins describes at length stories of working relationships between colonists and Zulu people in the late 1800s.[36] Miscommunications and mismatched expectations deepened the frustrations of both Zulu employees and colonial employers. In one example, colonists told Zulu people that they would be paid at the end of the month using the Zulu word for one lunar month (*inyanga*), which is also the Zulu word for moon. Colonial employers insisted on a pay period according to a Western calendar of 28, 30, or 31 days, which seemed to Zulu people like always demanding just longer than the real, lunar month of 29 days. Facing seemingly irrational or cruel demands from employers, many Zulu people organized to demand earlier payments or quit.[37] Other frustrations involved more direct injustice against African people. In the latter half of the nineteenth century, the European colonial government in what is now the province of KwaZulu-Natal authorized rounding up refugees and allotting them as employees on colonial farms, advocating slavelike apprenticeship of any children deemed orphans, sometimes even above the protests of their mothers. Such enslavement and trafficking of child laborers was justified in the words of one colonist: "It would be a great advantage to the black and white population, if the youth of the former could be induced to enter the service of the white employer and thus early acquire habits of industry."[38] Methods of forcing South Africans into formal employment further included demanding taxes payable only in wage-earned currency, as well as beatings and imprisonment. An eerie list of phrases compiled by Atkins from a nineteenth-century Zulu-learners' phrasebook offers evidence of the kinds of statements white colonists found themselves wanting to make to their black workers:

> Boy, I am tired of you.
> You are obstinate (bad, lazy, saucy).
> You are dirty (a fool).
> You are quarrelsome (you have much anger).
> I have warned you enough already.
> I now threaten you.
> If you do that again I shall dismiss you without payment.
> I shall keep part of your wages.
> I shall take your blanket.

I shall make you pay.
I shall put you in prison.
I shall have you flogged.
I shall stint you in your food.[39]

In South Africa today, employers often compare Zulu workers to other African immigrants. In one story I heard discussed in the Howick area, a local farmer laid off his entire staff of Zulu people and replaced them with entirely Malawian workers. I met multiple small business owners who insisted they would no longer hire Zulu people. Sometimes instead they resolved to hire foreign Africans, especially Malawians, Zimbabweans, and people of the Democratic Republic of the Congo. Often hiring foreign Africans meant waiving requirements for visas, and at the same time waiving legal protections such as minimum wages and contract laws. One Indian South African woman selling vegetables at a stand in the small business district of Howick pointed to the people employed at and managing small businesses along the street in Howick: "Malawian. Malawian. Malawian," she repeated as she pointed. "They come here for one reason, and that's to make money. Maybe ten sleep in one room, but they are working."

African foreigners themselves made use of the laziness myth to differentiate themselves from Zulu workers. A Congolese barber shook his head in disgust when I asked for his thoughts on South African unemployment. "It's a country of opportunity, but they don't use it. Everything is on the table. Just use it. Get an education. You can get a better life. But some, they like the quicker life." I asked him if people from his country like the quicker life, too. He admitted that yes, some do. A few minutes later, the Zulu man who had been in his shop for a haircut left, and the Congolese barber became more direct. "South African people are useless. They want someone to give you money." Another Congolese man in a separate conversation described his efforts to volunteer to improve Howick, criticizing Zulu people for not doing the same (despite evidence that many local nonprofits are staffed or led by Zulu people). "In South Africa, most of the people they don't want to work. The lazy people always will sleep hungry, because they don't want to work. Myself, I'm struggling to put food on the table. And I'm also struggling to even get funding to start this company, which can help people. And it can also create job opportunities. . . . We're trying to show them, guys, don't depend to government." He and others ignored the self-selection involved in undertaking the extreme risk of leaving one's homeland for a new place, and the ways that his people were pressured into cultivating a social image of better workers as their own strategy of survival in a land where whiteness pitted black and brown people against each other. As the one Congolese man hinted, there were undoubtedly people in their home countries, as in any country, who did not find the means or opportunity to start a business from the ground up or travel thousands of miles in search of work.

The prevailing assumption among employers was that foreign Africans would work harder and complain less than Zulu South Africans. Zulu people, in turn, saw foreign Africans as driving down wages and encouraging lax enforcement of labor laws by being willing to take whatever employers offered. The tension between immigrants and Zulu people erupted periodically in waves of xenophobic violence. The Congolese man cited in the previous paragraph was talking with me in 2015 only a week after people in Pietermaritzburg city had physically attacked immigrants and vandalized and burned their businesses. He and several others had temporarily fled the area or gone into hiding, locking their businesses and fearing looting. The distrust and antagonism between immigrants and Zulu people ultimately harmed both groups while benefiting white employers, who gained an immigrant workforce willing to forego union membership, minimum wages, and other legal protections in order to differentiate themselves from lazy workers.

Being forced into a hierarchy of competition for scarce opportunities has tended to fuel fierce racial hatred between Indian and black people as well. The apartheid system pitted one racial group against another, with Indians and colored people occupying a place barely above black people. "The bottom line is Zulu is lazy," one Indian man who ran a small business in Howick told me. He believed thievery also accompanied this laziness. "They don't even need to run. It used to be the Zulu could do two things, steal, and run. Now they don't even need to run." Another Indian business owner chimed in on the conversation to insist that every single Zulu person he had hired stole. I asked how many employees that was, and he estimated twenty. Then the first speaker added, "You can trust Zulu girls, but not Zulu boys. Never Zulu boys."

In this litany of quotations, we come face to face with the ways the laziness narrative intertwines with racial, ethnic, and gendered prejudices to deny people equal opportunities and blame them for the negative outcomes of that marginalization.

## Laziness Myth Part 4: The Solution Is Eradicating Laziness

According to the laziness myth, laziness is the source of social problems, so solving laziness should be central to solving social problems. The three hundred plus years since South Africa was colonized are replete with attempts to train, moralize, force, or starve the laziness out of African people. In the late 1800s, Commander Frere in South Africa offered the magnanimous statement that Zulu warriors could be trained to be valuable workers, as they "belong to the same race which furnishes the good-humoured volatile labourers and servants who abound in Natal, men very capable of being moulded in the ways of civilization and, when not actually trained to manslaughter, not naturally blood-thirsty, nor incurably barbarous."[40] The cause of reforming and civilizing indigenous people has often been central to justifications for colonial and racial domination. Similar hopes for reformed workers have also driven colonial governments, missionaries, educators, and development institutions through the centuries in attempts to indoctrinate black people with the morality of hard work.

Many colonists believed that Africans were culturally primitive and morally weak, so work could serve as a culturally transformative institution capable of molding a new kind of people.[41] These work-improved people would be dedicated, uncomplaining, and otherwise amenable to menial labor that would—as a sort of convenient side effect—generate wealth for colonial overseers. In the post-Enlightenment European ideology, individuals industriously pursuing their own self-interests could, through the invisible hand of the economy, produce the mutual good of all. If laziness was the cause of poverty and social ills, and laziness was inherent to certain people, then the way to help was not systemic change, legal rights, or respect for local economic systems. Instead, the solution was whatever compelled people to hard work. So unable were they to imagine any good life without a colonial-dominated capitalist waged-labor system that they justified poverty-inducing taxes, destruction of social and gender systems through migratory labor, below survival-level wages, beatings, and religious indoctrination all in the name of educating natives with a work ethic.[42] Colonists, in administering these supposed cures for poverty and immorality, could treat forced labor as a kind of paternalistic benevolence. They imagined employment as a humanitarian effort to mold better people.

Protestant denominations most prominent among European colonists tended to teach that hard work was evidence of a transformed Christian life.[43] At the same time, secularizing trends in Europe since the Enlightenment emphasized that the individualist pursuit of happiness through hard work was a means to the ultimate good of society.[44] When European colonists and missionaries arrived in Africa, they carried these deeply rooted assumptions that good people worked long and regular hours without question, saved much, and prioritized their own individual economic gain. While missionaries in at least some instances recognized oppressive labor practices and sided with Zulu laborers in disputes over worker exploitation, many joined in teaching a doctrine of hard work that benefited colonial overseers.[45] Many early schools for black Africans were run by missionaries, employers, or their wives, and the laziness myth came to seamlessly run throughout businesses, churches, and schools.

Sedentary farming has also been imagined as a whip to enforce good work habits. European settlers often assumed that switching from pastoralism into sedentary farming could make Africans into calmer hard workers. At the same time, they worried that if African agriculture was too profitable, Africans would not work for Europeans.[46] Apartheid-era relocations of black South Africans into Bantustans with low-quality, overcrowded, depleted land greatly inhibited agricultural productivity among black South Africans.[47] By the 1980s, people on rural land made so little income from agriculture that methods of tabulating official employment switched from counting rural Zulu people as employed (in agriculture) to acknowledging their status as unemployed.[48] Gardening in many Zulu communities today continues to be very challenging. Free-range goats and chickens eat what little compost people can collect, water taps are often far from gardens, soil is often hard packed with deep-rooted grass, and only the vigilant and strict can keep neighbors from taking ripe produce. Still, the push to make Zulu people into gardeners continues through the efforts of many development organizations, including at least three operating in Mpophomeni alone.

It is important to note that many efforts to reform Zulu people through agriculture, education, missions, and even labor from colonialism to the present have been seen at the time by both white trainers and black trainees as kindness. In my interviews, people who had gone through nonprofit work-readiness courses, even when they remained unemployed, were among those who talked most enthusiastically about the value of developing their character to become people who worked hard. But both educators and participants in these courses at times also revealed their cynicism as they tried to uphold a narrative based on prejudice and blindness to systemic injustice. One woman who worked with a work-readiness training organization complained that laziness stemmed from failures in how people think: "They've never had to think." She said she often had to train Zulu people to utilize their minds, or in her crass terms, "God gave you two ends, and you choose which one you're going to use."

At their ugliest, those who attempt to eradicate laziness sometimes envision poverty as a spur for better work ethics. Colonial state and business leaders made choices that went so far as to orchestrate poverty in order to keep black Africans working. The South African historian and anti-apartheid activist Norman Levy traced accounts of mining companies attempting to force black people into longer-term employment.[49] Rather than offer higher wages, which would seem the normal capitalist supply-and-demand method of inducing supply, they set wages insufferably low and taxes unattainably high so that workers would be too poor to leave their jobs.[50] The unapologetic end goal was not to improve African lives, but to mold them into a cheap prop for a white economy.

These arguments for impoverishment continue to creep into discourse in South Africa and elsewhere today. Historic accounts of companies attempting to force black people into longer-term employment through intolerably low wages bear an eerie resemblance to arguments for poverty-induced work ethics today. One South African former textile company manager gave her opinion about the reasons textile manufacturing moved from South Africa to Lesotho in the decades after apartheid. She said conditions in Lesotho textile factories were like "slave conditions." Then she added, "but at least they work hard," essentially saying that slavery was fine so long as it taught people to work hard.

The idea that poverty could drive people to a better work ethic also shows up in discussions about welfare. Both black and white people often complained that government grants (about forty dollars per month per child) encouraged young women to have babies rather than work. My interviews with young people who were working revealed that more likely the exact opposite was happening—having children compelled people to take whatever jobs they could get. When I asked individuals what had kept them searching for a job long enough to find work or staying in a disagreeable job, one of the most common reasons both men and women gave was having a child. Other researchers have further shown that child welfare helps people stay in the job search longer by providing the cushion of money necessary for travel, child care, and other job-search costs.[51] But the laziness narrative that permeates society says otherwise: give a person too much money, and they won't have the poverty factor that induces hard work. Without that, paradoxically, they supposedly won't find the right way to the good life.

## The Harm Done

As a reminder, hegemonies work not only because powerful people believe false and destructive things about less-powerful people, but also because less-powerful people are taught to believe those things about themselves. That self-blame contributes to deep psychological and social harms done by this narrative. In addition, the narrative reinforces societal systems that produce poverty. All of this happens while systematically shifting public attention away from the actual causes of inequality and unemployment.

Many of the most direct quotes I heard pinpointing Zulu people as lazy came from Zulu people themselves, though notably all came from employed Zulu people, including one who ran a small business and two who worked in positions of management. Two of the largest businesses in the outdoor marketplace in Howick were run by grandparent-aged Zulu people who complained about their inability to get their children to take over their business. One described his children's generation saying, "The problem is people don't want to work. . . . That's the problem of our people. They want things for *mahala* [free]. If they can put the effort, they can do that. . . . Why don't our people have children [help in their businesses], like Indian people do? If I die, this is finished. They don't want to learn. They want the money—'Please give me one hundred rand.' But they don't know how to work."

In conversations like these, Zulu people who considered themselves to be successful to some degree were distancing themselves from other individuals in their own ethnic and racial groups. This is an all-too-common pattern among groups that experience societal prejudice. To gain acceptance as successful, individuals from disadvantaged groups often find they need to define themselves as model exceptions, individuals who defy the characteristics of their group. The philosopher Pierre Bourdieu described the self-deprecating tendency of people climbing the class ladder: "Anyone who wants to 'succeed in life' must pay for his accession to everything which defines truly humane humans by a change of nature, a 'social promotion' experienced as an ontological promotion, a process of 'civilization' . . . but having internalized the class struggle, which is at the very heart of culture, he is condemned to shame, horror, even hatred of the old Adam, his language, his body, his tastes, and everything he was bound to, his roots, his family, his peers, sometimes even his mother tongue."[52]

For many South Africans, feeling true belonging in the middle class required reimagining themselves as something different from the people they might otherwise be grouped with, something exceptional and unusual. When people grow up without examples of people who have a unified identity as black, ethnically Zulu, *and* are successful in their careers, carving out that identity is not easy—though as we'll see in chapter 6, it is not impossible.

In addition to creating tension over class and racial and ethnic identity, the laziness narrative produces economic practices that reinforce poverty by labeling certain workers as undesirable and untrainable. When company managers perceive the available workforce to be low-skilled and transient, they locate businesses that require high-skilled employees elsewhere.[53] In regions with few highly skilled workers—or even a pervasive perception that most workers are unskilled—there is a disincentive to train workers on the job, because trained workers will have greater opportunities to leave for other job offers. The disincentive is especially strong when the workforce is seen as transient, which is true in South Africa because of the geographic segregation imposed under apartheid. Employers have shifted toward shorter contracts, and racial segregation often requires people to make unsustainable relocations away from their families.[54]

Under apartheid, black people were stereotyped as disloyal to jobs, even though their available jobs often involved risk, migration, and exploitation that inherently fostered that turnover. Over time, disincentives to invest in workers produce what the anthropologist Melissa Wright calls a "two-tiered system" in which supposedly "untrainable" and "disloyal" workers are distinguished from "trainable" workers.[55] Thus, black workers have been caught in stereotypes of laziness and disloyalty that render them untrainable, causing employers to hire them only for low-skill jobs, furthering their exclusion from higher-skill and higher-paid work and furthering their so-called disloyalty.[56]

## How Do We Know It's a Myth?

It should be clear by this point that people do in fact repeat this narrative blaming poverty on laziness, and that it harms certain people. But allow me for a moment to ask a troubling question: What if laziness *is* prevalent, and what if laziness *is* the cause of unemployment? After all, usually when a researcher finds person after person saying that something is true and giving evidence from their lived experience, a researcher would take that evidence seriously. So how is this different? Could all those people be right about laziness?

In my experience telling students and others about my research, I occasionally find someone brave enough to ask this question, usually with a genuine desire to better understand. In classroom settings, once that question is on the table, everyone perks up and listens. Most people at some level *want* to believe that marginalized people are not primarily to blame for their own poverty. In the United States as well as in South Africa, people learn that it would be politically incorrect or even racist to suggest otherwise. Yet, as I have shown, when people are afraid to ask questions about the causes of inequalities, they often fall back on explanations that blame the behaviors of the disenfranchised. Ignoring these questions does not make them go away. Silence allows ideas about poverty and blame to linger in the realm of unspoken hegemony.

Let me pause, then, to give some evidence to support the claim that this narrative of laziness as a cause of poverty is not just harmful, but unfounded.

## Reason 1: They are Working Hard, but the Myth Keeps That Work Invisible

Often when I fly into South Africa and arrive in Johannesburg, I spend a night or two with a Zulu friend who works as a prestigious lawyer. On one visit, she had just taken in a foster child, was housing a niece, and also financially supported countless extended family members across the country. She said of black South Africans, "We're lazy people. We are. We're not go-getters." But then, much like Jabu and the graduate student when they realized that this did not actually describe themselves or many others, this woman added significantly, "But there's a whole lot more that plays into it."

Among that "whole lot more" were all the ways that overcoming racial prejudice is itself hard work. This lawyer friend was the only black woman in many of her university courses. The effort necessary for minoritized people to overcome microaggressions and stereotype threats is often invisible to people in the majority. In addition, the basic tasks of life are harder in places that are disproportionately inhabited by poorer people. Public transportation eats up a huge amount of time. From the rural home where I lived, there was no public transportation at all. About four times a day, public buses passed on the main road, a grueling kilometer uphill walk from my home, a walk that farm and domestic workers on my road made daily. They would wait up to an hour for the bus to be sure not to miss it. If they got lucky, they might catch a ride in a passing car. In Mpophomeni, some streets had running water only a few hours a day in the middle of the night, so some people hauled water from friends or woke up in the dark every night to fill barrels. Many found ways to live on incredibly tight budgets by cooking slow meals from scratch, waiting in long lines on sale days, and carrying home heavy sacks of lower-priced bulk food when money was available.

Further, blackness and whiteness are socially constructed sets of ideas that have spatial elements. That is, certain spaces are imagined as black and others as white, and these separate spaces are imagined to have different characteristics. Among those characteristics are their relationships to work: white spaces are imagined as spaces where work happens, and black spaces are not. Thus, not only are black people seen as nonworkers; their very communities are imagined as nonworking. These spatial imaginaries are hegemonic among both black and white people. As George Lipsitz has argued, one way to trace antiblackness and its effects across a society is to observe the ways in which white spaces and black spaces are differently imagined. He writes, "Not all whites endorse the white spatial imaginary, and some Blacks embrace it and profit from it. Yet every white person benefits from the association of white places with privilege, from the neighborhood race effects that create unequal and unjust geographies of opportunity."[57]

Jabu was not alone when she overlooked activities in black spaces as if they were not real work. Often in interviews when I asked people to list their job experience, it seemed not to occur to them to report moneymaking activities happening in the township. One woman told me she had no work, then later happened to mention buying wholesale clothes in Durban and selling them in her neighborhood. "It's just a little business," she said, and then almost defensively she added, "I'm not too keen on it, but just doing anything right now." The same thing happened during one job-readiness training session when attendees were told to list on their résumés child care and other services they had offered in the township. Many young people sat with their papers blank, unable to think of any such activities in the context of writing a résumé for formal employment, even though I knew that several regularly offered neighbors this kind of help. These activities, while entrepreneurial and at times lucrative, took place in a spatial realm distinct from career.[58]

This invisibility of township work was similar to the contested distinction mentioned earlier between women's work with children at home and supposedly real work. By imagining domestic or gendered activities as nonwork, such activities can become uncompensated, unrecognized, low-status, and uncounted in statistical measures. Similarly, work in the township was often seen as not real work. One young black man who taught computer trainings in Mpophomeni pointed this out, saying that people running small businesses in townships "don't think it's work," and so they "don't take it to another level." In his assessment, not believing they ran real businesses also prevented people from taking their work seriously enough to expand it. "They just doing it, maybe you know for just for living, to make a living for that day." Evidence was everywhere of people working hard in housework, social relationships, jobs and entrepreneurship, but the laziness myth blinded people from seeing the pattern in that evidence.[59]

## Reason 2: The Causes of Unemployment and Poverty Are Systemic, but the Myth Keeps Those Reasons Invisible

Along with the evidence that Zulu people do in fact work hard, there are more causes for poverty and unemployment than the laziness myth tells us about. Among the deepest harms done by this narrative is that it hides what the Johannesburg lawyer called the "whole lot more that plays into it." As I explained in the opening chapter of this book and will continue to show in future chapters, the causes of unemployment in South Africa are complex and systemic. Companies can find cheaper labor in other countries, more technology is becoming available to replace human jobs, the government has failed to reliably provide necessary infrastructure like electricity, and the South African public educational system is among the most unequal and ineffective in the world. The relocation of black people under apartheid continues to distance them from places of employment and make job searches insurmountably costly, and staying employed often requires the money and opportunity to rent a separate home away from one's family. Under apartheid, black people were forbidden to run businesses, so white and Indian business owners cornered the markets and set up networks to retain market privileges today.[60] Black people are excluded from white social networks and viewed without the same level of trust that white people view each other, making job searches vastly more difficult than for white people.[61] These structures and imaginaries reveal the causes of poverty that the laziness myth disguises.

## Reason 3: Seemingly Lazy Behaviors Have Causes Other Than Laziness

Employers see the evidence that Zulu people do sometimes frown while they work, come to work late, or miss work without calling in ahead of time. This evidence, though, could support other possible explanations besides the laziness myth. Indeed, when white people behave in the same ways, their behavior is more likely to be explained as the result of an individual's poor choices or life circumstances than as a flaw across their racial or ethnic group.[62] In investigating causes of so-called lazy behaviors, I found that the reasons black people behaved in these ways usually had very little to do with disdain for hard work and much more to do with the social setting in which they worked.

Some behaviors of Zulu people had become associated with laziness because white people had refused to understand or appreciate aspects of Zulu culture, expecting Zulu people to assimilate to white culture rather than a mutual bending to include the cultural expectations of each other. For example, Zulu people often consider direct eye contact to be a signal of confrontation and disrespect when speaking to people of higher social rank or age. Zulu children learn from a young age not to look their superiors in the eye—to do so would be an insult and a sign of disrespect. Many people had also been taught that looking white employers in the eye was what white people expected, but found it a hard habit to break. Similarly, for Zulu women, walking slowly can be a sign of maturity and dignity, as well as a way to preserve energy, whereas white South Africans read slower movement as a lack of commitment to work. Smiling as well has different meanings in Zulu and white cultural contexts. Several Zulu women told me that they disliked being told by white people to smile. They said they preferred to smile only when they really meant it.

At other times, behaviors that seem like laziness were outright refusals to conform to white-privileging structures. For example, frowning could be more than a difference in custom, it could also be a means of exercising some personal control in jobs that demanded a great deal of conformity. As anthropologists have pointed out, many low-status service jobs demand that workers, in addition to their physical job duties, perform "emotion work" by performing outward expressions of emotions like happiness or concern.[63] Frowning meant refusing to do emotion work in addition to other duties demanded by employers. Frowning is one of countless examples of small and large refusals that black South Africans have used to resist and subvert the waged labor system. The sociologist Franco Barchiesi has traced how across history such refusals were often met with increased legal and cultural pressure to keep black people laboring in low-wage work.[64] James C. Scott, an anthropologist who studied employers and employees in Malaysia, used the term "weapons of the weak" to describe behaviors that people low in a hierarchy have used to push back against people in power, especially when they saw little hope of achieving any complete overthrow of those in power.[65] Weapons of the weak include gestures that belittle the dignity of the employer, like not giving polite greetings. They also include subtle ways of impeding the success of companies or people in power, like working slowly, coming to work late, going home early, or only working when the boss is watching. For people who had little choice but to submit to a racially discriminatory and extractive labor system, those behaviors expressed some pent-up resistance. But to employers, those behaviors looked a lot like laziness.

## Refuting the Myth

To Jabu and her father, not working "a day in his life" meant not working in white spaces. That refusal to work on white terms was what she respected, not some unwillingness to earn a living.[66] As she went on to show, he did earn a living, and did so in ways that gained the respect of his community and family. Recall that hegemony is threatened by its own inherent inaccuracies. Jabu's father's path confounds the laziness myth by challenging its inaccuracies in two ways. First, her account challenges the hegemonic assumption that black people (especially those not in the white-dominated waged labor system) intentionally and immorally avoid hard work. As she put it, he was working hard even though it may have been invisible to many: "You don't know how hard your parents are working, up until you actually stay at home with them." Second, the hegemonic laziness myth was inaccurate in its assumption that working in white spaces offers the single path to a better life. In Jabu's assessment, her father's life was well lived by both financial and social standards—not just because he made money, but because of *how* he made his money. Her father's older age, limited English abilities, township schooling, and black skin would earn him little respect in the white-dominated world of work. But in the black space of the township, he was widely respected as an older leader with diverse skills. He hired other employees and exercised considerable influence in the community.

In the course of our conversation, Jabu revealed both how difficult it is to see beyond hegemony, and also that it is possible. As the months passed and I spent hours sitting in living rooms and kitchens and on front stoops listening to people in Mpophomeni, I experienced what Jabu called "actually staying at home" with people and seeing how hard they were working. I saw the difference between the assumed narratives about these people and their real-life experiences. And I saw reasons that, for many of them, time in the township was closer to the good life than time in the jobs they could get.

The laziness myth exercises systemic violence against people, causing psychological, financial, and physical harm. My argument throughout this book is that to expose the hegemony of the laziness myth, we need to see the injustices causing the poverty and other life outcomes attributed to laziness, as well as listen to alternative narratives that people use to chart a path to the good life. In the next chapter, we'll see how relying on the laziness myth has left employers without feasible explanations for their workers' behavior. When workers made decisions according to narratives other than the laziness narrative, employers responded with confusion and frustration. Their antiblack assumptions and frustrations combined with the economic structural challenges of a globalizing economy to lead them into decisions that ultimately counteract the nation's oft-stated goal of creating more jobs.

2

# "YOU CAN'T UNDERSTAND IT"

Employers' Perspectives of the Unemployed

South Africans knew they were facing an unemployment problem: jobs were too few, qualifications for higher-paid jobs were too hard to get, and many people worked at wages that were barely enough for survival. Before we turn in the next few chapters to the question of how unemployed people and low-wage laborers dealt with these challenges, in this chapter we'll see that employers also saw themselves as facing employment problems. They were also exasperated. Many employers voiced their desire to improve the lives of their employees, but they found themselves unsure of how to do so and stymied by various challenges. Amid corporate conglomerations, global competition, and labor legislation, they felt their profits were squeezed and their interactions with employees restricted. In this chapter we'll see the ways that employers were also constrained—by social structures beyond their control as well as by their own narratives.

Nearly every white employer I spoke with voiced a complaint that they couldn't understand their workers' behavior. Many were perplexed and dismayed when workers dragged their feet on the job or when unemployed people seemed uninterested in employment. Many employers were eager to meet with me and thanked me profusely for looking into problems for which they deeply wanted solutions. They wanted to know what I could discover about the behavior of unemployed and low-waged laborers. They reminded me to share my findings with them, and when I sent them my first articles and drafts based on this research, several gave me hearty thanks and told me about ways they used those articles in meetings with employees and managers. On top of the economic challenges facing their companies, they wrestled with the challenge of how to make

55

sense of their employees. And when they failed to understand the behaviors of workers, sometimes they made choices that perpetuated the very problems they spoke about wanting to help solve.

In the final visit I made to South Africa before completing this book in 2019, I sat in a living room with the white couple from whom my family had rented a place to live in 2014–2015. We talked about the ongoing realities of racial segregation and inequality in South Africa. They had often talked with me about their intentions to use their white privileges well. They paid higher wages to their housekeeper than many employers did, and provided additional benefits like paying for a surgery for their housekeeper's son. They had been foster parents and planned to adopt a black child in the coming year. But they also admitted that employment, charity, and adoption were feeble solutions to deeper societal problems. As we waited for dinner to finish cooking, the woman leaned forward from her seat on the sofa and asked earnestly, "What could they *do*?"

In the conversation that followed, I told her that white South Africans, like people anywhere, have a limited social imaginary—a set of ideas, meanings, and actions that seem possible. If she were to hear a loud flapping sound coming from the sky, she might look outside expecting to see a helicopter, but not a dragon. This was because dragons flying past her home were beyond her imagination. Similarly, the problem she had bumped into was that the white social imaginary offered only limited solutions to racial segregation and inequality. In white South Africans' shared picture of how the world worked, black behavior would conform to the laziness narrative, and socioeconomic systems would follow white privilege and market capitalism. The limitations of these ideas ultimately exacerbated employment problems across the country, harming black people especially, but also producing undesired results for white employers.

My intention here is to humanize and complicate employers, avoiding painting them as clownishly racist, homogeneous, or explicable merely through the lens of their race. As I prepared to conduct this research, I found myself in several conversations with other researchers about whether to focus entirely on the lives of black South Africans or to also include ethnography of employers. In the end, I decided that to give a full picture of the society, it was necessary to attempt to portray the perspectives of white employers.[1] Since the 1980s, anthropologists including Sherry Ortner have noted that the Marxian roots of our discipline have sometimes led anthropologists to give strictly binary pictures of power, as if there are those in power who are motivated merely by retaining their power, and those without power suffering unmitigated oppression and constraint.[2] I hold instead that power is never simply binary. Power is threaded throughout society in complex and overlapping layers, such that each person exercises certain forms of agency and power, but is also constrained by certain societal limitations. These constraints are by no means equally distributed across society, but neither is any-one entirely free of constraints. The fact that whiteness exercises power does not mean that white people have unlimited powers, or that all their decisions are explicable merely through the lens of race. My intention is not to demonize white people or suggest that whiteness explains all that happens in a society, but neither is it to excuse antiblack racism and systems of whiteness that have exerted power and violence upon others. As anthropologists have long held, to document the complex social milieu of a group of people is not the same as to sympathize with them, but it is an act of understanding and bestowing dignity that all humans deserve, whether they have greater or lesser power in a society. And it is, for white South Africans like my former landlord, a start to answering the question: What could they do?

## An Employee Disciplinary Hearing

Joyce sat at the end of a long table with papers spread out in front of her. She flipped through pages, jotting down notes and occasionally glancing up as Greg, the human relations manager for a company of several hundred employees, delivered his statement. Joyce's job was to oversee the disciplinary hearing for employees that Greg was considering dismissing.

"We had hoped that by giving him a second chance he would prove to be a hard worker," Greg read. "But he has clearly broken the relationship with the company to the point that it cannot continue." He pulled out papers from a manila folder, checking notes as he read off the employee's offenses: "Fifteen days of work missed without notifying the company. . . . Repeated warnings unheeded. . . . A letter was hand-delivered to his house as a final warning." Greg read the relevant company policies: "Absence notice must be given not later than the first day of absence . . . three days without notification will be deemed to be deserted . . . cause for termination." His flat voice conveyed no hint of sarcasm or scolding, just an attention to procedural detail. He seemed tired already at ten-thirty in the morning. The three disciplinary hearings scheduled for the day began at 8:30 a.m. and would last until early afternoon. The company handled these hearings only once a month unless an emergency called for an immediate hearing, but the paperwork, preparation, and follow-up would take days more work for Joyce and Greg.

The rest of us at the table listened in silence. Our group included Richard, the employee in question; Fikile, a union representative serving as translator; John, a manager called in to testify; and me. As South African employers and their employees grapple with the growing complexity of legislation and bureaucracy and the rising economic stakes of mediating disciplinary situations like this one, they increasingly turn to professional labor consultants like Joyce. On this day, Greg's company had hired her, but employees could also hire consultants for company hearings or in court cases contesting decisions like this one. Joyce wrote notes on forms as she led the various participants through the steps of the hearing: detailed questioning of the employee, testimonies from coworkers and managers like John, a statement from Greg, and a time for Joyce's own private deliberation.

When earlier in the hearing Richard, the young male employee defendant, had answered a question with his hand in front of his mouth, Joyce had interrupted to scold him for speaking too quietly. Now as Greg finished his statement, Joyce turned to the defendant. "What are you expecting today?"

"Another chance." He was covering his mouth again.

"Do you want me to freak out right here at the table?" Joyce placed both hands on the table. Her voice was tense. "This *was* your last chance. The only reason you got another chance after your final warning was your hard work, not your begging. If the company gave second chances with every employee, it's just going to reduce this company to a circus." After a final summary statement, she sent the defendant and managers out of the room while she tidied her notes and formulated her recommendation—dismissal from the company.

The purpose of the careful procedures of these hearings, from the company's standpoint, was to cover their legal bases. South African employees who believe they have been unfairly dismissed or disciplined can appeal through the government's Commission for Conciliation, Mediation and Arbitration (the CCMA). The CCMA was founded in the Labor Relations Act of 1995 in the first year of Nelson Mandela's presidency, for the purpose of promoting labor relations that were less adversarial and more just. Labor laws have continued to evolve since, and employers have learned that court cases with the CCMA can be very costly, especially if the court decision includes covering employee back pay or rehiring an employee. For many employers, the CCMA is a looming threat that compels painstaking bureaucratic detail. Entire books have been written on "How to win at the CCMA." One such book tells employers, "You can't stop an employee from referring a dispute—you just need to make sure you are prepared to defend your position vigorously at the CCMA!" In an attempt at dry humor, the book explains, "Remember the meaning of conciliation? You and Joe Soap are supposed to bury the hatchet, love each other and go your separate ways so that he can go and buy his second-hand motor vehicle, with your hard-earned money!"[3] The same book offers signs to print and post in the workplace. One shows a picture of a person sleeping under a tree in a work hat and reminds workers of a list of unacceptable workplace behaviors that include dishonesty, absence without leave, damage to property, excessive demonstration of political ideology, and poor timekeeping.

In the next hearing of the day, a young woman named Precious faced charges of repeated absences without leave. As Precious explained her defense, Joyce broke in with questions about the reasons for her absences. Precious grew quieter with each question, and Joyce became increasingly frustrated. Fikile translated Precious's long explanation of missing two days of work to bring her sick daughter home from school, schedule a doctor's appointment, and bring the girl to the doctor, all without her own vehicle. When she finished, Joyce said loudly to the interpreter, "Can she hear properly?" Fikile nodded. "Then I need her to listen properly to me." Joyce delivered a stern warning that Precious could lose her job over this. "She needs to pay attention. She can't slip into a sulk. She steadfastly refuses to answer my questions."

Fikile passed along a softer and shorter warning in isiZulu to Precious.

Joyce raised her hands and turned to Greg as if looking for sympathy, then turned back to the defendant, "What was the sickness?"

Precious stared at the table in front of her in humiliation and murmured in English, "runny tummy."

Joyce made a note of the answer and mumbled, "She consistently doesn't answer my questions." Wrapping up the evidence for this hearing, Joyce listed off the offenses and the company's meticulously documented procedures: four expired warnings, two active ones including a final written warning, all for sicknesses without proper notification for length of absence, under four different managers. "She must have been dropped on her head as a baby," Joyce said to Fikile with a shrug. Fikile glared back without translating. Joyce went on as if she didn't expect her to.

Throughout the hearings, Fikile was translating accurately but using the third person, which added to the sense that the defendants were being talked about without being present in the room. At times Fikile and a defendant broke off into a brief conversation to clarify something one of the English-speakers in the room had said. After the hearings, Fikile would return to her own job among the lowest-wage employees in the company. In being here, she walked a line between building trust among the employees who had elected her as their union representative, and the trust of the managers who had chosen her to translate. Trust with fellow employees might mean the difference between respect or scathing complaints in her daily interactions; trust with employers might mean the difference between a promotion or another year at low pay. During one break when no defendant was in the room, Fikile turned to Greg and in a joking tone pointed out that Joyce, Greg, John, and I had all been served coffee or tea when we came in. She had not. Her direct and casual rapport with Greg drew a laugh, and a cup of tea, but the fact lingered unaddressed that it had not occurred to the white people in the room that the one black woman present had not been offered the same benefits.

"You're becoming very good at reading this." Greg changed the subject, keeping the joking tone as he gestured to the section on absenteeism that Fikile had read for the previous defendant. Two of the three hearings would focus on missed days of work. Greg and Joyce mentioned multiple times that these were the most common and most irritating offenses they had to deal with every month.

In between the second and third hearings, Fikile stepped out, leaving only white people in the room: Joyce, Greg, me, and John the manager who had come in to testify. They asked how my research was going and started talking about their thoughts on unemployment. "Family planning is a problem," John said. "They're always having kids." He told a story of an employee who kicked a woman in the head at work and then begged to be kept on because he had two kids. He followed that with the story of a man who was having two kids from different mothers born on the same weekend.

Protocol for the disciplinary hearings included asking each person at the end of the hearing how many people they support, and today's defendants supported four, six, and nine people. I had assumed that this question was designed to give the consultant reason to show leniency in her decision, but this conversation made me wonder if it had the opposite effect of frustrating the consultants. Their comments seemed to paint reproduction as part of the unemployment problem, as if people with fewer children made better employees because they had fewer commitments outside of work. They also exemplified what Shellee Cohen calls *stratified reproduction,* the prejudiced practice of holding people of differing social status to different standards regarding reproduction.[4] "They complain they're supporting nine kids," Joyce said. "They're still so traditional. It's going to take hundreds of years for these people to become sophisticated. To evolve. But it's their culture to go walkabout." The phrase "go walkabout," which I had heard at other times from South African employers, originated among white Australian employers as they mocked the supposed inherent cultural tendency of Aboriginal employees to skip work for spiritual journeys or other unexcused reasons.[5] It conjured images of wandering aimlessly for personal gain—images that seemed to have little in common with defendants' explanations of leaving work for funerals and their children's doctor visits.

John picked up the strand of conversation. "Lots of things are their culture." He described another example of a "brilliant guy" who didn't come to work for a week and didn't call the company. "You can't understand it."

"None of us understands it, and we never will because it's so basic." Joyce sounded exasperated.

"They hobble themselves," John added.

A few minutes later, John and Greg stepped out of the room, leaving Joyce and me alone together. I commented that these hearings must take a lot of time and resources. She looked me in the eye suddenly and said in a low voice, "Look, companies make a lot of money off the sweat of their backs. Make no mistake about it. And you have to factor that in. This is the price they pay."

I listened without responding. Then she leaned back and shrugged. "But you know, it's a free enterprise system. They can be creative and start their own business. No one's forcing them to work here. You shouldn't have to incentivize people to work properly. You are buying their time."

## Employers Seeing Something Wrong

In that little moment of conversation, Joyce did two things that emerged as a common pattern among employers. On the one hand, she admitted that something was not right in the relationships constructed between employers and employees. Companies are "making a lot of money off the sweat of their backs," and "this is the price they pay." On the other hand, she shifted responsibility away from employers by focusing on the employees, specifically their supposed faults of not working rightly or hard enough: "You shouldn't have to incentivize people to work properly." In interviews and interactions with employers, I was often struck by white employers' awareness that political and economic systems had long exploited black laborers, coupled with their exasperation that their efforts to improve black people's lives through employment did not seem to work. Employers saw that there were problems in their workplaces, but the dominant laziness narrative left them assuming that those problems stemmed from black laborers' behaviors at work.

As I examine employers' constraints and concerns in this chapter, I'll ask readers to consider some options for how to deal with complicated social problems like these. For employers, one way to deal with their exasperation would be to question what factors in the history and social structures of South Africa produced their employment problems. Another way to respond, which crept into the conversation between Joyce and the managers, was to shift the blame to employees and their culture. Like the comment from John, the manager at the disciplinary hearing—"Lots of things are their culture"—much of the employers' interest in my research was built on the assumption that something about the Zulu culture of employees must be causing employment troubles. At the same time, they assumed racial and cultural differences were an impenetrable wall, closed to mutual understanding: "You can't understand it." As we begin to trace out the structural challenges facing employees and employers, then, we'll consider what happens when people assume that the culture of a subgroup in society bears the responsibility for perceived problems. Ultimately, we need an approach that recognizes the influence of socioeconomic structures as well as the complexity of culture in order to avoid simplistically blaming culture for social ills.

In this book, I follow a two-pronged approach that social scientists have long used to explain social problems. It involves simultaneously recognizing the socio-economic structures shaping those problems, and the conflicting cultural explanations that people fall back on to make sense of those problems.[6] As we will see, the laziness myth offered people one cultural explanation for social problems, but it was marked by strategic misunderstandings that ultimately reinforced those problems.

Often when South African employers talked about overarching problems in South Africa's employment situation, they framed the problem using the sentence, *the cost of labor per unit of production is too high*. With this economics-based explanation, they pointed to two types of problems that they believed came together to make a bigger problem. First, costs of labor seemed to be rising. These costs included both government-mandated wage increases and other labor-related costs like disciplinary hearings. Second, employers perceived a problem of low productivity. They believed laborers were not working diligently, quickly, efficiently, or intelligently enough. With both of these constraints, we'll see that they directed their frustration sometimes at social structures squeezing them from beyond their companies, and sometimes to their own employees and the supposed culture of those employees.

## Employer Challenges: Squeezed in Supply Chains

South Africa had implemented laws between 1994 and 2014 to increase minimum wages in many industries by as much as 200 percent. Under South Africa's new constitution, minimum wages in many industries would be set by a government committee, the Employment Conditions Commission (ECC), which has the mandate to raise wages only to a point that will not cause job losses. The question of what that point may be—How high could wages go without causing employers to cut employees?—had no simple answer.

Several of the employers I spoke with had doubled their wages within the preceding three years. A poultry farmer named Scott increased wages from 60 rand per day to 114 rand ($6.00–$11.40), and a forestry manager named Adrian raised wages from 60 to 150 rand ($6–$15). Scott and Adrian both stressed that these changes were long overdue and necessary for the sake of people earning a livable wage. Both had doubts, however, about whether the net effects of enforced minimum wage increases benefited the broader population in the long run. Adrian's forestry company had laid off nearly 10 percent of its employees in the years since the wage increase. "In my opinion they kicked it up too much," Adrian said of the wage increase. He figured that while individual employees were earning more per person, companies were making up the cost by hiring fewer people to the effect that total wages per family were coming out about the same. From the employer side, he said, "It pushed us into modernization," and by "modernization," he meant replacing manual jobs with machinery. "Any machine that can replace a human, you use it," he said. "You don't worry about the cost now, because they expect the minimum wage will keep on increasing." In his opinion, the minimum wage had the opposite effect of its intention, making life harder not better in the communities his workers lived in. Likewise, Scott was introducing machinery in his poultry operation that reduced the number of employees he needed. "A lot of industry in this country is set up to employ people, but it won't be as things change in the direction they're going," he said frankly. Government and union talks were underway to double the farming minimum wage again, and he could not imagine how farmers would cope.

What tended to trouble employers about wage increases was not so much that employees earned more, it was that they—especially employers low on the supply chain—bore costs beyond their fair share and out of their control. Their frustration on this count was not toward the workers below them, but toward the powers above them. They were well aware that some players in the supply chain had greater power than others over whether or not to bear costs and risks. Scott explained wage increases from his perspective: "The government implemented the change, and the supermarkets said [to farmers,] 'That's your problem.'"

I met with Scott in his office, a room just off the kitchen in his own home. While we chatted, I could hear his wife talking with the family housekeeper, who was laundering the red cotton uniforms that every employee wore when they entered the poultry barns. Scott ran the business like a family farm. Employees walked in and out of his kitchen, and he knew many of their family members by name, as they did of his family. Many of his business decisions were not made by Scott and his family, though. Like nearly every farmer in South Africa's chicken industry, Scott contracted with one of only four chicken meat corporations that controlled the vast majority of the country's poultry production. His chickens' eggs, which would be hatched and raised at other farms for meat production, would contribute to the 1.5 million birds reaching supermarket shelves every week from the company he contracted with. Adrian, the forestry company manager, worked in a similar outsourcing relationship with one of the two forestry giants in South Africa. "Basically we handle all the wage-earning duties," Adrian explained. The big companies owned the land, while Adrian and his company hired, trained, and supervised the people who grew and harvested the trees on that land. In this arrangement, the subcontracting companies who managed labor had little control over their profit margins.

Scott searched for a phrase to describe the situation, "That thing—economy of scale. It's such a big thing in our lives nowadays. Most farms are three to five times my size." As a farmer of fewer than forty thousand birds, his farm was small for the industry. "In farming today, it's all about small profit on big turnover. The corporate guy turning a million chickens per week only needs to make a couple of cents per chicken." Small companies could not compete with the prices these giant companies could offer to supermarkets. Scott listed off the names of farmers he knew whose companies had once been considered big at a provincial level but had since gone bankrupt or taken his route of contracting with these ever-bigger companies.

Working under the central ownership of the farming corporation kept his farm alive, but barely. "It's all very nice having the contract [with a larger company], but they control everything, and they have the money. You know what the Golden Rule is?" he asked rhetorically, and I assumed he meant the biblical injunction to love your neighbor as yourself. He answered cynically, "He who has the gold makes the rules."

By way of example, Scott described a farming friend who had invested millions of rand into a vegetable packing plant with refrigerated buildings and more than fifty employees. A well-known supermarket chain rescinded their agreement to purchase that farmer's vegetables, and the farm failed, sending 75 percent of its employees back home unemployed. "Supermarkets make it so onerous about what they'll take," he said. "The industries we support are extremely particular about what they'll buy and how it's produced." It struck me that Scott described himself as supporting the corporation, not the other way around. I noticed many Zulu employees spoke of themselves similarly, as supporting people they worked under. The corporations and employers who did the hiring and managing often saw the relationship in the opposite direction. A corporate investor in the food industry once proudly told me he supported three entrepreneurial farmers, and the leaders of one of the largest forestry companies in the country spoke at length about the support role they played for the smaller contractors who managed their labor and operations on the ground. To middle-level employers, however, as to many employees, the relationship felt more like constraint from above than support.

Economists and labor consultants I met with confirmed that, in South Africa, the agricultural sector had little room to raise wages because their profits were squeezed by national chain grocery stores and large retailers. South Africa's small number of grocery companies and chicken meat companies purchase from vast numbers of farmers. Grocery stores can command a larger share of the profits per unit because they form what economists call a bottleneck or an oligopsony—a place in the supply chain where many producers and many customers have to funnel goods between just a few competing middle-level traders. Farmers selling their goods to an oligopsony have few alternative buyers, allowing those few buyers to control the market and command lower prices from farmers. Farmers who don't like the price a major grocery store chain offers can't easily take their produce elsewhere, and their only feasible short-term option is to let produce rot.[7] Farmers in South Africa (as in the United States and much of the world) typically receive only about 10–20 percent of total profits earned as a product changes hands up the supply chain until it arrives at a final customer. For lower-level suppliers in the supply chain, like Scott and Adrian, this meant the costs of higher wages squeezed their own profits, not the profits of their buyers.

Industrial farmers carry a heavy load of debt and expensive assets, but have very narrow profit margins. That adds up to high risk. Oligopsony buyers with gold also made rules that transferred risk downward toward farmers like Scott and Adrian. "If something goes wrong, it implodes very quickly," Scott said. "All of us are about thirty days from disaster." He gestured toward his home, his car, the sheds, saying he might look settled, but if he didn't get paid for just one month, it could all go. The same, he said heavily, holds for his staff. If his farm were to fold, how would they eat? He described an incident when he missed one of the several vaccinations carefully scheduled over the life of birds. Eleven months later, sickness broke out among chicks hatched from his eggs on other farms. Birds had to be culled by the hundreds of thousands. A major buyer opened a million-rand lawsuit and stopped taking his eggs for a time. Scott paid the damages by taking on debts that would take him years to repay. His face was sober as he described making that decision, knowing the risks he was balancing not only for his own family but also for his employees' families.

Because the future of his company could crumble with one mistake as small as a mis-scheduled vaccination, Scott knew he needed reliable employees. With his wage budget already expanding by 50 percent or more in some years due to government-mandated minimum wage increases, and his buyers taking on little of those costs, he faced the predicament of needing to find workers with skills beyond their pay grade. "It's no longer all you got to be able to do is pick up an egg and put it in a box." I spent a day shadowing workers you'll meet later in this book. I met employees who sorted birds by weight calculated to several decimal places, others who could walk through a sea of white chickens and spot an unhealthy bird, and those who explained the importance of bacteria counts. He needed employees with high school or even higher education, but in his industry, he could barely pay them twelve dollars a day. "We're battling to find the trainable people," Scott said. "It means we're going to have to pay a better salary to that person. I'm just gonna have to make a plan. It's a serious challenge."

The profits of farmers like Scott were further pressed by factors even beyond the control of the massive meat companies and the grocery stores buying their goods. The national poultry industry in South Africa has recently locked horns with the powerfully lobbied poultry industry in the United States. In 2013 South Africa charged the United States with dumping below-market-priced chicken into their market. Tension over tariff negotiations between the two countries heightened again during the months I knew Scott. The United States began threatening to remove South Africa from its African Growth and Opportunity Act (AGOA), which allows South Africa to sell certain products to the United States tariff-free. When the clash resolved, it was clear who made the rules and who held the gold. Incurring exclusion from AGOA was too high a price for South Africa to pay, and so the South African government set generous quotas for poultry imported from the United States. As the South African minister of trade readily admitted, the quota "will place the United States as a very prominent importer, and . . . it will have an impact on local production." In a spin that portrayed the South African poultry industry as willingly offering a noble sacrifice, the minister announced, "It's important to say that the South African Poultry Association, which had nothing to gain, came to the party and was a participant in this negotiation and played a patriotic role in terms of looking to the bigger national interest and making a concession."[8]

The United States bolstered its image in the affair by broadcasting the opportunities they made for farmers to travel to the United States for training. This rhetoric played into the image of Africa as intellectually behind and in need of someone to "teach a man to fish," skirting the issue of fairness in the market in which such fish could ultimately be sold. Observing the efficiency of Scott's farm, I could not imagine him gaining much from a training trip to the United States, even if he could somehow find the time to travel. Such training would offer no solution to the impossibility of competing with ever-lower international prices. The United States could afford to export cheap chicken while paying wages that vastly exceeded South African wages because the US government subsidizes the corn and soy that feed the chickens, and because it makes surplus-removal purchases when the supply of chicken meat exceeds demand. Surplus poultry from the United States, Europe, and Brazil has been dumped abroad—that is, sold for below-market prices in other countries including South Africa.[9] By artificially dropping the supply in the United States and boosting it in South Africa, prices in the United States stay high enough for farmers to stay viable while prices in

South Africa drop below any farmer's production costs. Three years after South Africa lost the negotiations to stop the US chicken-dumping practice, chicken producers in Scott's province of KwaZulu-Natal were laying off employees by the thousands.[10] "It doesn't matter how good you are, you're not gonna cope," Scott predicted when I met with him in 2014.

Scott knew his business could go under with a shift in any of the many economic factors that were out of his control, but paradoxically one of his few options for managing those risks was to take on still more debt for his farm. His company encouraged farmers his size to double up, meaning build more sheds, take on about ten million more rand of debt, and hire about ten to twenty more people. This amounted to close to a million rand of investment per new job created, a proportion that did not bode well for job creation prospects. Scott said maybe he would take that route if he were younger, but not now. For him, the decision was not about profit, it was about how much risk and stress he could take, and he had more than enough already. "I never really enjoyed poultry in the first place," he admitted. "It wasn't really my passion. But I had to realize that I had to do what was necessary, not just what I loved." After his early years struggling financially in other kinds of farming, he followed other farmers' advice to go into selling eggs because it offered a more steady cash flow than seasonal operations like grain, hogs, or cattle. "The wise decision is not necessarily the easy decision."

## Relational Fatigue

When employers talked about low productivity, they pointed in part to the challenges from above that we have just seen: the challenge of paying more for labor when they were offered nonnegotiable prices for their products because of corporate conglomerations, oligopsony distributors, and international trade disadvantages. Another piece of their frustration, though, was the challenge of having to coerce low-paid workers to produce more for less. Like the statement Greg the manager made in the disciplinary hearing, they had hoped that by giving employees a chance they would prove to be hard workers, but clearly the relationship between employers and employees "is broken." Scott and Adrian saw their profit margins and risks determined by companies higher on the supply chain, but they were the ones who had to look employees in the eye and interact with them daily. Such employers worked alongside some of the country's lowest-paid workers, knowing that their employees deserved better but not knowing how to give them more. When their employees expressed dissatisfaction with working conditions, these were the people who bore the emotional weight of responding. Many employers said they wanted fewer employees not because it would save them money, but because of the relational fatigue of dealing with these pressures.

Every employer knew that workers would not always passively accept the low wages and benefits that trickled down to their end of the supply chain. Scott had never had a strike on his property, and the workers I talked to at his farm seemed satisfied with him and their jobs. But even with relatively little labor conflict, Scott described the emotional drain of trying to create an environment where workers would contribute positive energy to the workplace. He knew that they were likely to see the job as little more than a way to put food on the table, a transaction they were trapped into by dire necessity.

A desire to create better lives for their employees despite limited budgets drove some employers to creative efforts intended to help employees. Scott had volunteered with more than one local employment-training program, and he recounted many attempts to build good relationships with staff. He had hosted employee braais (South African barbecues), taken employees and their families to a soccer game, invited pastors to lead church services on site, and taken staff to an all-you-can-eat meal at a casino. Many of the stories ended in discouragement. "I'm battling with how I interact with staff on a social level without alcohol," he said. "They won't come if there's no alcohol, but when there's alcohol they get drunk and attack each other." He recounted a change he made to stagger staff bonuses across the year because staff would all disappear on what he feared were partly drinking sprees for three to four days after the bonus. In another attempt to help, he paid into a retirement savings plan for staff. Staff members kept their accounts only just until the minimum time had passed so that they could take out the lump sum of their savings. The penalty for early withdrawal from the savings plan defaulted all the money he had contributed for them. He described these things matter-of-factly: the loss of thousands of rand in pension contributions, the drunken brawls, his intentions to help his staff somehow. He was well aware of the inequalities that ran through his farm, the chicken industry, the country, and the world, but he did not know how to solve them. On the one hand, market forces constrained the wages and benefits he could pay workers. On the other, he lived within a society marked by antiblackness where everyone he knew had seen few examples of equitable relationships between black and white people.

Disciplinary hearings like the one I described earlier played out month after month in companies across the country. Nearly every employee I spoke with offered stories of employees being let go for failing to come in on time, failing to notify managers of absences, stealing from the company, or expending minimal effort. The offenses that bothered employers were often difficult to quantify, like mumbling or spending too much time on a task. Such complaints rarely constituted grounds for firing. Employers complained bitterly about staff who had refused to increase their productivity despite any incentive schemes they tried.

One survey in the city of Durban (the largest major metropolitan area within two hours of Howick) asked employers for factors constraining job growth in their industries. The employers' most common answers were competition from established firms, slow national economic growth, and high energy costs—all systemic factors beyond their companies. But their fourth most common category of answers had to do with workers. These responses were from employers who said they did not create more jobs because their workers lacked a work ethic, reliability, and a good attitude.[11] Another study conducted by a nonprofit organization interviewing over fifty employers in the Howick/Mpophomeni area found similar results. Employees' personal traits topped employers' lists of concerns, including "good work ethic (willingness to learn, dedication and self-discipline)" (55.7 percent of respondents); "reliability (punctuality, attendance and commitment)" (39.3 percent); and "customer service" (18 percent). Many employers described a need for better employee "attitudes," including eliminating the problematic "entitlement attitude" and building an "ethic of working your way up."[12]

Economists and employers sometimes refer to skills like numeracy, literacy, or the ability to drive a tractor as hard skills. In contrast, soft skills include habits like punctuality and nonverbal communication methods. In the above surveys, employers were far more interested in soft skills than hard skills, the latter coming up in only 16 percent of Howick employers' responses. The very term "soft skills" rather than, say, "style of interpersonal interactions," implies that workers simply lack the training or know-how to behave properly at work. That assumption masks the possibility that workers might have real and logical reasons for their behavior at work. When employers' efforts to train workers in better soft skills failed, they often fell back on explanations like that of the manager at the disciplinary hearing described earlier, who believed that workers just chose to behave badly or had something inherently wrong with their culture or racial group.

Distrust between white employers and Zulu employees was also fueled by the ways that other events across South Africa were being interpreted through an antiblack lens that treated blackness as a threat to the supposed control and competency of whiteness. Conversations among white South Africans often turned to rumors of impending racial and class conflict. In 2014–15, the topics of conversation around town included the news of President Jacob Zuma's misuse of millions of rand on his personal estate, the country's failing public electric company costing businesses across the country millions in monetary losses, and killings and beatings of foreign Africans by Zulu people. Conversations on these topics fueled distrust not only toward the Zulu-led government, but also toward Zulu people in general, including their workers.

The most vehemently pessimistic statements I heard about South African workers came from Willem, the employer mentioned in the previous chapter who hired workers for just three dollars a day. He traced his nation's economic troubles to the low motivation of employees. In the conversation we had in his office, he said that the reasons major business investors were backing out of South Africa included unions wanting more wages for less work, black government leaders who set an example of laziness, and unmotivated workers. "It's not easy to motivate them. And that's why people are reluctant to start new businesses."

His frustration was palpable. From his perspective, people's laziness was hurting his business and him personally. He said black workers had no appreciation for the hard work white people did in the country, and their behavior toward whites caused unhealthy stress among managers. "What country has the highest rate of heart attacks among white people?" he asked rhetorically. "South Africa." (I later found no verification of this statistic). Willem's stress over worker behavior was exacerbated by the fact that he envisioned himself as someone on the "good side." He expected people to be grateful to him for his contribution to employees and the nation. With that mindset, he saw strikes and poor worker performance as belligerent ingratitude and an obstruction to his aim of a better economy.

Willem listed business owners he knew who had left the country out of frustration with workers and thieves. "We get cross," he said, expressing a sentiment I heard from many employers. "We're not scaling up, because we get fed up." Because of problems with workers, he said, "we're not looking at investment opportunities anymore, we're looking at how to get our money out of the country."

Willem's racism was blatant in this conversation, but the embittered and cynical antiblack narrative that portrayed black people as the cause of white people's stresses ran more subtly through many conversations with employers. When most employers talked about the cost of labor, like Willem they were not just talking about wages. They also considered the financial and emotional costs of preventing laborers from seeking rights that were routinely offered to white and upper-level employees. Those costs included hiring labor consultants, offering personnel training to teach employees the value of teamwork, hiring external human relations firms to manage employment contracts, and keeping up to date on the complex and shifting legal rights of employees. Employers put significant time and emotional energy into keeping up to date on labor laws and managing their interactions with employees to avoid lawsuits and much-dreaded strikes. As many research studies on social trust have shown, the level of trust in a society is often underappreciated until it is lost, at which point it can become very expensive to put props in place to hold together distrustful relationships.[13] In South

Africa, the combined emotional costs of relational fatigue and perceived risks of labor unrest, together with financial costs of mitigating those risks often made the difference between hiring laborers or mechanizing.

Unions appeared often in the news while I was in South Africa, and employers sometimes alluded to assumptions that unions were continuing to grow in number and power. Actual numbers of union members in South Africa had risen from 1994 to 1997, but then fell gradually in the following years, and by 2014 the total number of union members in the country was lower than at the end of apartheid.[14] The national percentage of contracts negotiated through unions and bargaining councils was also declining at the time I met Greg and Joyce.[15] These numbers reflected a trend of declining trust in unions by employees, due largely to some heavily publicized failed strikes and corruption in union leadership. But the trends of declining union membership were probably also evidence of the power of employers to temper the effectiveness of unions.[16]

Adrian described the measures his company was taking to move toward mechanization. They had already replaced jobs with machinery by using tractors to break up soil instead of picks and spraying pesticides from airplanes rather hiring people to carry backpack sprayers. They made these changes despite knowing, he said, that these methods were "definitely more expensive than labor."

Greg, the human resources manager in the disciplinary hearing, told me later that his company was also investing in automation that would reduce labor needs even though "cost-wise it is probably cheaper to use labor than automation." Speaking of the company's choice to focus on automation, he said, "Really it depends on labor unrest." In his opinion, South African labor laws were already "the most complex labor law in the world," and recent changes tended toward "aiming to protect the laborer at all costs, not the employer." He gave examples of how his company tried to build positive relationships with laborers but admitted that ultimately the relationship between employer and employee remained "an us against them mentality."

An employer at a large farm put it more bluntly. "The general trend is to automate and employ fewer people, the reason for that being machinery doesn't go on strike, machinery doesn't come to work drunk, machinery doesn't cause problems. I can keep a spare one in the storeroom." He spoke with a hint of sarcasm, but his bitterness was clear, and so were his choices toward hiring fewer people. When I asked this man what makes a good boss, he told me, "Probably not the one I am. I'd like to be more patient, more long-suffering. I think I'm fairly understanding, but I'm pretty intolerant and impatient, and that's what I don't want to be. But it's where I've become because of who I've worked with. It's something I've been forced into in a way, a survival mechanism, looking fierce and mean."

Employers like this farmer described themselves as being pressed into choices they did not like—to be mean bosses, to mechanize rather than hire, to use intermediary companies that distanced employees from company managers, and to hire people on short-term easily revocable contracts. Both in South Africa and globally, there are notable trends toward shorter, more casual, less binding work arrangements.[17] At times, employers took more drastic steps. I heard of three businesses in the Howick area that had decided to stop hiring Zulu employees— one that stopped hiring altogether, and one that hired only immigrants from other African countries. At least two people I met said they had gone so far as to disband a profitable business because of the stress of working with employees, and stories abounded of those who had emigrated from South Africa for related reasons.

"We are not capitalist pigs," said one white woman who started a company selling crafts made of recycled items. She said she had started the company because she was concerned about high unemployment in a township and wanted to help provide living wages. "I'm trying to hang on to my enthusiasm," she said, "but quite honestly I'm tired." After several incidents she described as being betrayed by employees, she had redesigned the company to reduce staff. She was also going to try hiring only Zimbabwean immigrants in the hope that they would make better workers than Zulu South Africans.

## Deteriorating Work Relationships and a Social Imaginary

The growing distrust between employers and employees has caused many employers to take actions that ultimately worsen the situation. At one manufacturing company I'll refer to as Intertech, I was sitting drinking coffee in the office of a human relations manager, a white woman named Alice, when another white manager named Jim walked in to ask Alice a question. She introduced me as "a woman who has come to talk about Intertech employees and strikes." Jim raised his eyebrows and made a sour face. "I'm just telling her about the soccer team," Alice said.

"Oh, I could comment!" Jim said with a sarcastic tone that drew a laugh. From what I could gather from their explanation that followed, Intertech had spent around five thousand rand to buy soccer jerseys for a team of local young people. They were in the process of preparing the ground for a community soccer field in a nearby neighborhood. After their work had begun, someone in the community had dug under the field to install an electrical cable—possibly illegally, though it was hard to place blame when the government had chronically neglected to provide water, electricity, and other services to the area. Jim said other people had then dug up and stolen portions of the cable. Alice pointed out that now children were running on the pitted field where there were potentially live power lines. Jim had met with local officials to try to decide who would cover the cost of cutting the grass and resurfacing the field. "There's quite a few issues," he said. "We've closed the door because they [the local government and community leaders] don't give us any support." The money they spent would count as corporate social responsibility funds, meaning it could earn various incentivizing tax cuts and benefits for the company, but he did not mention that. Instead, he talked about his personal willingness to help and his frustration over the seeming lack of cooperation from local government officials, neighbors, and employees. "We're willing to do it," Jim said, "but we're not willing to do it if they continue to come under our fence and steal our stuff."

That comment led into a long list of the ways people—presumably from the community surrounding the soccer field—had stolen from Intertech. Alice said people stole "basically anything, anything that can be resold . . . and copper wire is a big thing."

Thefts of copper wire from city street lights and power lines were not uncommon. Jim brought up a story from just that week in Intertech. "On Tuesday morning, we were busy putting in a new cable to [a portion of the factory]. A brand new cable, cost us R160,000. On Tuesday some youngsters from there came and cut the cable. So it's cost us R36,000 to repair the cable. So the message I want to say to them is, if we take some of that R36,000 to fix the field for the soccer kids instead of wasting it on something that we don't need to spend money on . . . ," he trailed off. "So it's quite a vicious circle because they're trying to generate an income but unfortunately they're trying to generate an income from *our cable*," he emphasized the last two words, and he and Alice laughed.

Alice and Jim knew that people had reason to be angry with their company. They had been with the company through more than one strike, and the negotiations rarely ended in favorable decisions for employees. Starting wages at the company were around twenty-two rand per hour (about two dollars), and much of the work was dangerous and exhausting. According to Alice, "We have strikes all the time and that really does nothing for the economy or anything like that. And the problem is that the employers react to it in a way that is to the detriment of the employees." The employees had been off work without pay for about six weeks. At the end of it, they got about a 5 percent pay increase, but the company docked their pay for their days off work, leaving them with a net loss in pay for the year.

Besides, Alice said, "a strike is so bad for the relationship. At the end of the day, both sides have lost. So management will sign, but they come back to work and there's still a bad vibe." Alice was well aware that the amount of theft their company experienced was related to that "bad vibe." "I think there's a lot of resentment within the community toward Intertech," she said, "and I think people are often still looking for compensation." The company was one of many I visited that had implemented a company-wide incentive program aimed at building a sense of teamwork and company loyalty. A sign near the entrance to the factory told workers they were stronger as a team. In at least two other companies I visited, employers told stories of frustrating relationships with employees even while their factory floors were decorated in motivational slogans about teamwork and company loyalty.

Jim and Alice shrugged off the stories of theft and wasted social development funds with laughter when we talked, but these stories had real consequences for how their company interacted with its employees. One way they dealt with concerns over rising hassles in interactions with employees was by outsourcing their human resources management to an employment contractor. From 2000 to 2015, use of employment contractors among companies in South Africa grew exponentially.[18] These companies, often referred to as labor brokers, neatly cater to employer concerns about employees. They manage short contracts to allow for flexible hiring and layoff schedules. They keep abreast of the labor laws in order to manage disciplinary hearings, and they bear the risk of law suits filed by employees claiming unjust treatment or termination of work. They likely hire the same people that employers would have hired, but the difference is that they take the responsibility of playing the bad cop role when mediating disputes between employer and employee. In a growing number of companies (including three that I visited), they act as the long-term legal employer of low-skilled laborers, who are merely situated at the company where they work. The website of one such company used by some businesses in the Howick area, Capital Outsourcing Group, advertised that it employed over twenty-six thousand temporary staff in 2015. This company promised employers "the flexibility to quickly tailor the workforce to meet fluctuating operational requirements," as well as the "best staff, that will improve your productivity and service to enhance your profitability." The website offered "a full range of psychometric tests" and "a personality profiling system to assess role behaviour and personality styles: i.e. motivation level, distortion levels for honesty, adaptation, communication, decision-making skills and stress tolerance."

I talked to Alice at length about labor contractors. She spoke openly about how contractors benefitted Intertech. Throughout the conversation, she made it clear that she did not think that labor contractors were good for employees or even necessarily for the long-term sustainability of a workforce, and yet this seemed to her to be the only option the company had left to avoid strikes and disciplinary hearings.

The labor contractors acted as the actual employer for all but a few critical higher-skilled long-term positions that Intertech hired directly. If an employee came to her with complaints about their job, she simply referred them to the labor contractor. "If we perhaps have to downsize for operational requirements," she said, "they'll go in and do our negotiating and all that sort of thing." Labor contractors made it easy for her company to let workers go and pass along worker complaints to a third party, but that also meant that workers had fewer options to negotiate their circumstances. "Can workers who are coming through labor brokers unionize?" I asked.

"There's nothing that says that they can't," she responded. "But it's quite difficult for them as well, because generally speaking, a lot of their contracts are short term." She explained that workers often stayed at the company for years, but always with short-term contracts that had to be renewed every three months to a year. Unions were less interested in representing workers on short-term contracts. After years of having union-led strikes during contract negotiating seasons on a nearly annual basis, their company went with a labor broker. "Ever since we've gone through labor brokers," she said, "we haven't had strikes." She said this matter-of-factly, but with a sort of shrug and an expression of concern.

"It is a bit unfair," she said about workers who continue there for years on contracts lasting only a few months at a time. "You know, because they don't have that security." She said from her perspective, "it's bad" that the arrangement took away some of the connection between the company and their employees. "It's almost like a commodity, if you know what I'm saying. You miss that personal contact in a way." She concluded with a tone of resigned disappointment and a glance toward the door as if expressing a controversial opinion, "I prefer to have our own employees, just from a belonging and loyalty perspective. But this is the decision that's been taken."

For workers, dealing with a labor contractor could mean the convenience of applying in one location rather than to dozens of companies separately. Once hired, though, it also generally meant little certainty of permanence, less take-home pay, and a thicker bureaucracy to navigate with questions or complaints about the workplace. As Alice herself recognized, the arrangement served to further dehumanize and commodify the work experience.

The turn toward labor contractors that distanced employers from employees was part of a larger cycle that breaks down the trust between employers and employees. Employers saw themselves as attempting to treat workers well, but succumbing to overwhelming factors pushing them to do the opposite. As a result, they built systems that protected themselves from costs and risks, but these systems further distanced themselves from employees and increased worker dissatisfaction. As they reduced staff through mechanization, shortened contracts, and fended off worker complaints through labor brokers, they weakened the regard that employees had for employers. In their attempts to avoid the bargaining, complaining, and lack of motivation they perceived in workers, they created situations where workers had every reason to bargain harder, complain more, and devote less energy to their jobs. Frustrated employees, frustrated employers, and broken trust formed a perpetual cycle of weakening employee-employer relationships and lessening incentives to hire, despite the stated intentions of many people caught in this cycle who wanted to improve various employment problems in their country.

Throughout our conversation, Alice seemed to dislike the systems of labor relations she operated within, and yet she seemed at a loss for better alternatives. She, like most employers I met with, saw themselves as choosing between a very few disagreeable options. Not only were their options constrained by profit margins in a competitive global market; they were limited by what social scientists call a "social imaginary"—the range of shared ideas, values, meanings, and systems that define what is possible and real in a given social group. A social imaginary is like the space in which a person's ideas can roam, beyond which thoughts simply do not go. A particular conception of reality can seem ridiculous to one group, while it seems quite normal in another time or place—like the idea that humans are reincarnations of other species, or that white people make better managers. The laziness myth offers insights into some aspects of the social imaginary among white South African employers. A market capitalist economy and the privileging of whiteness are also firmly embedded in that imaginary. The issue I heard employers describing wasn't that they didn't want black employees to have good lives, it was that they simply could not imagine any acceptable way for that to happen.

A social imaginary is not neutral in terms of power. Humans create and maintain shared conceptions of reality in ways that involve strategically refusing to believe certain alternatives as possible, often when those alternatives seem threatening. As John Thompson writes, people are constantly involved in shaping social imaginaries and, in the process, are "thereby also involved, knowingly or not, in altering, undermining or reinforcing our relations with others and the world" in ways that "serve to sustain social relations which are asymmetrical with regard to the organization of power."[19] The options employers imagined included employing black people for bare-minimum wages, laying off black people who seemed not to profit the company, and offering some charitable benefits to black employees and neighbors on the side. Their accepted conceptions of society did not include significantly breaking down the antiblack structures and mindset that permeated society.

# Considering the Options

It's worth pausing for a moment to consider what to make of this situation. Clearly, many people were experiencing a problem here. Employers were frustrated, and, as will become even clearer in coming chapters, employees and unemployed people were, too. Sometimes these groups were troubled for similar reasons and sometimes for very different reasons. From the perspective of the employers, the problem was that workers did not behave in ways they wanted, and they could not imagine effective ways to pay more or otherwise produce that behavior. At this point we might stop to consider how their imagination was limited and whether there are other possible solutions that might be imagined.

For nearly two centuries, a sort of debate has been lingering among social theorists over a question that is at the heart of employers' concerns about worker behavior. The question is this: What drives human behavior? For employers in South Africa, this question factors into attempts to understand what causes workers not to behave in ways that employers want them to behave. And the answers they come up with shape the solutions they pursue.

On one side of the debate are theorists who argue that *culture* is a crucial factor—if not *the* factor—driving people's behavior. One of the earliest theorists to formulate this argument was Max Weber, author of the book *The Protestant Ethic and the Spirit of Capitalism*.[20] In it, Weber outlined two different ethics, or ways of thinking about work evidenced in Europe and the United States from the sixteenth to the nineteenth century. Weber calls one way of thinking about work an "economic traditionalist" mindset and the other a "modern capitalist" mindset. Weber writes that before the spread of capitalism, people with the economic traditionalist mindset worked only so much as necessary in order to fulfill their daily needs. Higher wages would make it easier to meet those needs, so higher wages would lead people to work less, not more. Weber contrasts that economic traditionalist mindset with the "modern capitalist" way of thinking about work which was founded on "perceiving work as an end in itself."[21] Weber traces how the new mindset—the "spirit" of capitalism—was made to seem inherently rational through a long process of historical circumstances. That mindset became woven into Western culture through religion, education, and socialization. Weber offers the important argument that capitalist ways of thinking about work were no more or less inherently logical or rational than the traditionalist ethic. From the point of view of the traditionalist mindset, he noticed, the capitalist idea that work is an end in itself "must appear fully irrational, . . . so incomprehensible and puzzling, so vulgar and repulsive."[22]

According to Weber, economic and social structures come about because of shifts in cultural elements such as values and religion. The way to understand economic behavior, then, is to start with culture. This culture-driven view of behavior would suggest that any analysis of South African employment should examine the potentially clashing cultural beliefs of employers and employees. We would follow the trail from John the manager's comment that "lots of things are their culture" and try to understand why the cultural differences between John and his employees make their work lives so strained.

On the other side of the debate over the impetus for human behavior, social theorists in the tradition of Karl Marx see *economic and social structures* as the driving force behind behavior, not culture.[23] For Marx, any search for an ethos of capitalist worker mindsets would miss the true course of history and society. Humans are not primarily guided by cultural beliefs; rather, humans are caught in structures that include economic systems and class divisions. Cultural beliefs come into being to uphold economic structures, not the other way around. In South Africa, such structures include the history of racialized privilege and the fact that employers can reap profits out of low-wage laborers who will never be able to afford companies of their own. This type of analysis would center on what Joyce admitted: "Companies make a lot of money off the sweat of their backs. Make no mistake about it. And you have to factor that in. This is the price they pay."

Looking at the employment situation in South Africa, then, one could come up with two very different explanations for the problem. In the Weberian culture-as-driving-force camp, we could say that employers and employees simply do not share a common set of cultural beliefs about how to conduct oneself at work, so it's no wonder they clash. Solutions from this side might suggest educating one or both sides about the culture of the other, possibly even training each side to adapt to the culture of the other. This was not an uncommon approach in South Africa. In the Howick and Mpophomeni area alone, I found and met with twelve different organizations with programs that trained employees and unemployed people to adapt their culture to fit the culture of the workplace through behaviors like smiling more often, making eye contact, and coming to work five minutes early.

But this way of understanding behavior can easily slip into blaming culture for poverty. Because whiteness has historically been treated in much of the world as normal, right, and as if it has no culture of its own, attempts to solve social problems have often focused only on correcting the supposed culture of people in nonwhite and other marginalized groups. These so-called solutions ignore the ways in which cultural behaviors within oppressed groups come about largely in response to systems of oppression in the broader society. And they ignore the fact that dominant groups also have culture and, as we saw above, social imaginaries. If you take economic and social structures out of the analysis of unemployment, you will end up with warped and prejudiced views of culture.

The other very different explanation for the employment problem would focus on the structures to blame for the present inequalities rather than culture. This approach would ask not what resulted from people's beliefs, but rather what has resulted from the systems people create to live in. How has systematically depriving black people of meaningful work experiences for at least a century produced a situation in which black people—not surprisingly—might be wary of work and distrustful of employers? This approach has also been used to seek changes in South Africa. The social movement that eventually toppled the apartheid regime and that continues to push for improved labor conditions has been driven largely by people who saw how unequal social structures powerfully affect every aspect of people's lives, and who fought to change those structures. Throughout this book, we will see many ways in which workers' choices are dramatically shaped by racialized double standards, class power dynamics, and systems (like labor-brokering) that alienate low-wage workers from the products of their own labor and from flourishing relationships with other human beings. But this approach on its own fails to take into account the ways that historically distinct cultural systems come together in South Africa and the world to interact with each other, adapting and shifting in ways that produce ideas about, among other things, how to achieve a good life.

Neither of these two approaches is adequate in itself. Even if we look carefully at people's cultural beliefs and then look carefully at the economic structures they operate in, we miss something important: the ways each of these affects the other. How are culturally replicated beliefs among various groups shaped by their involvement in certain class positions and economic roles? And how are economic systems being constantly reshaped according to the cultural beliefs and values of people in society? How do social imaginaries create systems, and systems create social imaginaries?[24] By examining how culture and structures interact, we can also begin to imagine how these *might better* interact.

One method of looking at socioeconomic forces and cultural forces at the same time is by examining people's narratives of a good life. This involves asking two questions: What are the narratives people follow in pursuit of a good life, and how are those narratives both recreating and created through social structures? If you ask someone what they think it takes to live a good life, you will discover evidence of the privileges and constraints that surround that person in a socioeconomic environment, and you will find moralities and values that made sense in that person's cultural context. Recall how Bullet was born into geographic and economic structures that excluded his parents and most of his neighborhood from accessing an opportunity like going to a top university. Those structures were upheld by the dominant narrative and a social imaginary that privileged whiteness by blaming inequalities on laziness. But culture is not homogeneous, and Bullet and his peers also accessed different narratives. Those narratives shaped his decision not to study law, gave him ideas about what kind of person he should be at age fifty, and also motivated him to write music about social injustice. Narratives are shaped by, perpetuated through, and productive of both structures and culture. My approach in this book is to trace out the competing narratives that circulate in society in order to draw together both culture-based and structures-based perspectives to understand a problem.

What does this mean for the employers we have seen in this chapter then? As for the comment from the manager about "their" culture that "you can't understand," it does seem that there is much he does not understand. That lack of understanding, though, is more than a personal failing—it is a product of the society in which he lives. As George Lipsitz writes, "Condemning whiteness is not the same as condemning white people. Whiteness is a structured advantage subsidized by segregation. It is not so much a color as a condition. Yet because whiteness rarely speaks its names or admits to its advantages, it requires the construction of a devalued and even demonized Blackness to be credible and legitimate."[25] The laziness myth has served to do precisely that—to demonize and devalue blackness, treating black people and their inherent characteristics as the causes of their own disadvantages. But social imaginaries are never fully stable, and hegemonic narratives are threatened by alternative narratives that exist in a society. This book is an attempt to destabilize a social imaginary, and in effect to prove John wrong—not to prove that you can fully understand another person's culture and social circumstances, but to show at least why the attempt to understand is worth it.

Just understanding culture would not be enough, however, either for employers or readers. We also need to see economic systems for what they are. Employers like Scott are in an economic crunch between larger producers they contract with, buyers' demands, international trade agreements, legal shifts, and rising costs. And the reasons employees like Precious end up dismissed for taking a child with runny tummy to the doctor can be traced back to a far wider system: an apartheid system locating the best hospitals farthest from black neighborhoods, long waits at understaffed public hospitals, import taxes and low wages making cars too expensive for black people to own, taxi cartels keeping transportation schedules limited, possible limited access to clean water leading to digestive sicknesses, lack of access to cell phone coverage or electricity to charge phones preventing employees from calling in their absences, lack of access to an English-speaking school in order to grow up comfortable communicating in English with managers, systems that have privileged English as the language of power, and the list goes on. These examples point to the ways people are constrained or privileged by their positions within various economic systems. People navigate life within economic structures and cultural settings using a variety of narratives, even as those narratives guide the ways they cocreate those very structures for themselves and future generations.

As we saw in this and the previous chapter, the laziness narrative is pervasive. It upheld apartheid, colonialism, and slavery, and it has also outlasted those systems. It continues to leave employers frustrated and perpetuate prejudices that hinder many people from accessing the good life. But the laziness myth is not the only narrative. What, then, are the other ways that people seek the good life? Can people who struggle to find good work, or any work at all, still achieve what they consider to be good lives?

# "I NEED TO RESPECT THAT PERSON AND THAT PERSON NEEDS TO RESPECT ME"

## The Respect Narrative

Nomusa was not just one of my best friends in Mpophomeni; she taught me what was wrong with my research plan. A neighbor took me to meet her at home for the first time, walking me through her gated fence up to her pale yellow cinder-block house to the large front window where customers could purchase bread, cigarettes, matches, and other supplies. As we approached, I thought I heard someone talking or laughing inside. Then a hand darted out the window, pointing straight at us and holding what looked like a black handgun.

Before I had time to think clearly, the person holding the gun—a middle-aged woman with curly hair pulled back in a loose ponytail—appeared in the open window and burst out laughing. The neighbor with me laughed too, and I figured I was also supposed to be laughing. The gun, which the woman tossed onto the window sill, was a toy squirt gun. She didn't explain the reason for her practical joke, but I got the impression she was not shy. When the neighbor introduced me as an American doing research on businesses, she raised her eyebrows and looked me over with an expression I couldn't decipher, either admiration or playful mocking. She laughed again when the neighbor said I would like Nomusa, first because she spoke English and second because she loved to talk.

These descriptors proved true. Nomusa invited us inside to join another young woman in her living room where a television was playing music videos on low volume. We sat together on a velvety couch wrapped in the manufacturer's crinkly clear plastic to keep it looking new. After a few minutes of small talk, Nomusa turned to me. "Well, do you want to interview me or something?" With the other two friends still in the room, I turned on my recording app and began, "How about you start by telling me about your work experience?"

"I didn't finish matric," she began, referring to the last year of high school. "I went to matric like three weeks, and I stopped because of"—she hesitated just slightly, then continued—"I didn't have a mom." When her mom died during Nomusa's eighth-grade year, she "had to do the things a mom does." Besides, she continued, "You know, my father kind of like abused me, hit me, all the small little things. You get a hiding and going to school with those blue marks." One of the friends had her gaze calmly fixed on the muted television. The other twirled a strand of hair between her fingers. They seemed hardly to notice this story of physical abuse. "And then besides," Nomusa continued casually, high school required "a whole lot of extra moneys like excursions and exams and things. So then that's how I dropped out." In a few years, she fell in love and moved in with a man who became the father of her first child.

That was Nomusa's answer when I asked for her work history. I still had not heard anything about work, and in the hour-long conversation that followed, she wouldn't share much more about work. Next she told me how that first husband began to cheat on her because another woman had secretly inflicted him with *muthi*—an herbal medicine used to influence bodies, spirits, and the material world, sometimes for good and sometimes for ill. Like many South Africans, she talked about muthi at first a little hesitantly. "I don't really believe in it but some people do," she said, watching me closely as if gauging my opinions on muthi as a white foreigner. As I got to know her better, she talked more about muthi, and it became clear that muthi and its role in relationships with her family and the spiritual mattered very much to her.

Nomusa went on to say she eventually divorced her cheating husband. She spent long years in negotiations with relatives and social workers trying to maintain custody of their child while she moved from one sibling's house to another. She asked a pastor to pray with her that God would give her a new husband, and he wrote down some words of prayer on a paper she kept in her Bible. Not long after, the prayer seemed to be fulfilled when she met the man who now lived with her as her second husband.

All this came out on that first day I met Nomusa. We talked for over two hours, long after her other two guests had quietly excused themselves. Because Nomusa's business depended on being home for customers, I could easily stop by without planning ahead. Often I would find her with a few friends watching television, braiding hair, or chatting while she cooked in the kitchen. If there were just a few of us, she might pull out a cold drink from her shop or hand me a bowl of whatever she was cooking. Once she mentioned with a nervous laugh that her neighbors probably thought she was using witchcraft to keep me coming back. I didn't ask whether there was any truth to their suspicion. She seemed genuinely welcoming of my visits, and I sometimes wondered what use she might find in our conversations. I made it clear, as with everyone involved in the research, that I couldn't pay her, and she never asked for money. Occasionally she took me up on my offer to give her a ride into town to restock her shelves, but it seemed to me she spent more monetarily on our relationship than she gained. She was a constant help to me as I learned about life in the township. She taught me tidbits of the beliefs she grew up learning, like that women should not garden when they menstruate and that eating burned cornmeal gives people body odor. Most of all she taught me that relationships mean life or death in the township. "People fight for love here," she said one day. "They kill for love." Another day she said that a person who wrecks a relationship with a neighbor is like one who "shits under her shade tree. When she needs it for shade, now she's going to be smelling her own shit."

Nomusa never seemed to mind answering my questions about her business or her previous jobs, but neither did she volunteer information about her work experience as if it were an important subject. When I asked how long she had run the shop in her home, she said vaguely "a few years." By her estimate, her profits from the business were only a few rand a day, which seemed in line with what I'd heard from other owners of businesses of that size. She tried to keep her money out of reach of her husband because spending even an extra hundred rand (ten dollars) to replenish the shelves could send her in a downward spiral of a shrinking business. A young man next door had recently opened a shop selling many of the same items she sold, which she found to be disrespectful, but her business did not appear to have suffered. A few weeks later, she told me the neighbor was too badly addicted to drugs to keep his shop stocked. The real threat to her business, she said, was customers who ran up credit and then left town or avoided her. Like every township business owner, she negotiated a careful coexistence with her clients. For them, the goodwill of a local shopkeeper could mean the difference between food or hunger at the end of the month. For shopkeepers, surviving in business requires convincing indebted customers to pay their bills when paydays and welfare-disbursement days come.[1] Both need to persuade the other without breaking the long-term relationship.

Sometimes, as Nomusa talked about her past, I would ask questions like, "And were you working then?" She had once worked as a sales clerk, but she wasn't interested in telling the type or name of the store. Instead, she brought this up to tell how the Indian shop owner's wife kindly smuggled food to her. Another time she mentioned a job cleaning the home of a young couple, a story she brought up to describe the dilemma she faced when the man made sexual advances toward her and she quit to avoid wrecking the couple's marriage. Always the topic of work was subsumed by talk of relationships. Relationships nearly killed her, relationships kept her alive, relationships could mean hate and fear, and relationships brought her purpose and meaning.

Not all of the relationships she spoke about were with the living. Like many Zulu people, she considered the spirits of her family's ancestors to be active agents in her life. Since moving into her second husband's home, Nomusa had never been certain that her late father-in-law's spirit welcomed her there. As we got to know each other, she told me about various hardships that she attributed to troubled relationships with her deceased father-in-law, as well as her deceased mother. Her mother had trained as a *sangoma*—a person who consults ancestors to determine causes of events, thereby acting as an advisor through any sort of hardship. Like many sangomas, Nomusa's mother also had gained skills as an *inyanga*—one who specializes in herbal and spiritual techniques of healing. Before her death, Nomusa's mother told her that she had bequeathed her powers to Nomusa. Nomusa feared and avoided her mother's bequest. Training as a sangoma can require years of time and thousands of dollars. Many Zulu people believe that when ancestral spirits select someone they want to become a sangoma, the spirits inflict that person with sicknesses and other misfortunes until that person complies. When I met her, Nomusa was considering paying the equivalent of several hundred dollars to another sangoma who had offered to conduct a ceremony to free Nomusa from the call to become a sangoma.

Early in our conversations, Nomusa told me about a time years earlier when her second marriage nearly ended. She explained, "Me and my husband weren't getting along. He was abusive—drinking, fighting, chasing me with the knives on the road, even when I'd run out with petticoats and bra down the road." In her typical style, she would drop little details like this and let out a laugh even in the middle of stories of the hardest points in her life. "And that's when things got really out of hand. I almost got killed right here. He was drinking that time, my husband. He hit me so bad, he stabbed me. And because I was attending counseling, and I knew the lady's house, I went to her and I cried, 'I'm dying.' I was with my daughter and my two sons. I said 'I'm dying. Can't you help me do something?'"

This counselor immediately phoned a social worker and they took Nomusa and her children to a safe house. After several weeks of intervention and phone calls, during which she nearly divorced her husband, she went back to live in a small building along the side of their home. He was still drinking, and little changed. "He was sleeping all the time. In the time he was sober, it was like two or three days a week at home, then away. And when he does come home he's angry. I'm wondering is there another woman. When he does get money he drinks it. He doesn't give me money to buy food and all that."

Finally, she decided what she had to do. "I said, 'No, this won't stop until I make it stop. It's up to me what I have to do. I'm a forgiving person, but I had to live with this for so many years, I can't anymore." Desperate and furious, she grabbed a butcher knife and waved it at her drunk husband, shouting, "I'm tired of this! You're not respecting me as a wife! I'm leaving now. I've had enough."

She took her children and fled their home with her savings of about R600 ($60).

## Inequality and Respect

I thought about never publishing Nomusa's story because it's messy. Like any life account, it doesn't have a single theoretical lesson, and I resisted telling it in a way that might have too simplistic a point or narrowly portray her as either heroine or victim. I had also become entangled in the story. Our friendship raised the kinds of ethical questions anthropologists often wrestle with during fieldwork. What should I have done when I heard about her past domestic abuse and the possibility of her becoming abused again? What did my relationship mean to her? Was I taking advantage of her kindness? What did it mean that she had begun to see me as entangled in relationships of both her living and deceased relatives? What problems might it create for my research if I allowed the boundary to blur between friendship and research, and what problems might it create for her? Aside from these ethical questions, I could easily have dismissed her experiences as irrelevant to a book about work. After all, she didn't seem remotely interested in talking about work.

Ultimately, I chose to include her story because she asked me several times to write it, though I insisted on disguising her identity and using a pseudonym. Her friendship helped me see the complex layers of unequal power relationships that surrounded the working lives of South Africans and others around the world. Social scientists have often pointed out that economic conditions shape domestic relationships. Breadwinners, for example, often have an easier time ending a relationship than those who are financially dependent on a domestic partner.[2] Nomusa's story points to a causality that moves in the opposite direction as well: domestic and interpersonal relationships shape economic conditions. People's possibilities for work are affected by what happens among people in their homes and workplaces. The hopes, priorities, and values that shape their domestic lives also reveal a lot about what they want to get from work. If we want to understand how work fits into people's narratives of the good life, we would do well to learn what the good life means outside of work. As my conversations with Nomusa showed me, the problem with my plan to do research on work was that I was asking too many questions about work itself.

Buried in Nomusa's retelling of a key turning point in her life, she used one word that tells us a lot about what she and many South Africans wanted both in and outside of work: *respect*. When Nomusa swung a knife at her husband and told him she'd had enough, the words she shouted at him were "You're not respecting me as a wife." Caught in a social position with less power and status than his, she called him to account with a moral code he would understand: he had to respect her.

This kind of situation—when someone with lesser power has to figure out how to demand better treatment from someone in power—happens all the time. The history of work in South Africa is full of such arrangements. People need to survive—they need to meet basic needs like shelter, food, and the means to raise children. But the options available for meeting those needs are often like a bad marriage. Someone else in the relationship has the control. As long as the one in control gets what they want, that person can ignore the needs of the one being controlled. Often those without the control are women and people of historically marginalized ethnic and racial groups. This kind of power inequality and lack of incentive to care was built into the apartheid system, and it continues to be the default relationship for many businesses in South Africa, if not (as some would argue) anywhere in market economies. The world has wide inequalities that are not going away.

South Africa and Lesotho, a small country surrounded by South Africa, are the two nations with the most unequal distributions of incomes in the world.[3] The richest 10 percent of South Africans own around 95 percent of the country's wealth and earn 99 percent of the country's investment income.[4] What's even more startling is the fact that when you compare the wealthiest to the poorest people across the globe, rather than within the boundaries of a single country, the distribution of wealth is even less equally divided.[5] Not only that, wealth distribution is getting worse—in South Africa, in the United States, and in the world as a whole. The past century has seen some major improvements in decreasing the percentage of the world's people living in absolute poverty and eradicating some diseases that disproportionately affect the poor, but governments have not done well at creating a more level playing field when it comes to household incomes or assets. With inequalities in wealth come differences in the power people have—the power to hire or fire, and the power to choose a school, a job, health care, or a home. We live in a very unequal world, and situations in which someone gets exploited, beaten up, ignored, mistreated, or cheated are not uncommon. The question to consider when it comes to work, then, is not just how to get more people jobs. We also need to consider how people can maximize the well-being they have while they live in situations of unequal power and wealth.

The answer for Nomusa, and for a lot of Zulu people, included demanding this thing called respect. Being respected is not the same as being powerful, benevolent, wealthy, famous, or even employed. Nor is respecting someone the same as meekly allowing them to do whatever they like. In fact, what I found to be so profound about the ways Zulu people talked about respect was their insistence that respect was not—and must not be—something you earn by having high wealth or status. Instead, you need it more than ever when you *cannot* get status, power, wealth, or success. It is not something you deserve by marketing yourself as valuable; it is something you deserve for being human. When respect runs throughout a relationship, the relationship becomes what people call "lungile," or "right." This quality of relationship was what people wanted at work, and it also shaped the lives they formed outside of work. But it is not just in people's heads as a way of regarding other people, it is lived out and confirmed through practices that often involved redistributing material resources. When people said they wanted respect, they were acknowledging that social hierarchies are inevitable, even as they were demanding that powerful people have moral responsibilities including treating every human being with equal value regardless of their place in a hierarchy.

Many Zulu people described respect—in isiZulu, *inhlonipho*—as something closely tied to their own culture. In a sense, Zulu people were world experts on respect. There were aspects of *inhlonipho* that differed from understandings of respect in other cultural settings but also parallels. Listen to the music, media, and literature of people who have experienced oppression nearly anywhere in the world, from African American hip hop to American Indian poetry to interviews with white-collar workers in cubicles, and you are likely to find people calling for respect.[6] Or take Aretha Franklin's 1967 hit song with the famously spelled out R-E-S-P-E-C-T. The lyrics voice a demand for domestic equality, but given Franklin's position as a black woman—praised by Martin Luther King Jr. as a "devoted and consistent supporter" of the civil rights movement—the song took on a political significance for black Americans and black women in particular.[7] In another direction, people frequently mention a lack of respect when explaining what led them to commit crimes.[8] The former neo-Nazi skinhead Christian Picciolini reflected that he "readily took on" a leadership role in a hate group because he grew up socially ostracized, bullied, and "always searching for that feeling of respect."[9] What he meant by respect and the ways he went about seeking it differ from Nomusa's demand for respect from her husband, but there seem to be common trends globally that people who have experienced marginalization in many diverse settings feel an absence of something commonly referred to as respect. When marginalized people have already had their jobs, schools, opportunities, families, communities, land, and freedom taken away, don't you dare take away their respect. And if you want a starting place for change, respect is a pretty useful place to begin. I argue that the calls people made for respect were not a substitute for structural change in society, but rather the central focus of one path to structural change, as well as a defining characteristic of the good life toward which that structural change was aimed.

## Troubling Talk about Hierarchies

Duduzile was a woman in her mid-fifties with a calm manner of speaking that nearly always seemed to end in optimism. She exuded a quiet contentment, even when she described difficult circumstances like having only an intermittent water supply at her home, living HIV-positive, and caring for terminally ill neighbors. As I'll describe in chapter 6, despite being currently unemployed she was one of only a few people who told me they were currently living a good life. I visited Duduzile every few weeks and came to appreciate her insightfulness about township life.

I found it troubling and surprising, then, when Duduzile told me one day, "White people have a cleverness. African people, we have power, we have strength to work." She tapped her head to demonstrate cleverness, then flexed her arms to show physical strength. That's what God gave each of them, she said. She offered what she took as evidence, saying that if a black person runs a company, it won't go well because the person doesn't have cleverness.

We were relaxing on her front steps drinking tea as we talked. I had known her for nearly a year, but her outright embrace of this hegemonic view of white and black essentialism stunned me. I suddenly faced the reality that she had, after all, been raised in an era when even public schools for black children were designed to teach the inherent inferiority of black people. I questioned her directly, asking whether perhaps things just seemed this way in her country because black people did not have educational opportunities. She defended her position, leaning forward with an intensity in her voice as she spoke. When white people have control over funds for farms or businesses, she said, everything "runs properly," but when Africans gain control of funds, things go poorly. The reason, she said, was because for Africans, "even if you are well-educated, . . . it's not in your blood." She laughed a little uncomfortably. "I don't know if I can put it that way. But because the whites, it's in their blood." The more we talked, the more amazed I was that she seemed to accept this view of society.

I tried to gently question her further. I told her honestly that her words concerned me and that I thought that what she was actually seeing was the result of historic racism in South Africa. "When I think about the world that way," I said, "then I wonder if there's hope for Africans, if all they can do is work with their hands. That doesn't earn very much money. Those are usually the jobs that earn the least money. What do we do about that then?"

She responded with a patient tone as if trying to help me see some hope in a sad situation. "I'm not sure in that part," she said. "But you know, as I've said before, we are on the different levels of life. And I think God made it purposely that we are not on the same level. Even if you try so hard, if God don't want you to reach that kind of level, you not going to reach it. So you need to accept it"— here she paused to clarify—"but not that you can accept living in a shack, or not having the proper furniture, you know." Sometimes, she said, a person is at a level that is not right for them, and they don't have peace at that level. That means they have to do something about it—go earn money, get a better education, look for a different job, or start a business. In those cases, "You not supposed to be where you are." But being at a low level doesn't necessarily mean you need to change your place in society. "At any level you can have peace," she said, "any level."

"OK," I said, trying to approach the issue from another angle. "So are there certain things that people at a high level must do?" Now her tone became even more insistent, articulating each word in English as she explained: "God puts you on that level for you to"—she repeated the words with emphasis—"for *you* to take *care* of that person who's at that low level." She said people at high levels have more things than they need, and that's because those things are not meant to belong to them. People at high levels are there for the direct purpose of giving their extra things—whether money, belongings, or opportunities—to those with less. Later she would explain this with herself as an example, saying that if she had an extra ten rand or hundred rand one week and a neighbor needed it, then those rand were not for her, it was for her neighbor. I had heard Duduzile talk about a neighbor child for whom she was paying school fees, and I had witnessed plenty of incidents in which someone requested a few rand from a friend and if that person had it on hand, it was handed over. From what I could tell, Duduzile meant quite literally that, whenever possible, her money was and should be available to those who needed it.

As I listened to Duduzile explain her perspective on hierarchy, I felt an inner conflict. On the one hand, I recognized in her explanation a hegemonic set of ideas that essentialized white and black people as inherently good and bad workers. She had been taught through the apartheid education system and a thousand subtle messages that white people were inherently smarter and better at business than people of her race. As I explained in chapter 1, hegemonic ideas become accepted not only by those in power, but by people like Duduzile who are raised in powerful structures designed to keep them subordinated. Her words echoed a deeply persistent lie that claimed that white dominance stemmed from something unique in the so-called white bloodline. Yet Duduzile was also making another point about that hierarchy, a point about how to live within it. She was challenging much about the racist society that had grown out of apartheid. She was not saying that white people were better human beings than black people, or that they deserved to keep more wealth. Quite the opposite. For Duduzile, the fact that hierarchy existed necessitated that society must follow a certain moral order. When white people, managers, wealthy people in the township, or anyone else had power and wealth, their job was to respect the people with less, and that meant taking on certain responsibilities to shape society for the good of those with less.

Part of the reason I found this conversation so difficult to process was that I grew up as a middle-class white person in the United States, where the history books I read, the songs I memorized, and the holidays I celebrated tended to laud equality as an interpersonal and national value, and yet equality was often presumed to happen automatically somehow without people actively redistributing money to make it happen. Circumstances for people in the United States are far from equal or equitable, and yet our dominant culture claims to value equality. Like many American researchers, I took for granted that people anywhere must want equality. And let's be clear—greater inequality usually makes a society worse by many standards. Countries with greater inequality tend to have lower levels of education and trust, higher rates of violence, and higher rates of physical and mental illness.[10] When inequalities are patterned along racial and ethnic lines (as they often are), treating the causes and effects of those inequalities as acceptable would be outright unethical.

So it is with great caution that I describe a kind of response to inequality in which people admit that inequality is not going away, and even that inequality itself might not be the enemy. To suggest that people in poverty want something other than equality is to risk having one's words twisted. In all honesty, at times as an ethnographer I would have preferred to ignore portions of interviews like Duduzile's comments implying that black people accepted or even appreciated systems that remained racially hierarchical. I know some readers could interpret those quotations as nonchalance toward racism. I wrestled with the tension of presenting the words of people who at times seemed to express acquiescence to, even a desire for, societal conditions that predicated a racially hierarchical society. One person who read a draft of this chapter expressed their concern that it could be interpreted as suggesting that social structures can stay as they are as long as people regard each other in interpersonal communication with a kind, respectful attitude. To be clear, that is not my argument, nor was it what Nomusa, Duduzile, or others who are mentioned in this chapter meant by respect.

The task of an anthropologist is not to choose a theory and then string together bits of evidence that support that theory. It is to listen long, watch closely, and draw upon the full range of previous scholarship on human behavior in a shared "commitment to making an impact on the quality of life in the world."[11] I used an iterative process, changing my line of questioning to adapt to what people brought up over many months of fieldwork, and returned again and again to questions of hierarchy, respect, and social levels because these ideas were surprising and troubling to me as a social scientist committed to racial equity and workers' rights. Thankfully, I am not the first to have wrestled with questions of how to understand the ways that less powerful people sometimes want other things besides a more equal society.[12] Living in the most economically unequal society in the world, black South Africans have many techniques for dealing with inequality. Those techniques are worth paying careful attention to for their implications in South Africa and beyond. And as the people in this chapter explain, those techniques are anything but complacent toward racism.

## How to Live in a Hierarchy?

One of the people I talked with several times about hierarchy and respect was Bullet. Like Duduzile and many other black South Africans, Bullet used the word "level" to talk about different life stages and statuses that people experience. People often used the phrase "finding your level" to describe a process of settling into a place on the social ladder that fits your life circumstances. Like Duduzile, Bullet was more interested in living at the right level than the highest level. When I asked Bullet to explain what he meant by "levels," he said, "I think it's about being comfortable. We don't know who we are, and when you don't know where we are, you need to find somewhere to fit in. I think it's basically trying to find yourself." Another day, when I asked him what he thought the word "development" meant, he said it meant finding your level in society and living at that level. He compared it to the feeling of being assigned to the right class in school—A, B, or a lower level—in accordance with your ability, a common practice in South African schools. A good life involved finding a place where you and the people around you agree that you fit, no matter where in the social hierarchy that is.

One of the first few times he brought up the idea of there being hierarchies in society, he was giving a playful retelling of history. "Old Zulu" culture, he said, had a hierarchy from kings and chiefs, then "all the way down to the person who has to die just because the king dies, just because you were at the level of, 'Homey, that's your job—you were brought into this world to die for the king, now die with him." Historical accounts corroborate this interpretation. Inequality reached new heights and took on racialized characteristics under colonialism and apartheid, but it did not begin in South Africa with European settlers. Historical accounts suggest that Zulu society was hierarchical even before colonists arrived. While Zulu people have lived with hierarchy since before colonialism, they have also found ways to criticize and resist misuse of power for at least as long.[13] And some of the most foundational stories told about Southern African kings of early colonialism are about people who changed levels, like the Masotho king Moshoeshoe, who were born in obscurity and became powerful leaders mainly by the force of their character.

Moreover, people spoke with admiration and nostalgia for a time (real or imagined) when African leaders created cultural and structural systems that kept people from becoming stuck in a lower economic and political status. "A king before would have so many cows that if he sees a man he don't have any cows, he give you two cows," Bullet explained. Another thirty-something-year-old man talked at length about how an *umfokazana*, a person who found himself destitute for lack of family or property, would in the past have been provided for by a community with a gift of a cow from someone of higher status.[14] This, Bullet said, was what was missing in society today—people took on political leadership without having to prove they respected others and were worthy of respect. It wasn't just those individual leaders who were flawed, it was the entire system and beliefs surrounding those individuals, making ascent to higher levels dependent not on respecting those around one, but on personal advantages like wealth and abuse of power that used rather than helped others.

Bullet wasn't bitter about living in a hierarchical society, but he did care how people behaved within a hierarchy. After I had already written most of this chapter, I told him what I had written and asked him directly for his thoughts on hierarchy, respect, and racism. "We all want hierarchy," he insisted. "Where there's no hierarchy, there's no organization, there's no leadership, and there's just no way forward. We can't all lead no one." He gave example after example of how hierarchies inevitably formed: on playgrounds, and in school friend groups, gangs, jails, families, and dating relationships. I asked him—based on the concern I had heard from a person who had read an early draft of this chapter—"Is saying you want to have a hierarchy the same as supporting racism and apartheid, then?"

"No! No!" he responded. "Apartheid only forced you to choose a leader. It said, 'This is your leader,' and that's not nature. That's the reason it was wrong. Because it was forced. But everybody in this world needs leadership." Apartheid wasn't wrong because it was political, it was wrong because of the ways it shaped politics, determining who would be at high and low levels based on race. Instead, Bullet said, people should be able to choose who will lead others based on elements that make "natural" sense, like "character," "years of service," or "qualifications."

Bullet called for a world in which people could move between levels according to a range of factors accessible to anyone, including moral character and stage of life, not skin tone. When Bullet described "development" as people each being in their own school "level," he spoke as someone who had often been an

A student in a predominantly white school. He would have experienced people respecting him—acknowledging the level his capabilities put him in—as well as not respecting him. But capabilities were not the only factor determining levels. When I asked people questions about how people moved through levels in society, they listed life stages and demonstrations of character: marriage, building a home, caring for the needs of the community, and simply aging. A society marked by respect, then, included structures and cultural practices in which people acknowledged the status of others not primarily by racial privilege, but by their character, qualifications, and their progression through stages of life.

## Managing Precarity

Nomusa once explained that when Zulu children learn how to show respect, they learn how a person at a lower level should approach someone at a higher level. When a child walks toward an elder, a wife toward a husband, or a commoner toward a chief, they move in ways that communicate something about their relationship. The subordinate person should bend down, avoid eye contact, bring gifts, and approach on their knees. I had heard these practices described but had never seen them, and I doubted how often this happened in recent generations. I found it hard to envision Nomusa treating her husband or anyone like this, given what I knew about the ways she had stood up to her own father and two husbands at difficult times in her life. I asked if she ever treated her husband with that kind of formality.

"If I want to ask him for something, I do kneel," she said, then started to laugh as she recalled an example. When she wanted to go on a trip with her son, she had rubbed and washed her husband's feet, brought him a drink on a tray, bent her head down and made no eye contact. They both knew it was an act, but it was an act that communicated something, and he got the message. These behaviors, she explained, all signaled respect. She gave me a playful smile and said that when she does these things, she gets what she asks for. She got the trip with her son. Another time she got money to get her hair done. "It's like you gonna get his special recipe. It's like softening a person."

Respect, then, is something that a person of lower status in a hierarchy can direct toward someone of higher status. But notably, this isn't just for the benefit of the high-status person. This respecting of a high-status person calls into play a moral code that places demands on them. Nomusa could use respect for her own benefit because the moral code of respect says that when she respects her husband, he must respect her. He must treat her as a human. And he must recognize that because they are both humans at particular places in society, she can demand something of him. Respect was a tool for managing relationships, and relationships were crucial for survival in a precarious life. At least that's how it's supposed to work.

When Nomusa stood up to her husband and fled her home, according to the account she gave me years later, the only thing she could think to do was find people who could help her. She went first to her sister's home, but she knew that living there long term would put too much of a strain on their relationship. "So then I thought, 'I will find a job. God will give me a job.' I said, 'God you have to, you can see what I am doing.' And I spoke to him like I'm speaking to a normal person." At that point in the story, I expected her to tell me whether or not she got a job, but instead she carried on telling me about all the people who kept her alive and hopeful—the woman who gave her son a baked good on the street when she needed encouragement, the relatives she stayed with, the nights her children stayed cheerful even huddling in a leaky house in the rain, and the woman who told her about a job where she could earn five dollars a day.

Before she could start that job, Nomusa discovered she was pregnant. When she told her husband, he begged her to come home. She had not been able to transfer her kids to a school near the place she was renting, and she worried that she would not be able to keep them with her much longer. As her husband kept inviting her back and her plans for living alone floundered, she received help from a counselor, a social worker, and a psychiatrist who all intervened to figure out a safe plan for her and the children. A friend found people in the township to hire her husband for small jobs like gardening, hoping that keeping him busy and earning money would keep him from drinking. Then one day Nomusa's brother showed up at her husband's home and—in her words—"said he'd kill my husband with a gun if there was any problem." Her husband insisted he would change. "He says he'll even kiss my feet and I can lock him up if he does anything wrong." She moved back in with him.

That was about three years before I met Nomusa, and she said that for those three years God had answered her prayers and her husband had treated her well. But in the year I began visiting her, problems seemed to be mounting again. One by one she exhausted her possible solutions. Her husband's drinking was increasing. One day she walked into a friend's home to find him kissing another woman. In one of our most heartbreaking conversations, she told me he had contracted HIV from another woman and passed it on to her. He had apologized, but he also denied that the disease was serious. He had heard that drinking alcohol freezes HIV from spreading, and he preferred that option to seeking medical treatment.

Meanwhile, Nomusa's teenage daughter was disappearing at night, and Nomusa worried about becoming a very young grandmother. One day she found that several hundred rand had been stolen from her cash for restocking her store.

She accused her best friend of stealing it, cutting off their relationship for over a month. Their relationship was mended when Nomusa decided that another culprit for the lost money seemed more likely, namely, her husband. She also never ruled out the possibility that the thief used one of the most malevolent forms of witchcraft—an *utokoloshi*, a small dwarflike demon controlled by a greedy or vengeful person. As a shopkeeper, she managed many difficult relationships with indebted customers, and she knew any number of people who might find reasons to send an utokoloshi.

One day she told me she was worried there might be a demon inside her. She based this on evidence that she was sleeping fitfully and had found a knife mysteriously placed beside her bed one morning. This evidence could mean that demons were taking her spirit to do evil things while she slept. She asked around to find a church that could help dispel demons, and I accompanied her to one church service. Members of the church visited her home later to pray for her and her husband. In addition to consulting with a social worker and a police officer about her troubles with her husband and daughter, she regularly met with a sangoma on her street. She tried some of the sangoma's recommendations to conduct ceremonies to repair her relationships with ancestors who could be causing her bad luck. One day when I was visiting, she showed me the two chickens tied outside that would be slaughtered for her ancestors, and another day she was brewing a pot of homemade beer that she would place in a certain part of her home to give to her ancestors. Her husband had also begun saving money to slaughter a cow for his ancestors.

Her optimism came and went depending on the state of these rituals and the news from the sangoma. One morning she told me with some confidence that she was going to get a job. The sangoma had just told her about a number of signs that would occur before she got a certain job that she had applied for, and the last of the signs had appeared. When I asked about the job some weeks later, she had heard nothing. We did not bring it up again.

When I left South Africa after the first year of research, Nomusa's shop shelves had been bare for several months. The theft left her unable to restock. Her relationship with her husband was extremely strained. She moved out soon after I left. After a few months living with family members, she told me in an optimistic text message, "I'm meeting a lot of new friends." But the optimism didn't last. Another month later she moved back in with her husband. She needed to live in the area so her kids could attend the same school, and without any source of income she had run out of people with whom she could stay.

Much of Nomusa's life could be described as what social scientists call "precarity." Even when she had a source of income, a supportive social group, and a home to live in, she was always hovering just at the edge of losing those basic necessities.

Social scientists studying work in recent decades have pointed out that precarity is becoming more common in the world.[15] Job contracts are becoming shorter and easier to break, and job benefits like health insurance, pensions, transport, and housing are getting cut. Living with precarity means being unlikely to have a job at all and certainly not a job that lasts.

In a life of precarity, relationships matter all the more.[16] According to a Zulu saying, "If you want to succeed, get close to those who are succeeding." Nomusa talked about relationships all the time, even when I repeatedly attempted to follow my prepared research questions to steer her back to talking about work. Nomusa's line of conversation was not just due to some unique way she saw the world. Like nearly everyone I met in Mpophomeni, relationships mattered to her at least as much as a job. As one medical anthropologist pointed out, the number one predictor of whether you live or die of a life-threatening disease in Africa is not whether or not you have a health clinic, it's whether you have a good friend.[17] Friends and family help get you to a health clinic, pick up medicine, feed you and administer that medicine, and take care of your daily needs while you recover. The same goes for income. Being qualified for a job often matters less than whether you have relationships that allow you to get, keep, make sense of, and survive in that job. Relationships also determine how you keep on surviving when that job goes away. For Nomusa, showing respect for the people around her with resources and power was one way to secure those relationships for times when she needed them.

## Respect as a Moral Code

Social scientists have thought a lot about how people handle moral conundrums of sharing resources. Exchanges of goods do not happen in a realm separate from social relations—the two are intricately intertwined. Cultural norms about social relations shape how much people share, with whom, when, under what conditions, and more. As Karl Polanyi wrote in 1957, "The outstanding discovery of recent historical and anthropological research is that man's economy, as a rule, is submerged in his social relationships."[18] In the early twentieth century, anthropologists—including Marcel Mauss and Bronislaw Malinowski—studied the ways people exchanged gifts, pointing out that gifts are more than just a way to meet economic needs. Gifts bond relationships in ways that offer the security of long-term reciprocity.[19] In the 1980s, the philosopher Pierre Bourdieu pointed out that relationships are in some sense exchangeable for financial capital. He suggested that people's class position depends not just on income, but on gaining what he called social capital—meaning the connections people have to others—and cultural capital—referring to the behaviors people learn that gain them acceptance into socially ranked settings.[20] Social capital offers one way to describe what was happening when Nomusa went to stay with siblings, or when she convinced her customers to pay their debts. She was in a sense turning social capital into financial capital.

But there was more happening in her relationships: she was navigating cultural expectations of what constitutes moral exchange in various situations. Marshall Sahlins, building on the work of Marcel Mauss and Bronislaw Malinowski, attempted to classify the kinds of moral codes people follow as they exchange goods.[21] Sahlins presented a spectrum of moral codes ranging from situations where people expect to give without receiving anything back (**generalized reciprocity**) to situations where they give little and expect to get a lot back (**negative reciprocity**). Many relationships fall somewhere around the midpoint of that spectrum (**balanced reciprocity**), in which people expect to get back about the same amount as they give, at least over time. The economic anthropologist David Graeber more recently proposed another set of moral codes.[22] He said people often assume that most economic transactions simply follow a moral logic of market-like transactions, in which people exchange roughly equivalent values. Graeber argues that in seeing everything as exchange, we fail to notice the other moral logics happening all around us. As an example, he describes what he calls "**everyday communism**," in which people give according to ability and need, such as giving a stranger directions or helping clean up after a natural disaster.

Whether we try to fit situations into one of Sahlins's moral codes or one of Graeber's, the important thing is that when people exchange goods, they follow moral codes. Part of growing up in any cultural setting is learning its specific moral codes. People everywhere learn when to exchange, how much, and with whom. We learn what behaviors need to accompany that exchange, whether it's haggling for a long time over a price or placing a gift secretly in someone's mailbox without mentioning it. When someone doesn't follow those codes, the people around them will correct them with some kind of social sanction: a child whines that a parent should give more dessert, an employer posts a notice warning that tardiness is stealing time, or a union goes on strike to demand higher wages.

Respect is one such moral code of relationships and exchanges. It offers both a deeply indoctrinated sets of behaviors—a *habitus* that people follow without question, much like the habit some people learn of saying thank you to the host of a dinner party.[23] It also offers a standard people call upon when the code is broken—much like someone appealing to the idea that education should be a universal human right when they are denied free education. One of the main things the moral code of respect calls for—as Duduzile said—is that those with more must help those with less, especially if they have close social ties.

Church sermons were one of the many public settings in which people reinforced this moral order of respect and its implications about sharing. More than once in Zulu churches I heard part of Luke 12:48 cited: "From everyone to whom much has been given, much will be required."[24] One pastor told the congregants: "It's your responsibility not to close the door behind you, but to open it more widely." He asked, "Do you have the strength to meet the needs that arise from what you ask for?" Another pastor told the story of Esther, a Jewish woman who became a queen in a foreign country, saying "She knew who she was. She was a Jew." He compared Esther to Africans who become wealthy. "Don't forget you're an African. Don't forget where you come from." One pastor used a catchy phrase of warning: "The higher the level, the higher the devils." The moral of his sermon was not that **money or higher levels** were wrong, but that these came with responsibilities and obligations to dependents.[25] For people encountering hardships like Nomusa's, an important strategy of survival, then, is to hold others accountable to those obligations.

## Every Human Has Value

In the precarious world of scarce employment, strong relationships characterized by respect can help people access material resources that contribute to a better life, but respect is more than just a way to access good things. In an important sense, for many people respect itself is the good life. Respect is not just a moral code for requesting redistribution of resources, it also offers something that lessens the sting of inequality even when no resources change hands.

The sociologist Richard Sennett wrote about what he learned from his own experiences living in low-income housing in the United States. He points to respect as a way to overcome inequalities, not because it might lead to changing the actual inequalities of wealth, but because it is a kind of performance. When people show respect, they behave in ways that **reach across the boundaries** of inequality to transform the experiences of inequality for the better. Sennett argues that especially in situations of inequality, we need to recognize the ways in which performing respect turns people outward to mutually acknowledge each other.[26]

In believing the dominant laziness myth discussed in chapter 2, many Europeans and Americans have increasingly come to think of dignity as inextricably tied to labor. In this narrative, labor leads to dignity either because the sort of labor people do is socially constructed as dignifying, or because people use the wages of their labor to buy things that show their status. People who do not have the kind of work deemed dignified are treated in such a cultural setting as having little value at all. One remarkable aspect of the Zulu concept of respect is that it outright contradicts this way of thinking about labor and human value. In the narrative that puts respect at the center of a moral code, every human being deserves respect and dignity. Human value is performed into existence by interactions between people, regardless of their employment status.

One of the workplaces I chose to study was a gas station (or petrol station, as South Africans say). South African law forbids self-service petrol stations, so as a car owner, I interacted regularly with people who pumped petrol. We would exchange brief conversations as they checked the oil level and washed the windshield, and I often observed similar friendly banter between employees and other customers. In an interview with a young man working at a gas station, he admitted he saw pumping gas as a low-level job and hoped not to work there for long, but he said his job satisfaction depended on how customers treated him. I asked what he wished customers knew about work as a petrol station attendant, and he responded: "What I can tell them is *respect*. Respect is the most important thing. You have to respect someone, even if he's poor, if he doesn't have money, because he's a human being. If they can give us respect and don't take our job as just a stupid job, because they taking us for granted."

One aspect of performing respect that several people mentioned was the simple act of greeting someone according to Zulu custom. Multiple Zulu people had warned me, knowing mistakes other white and foreign people have made, that in South Africa you *must* greet people properly. Not to do so is an egregious signal of disrespect. More than once over my years in South Africa I made the unfortunate mistake of forgetting to greet people with the Zulu words for "Hello" and "How are you?" I was treated in response with deliberate aloofness. As I came to understand respect, I understood why ignoring the greeting process was considered so rude. The very word used like "hello" in isiZulu is *sawubona*, literally meaning "I have seen you." To greet someone saying sawubona is to perform an act of respect that communicates "You are a person before me; I see your humanity."

This emphasis on treating others in ways that acknowledge their value also intertwines with another term that people associate with being Zulu: *ubuntu*. People often explained this word as expressing the idea that "a person is a person through other people," or "I am because we are." When I asked one woman what she meant by ubuntu, she responded simply, "Ubuntu is respect." The word "ubuntu" is a combination of the stems *ntu* referring to "person," and *ubu*, a noun-marking stem that is similar to the English suffix "ness." Thus, ubuntu might be translated as something like "humanness" or "being human." While ubuntu is sometimes over-romanticized by tourists and debated by scholars who are cynical about its actual influence, people I spoke with brought up ubuntu as something deeply entwined with Zulu identity and something that society would be worse off for losing.

It is no accident that two words people used to explain performances of respect—sawubona and ubuntu—are words that cannot be easily translated from isiZulu to English. Zulu people emphasized that respect is not something that everyone in the world learns in the same way; it is a moral code that their ethnic group is especially good at teaching. In multiple conversations about what is unique about being Zulu, people stressed that to be Zulu is to know how to use this code. One young woman told me she was glad she was Zulu because "Zulu people are respected; they respect everyone." On two occasions, middle-class South Africans who had moved away from the township told me they wanted their children to grow up back in a Zulu township because a Zulu community is where children can best learn respect.

Because this moral code is so deeply rooted in a cultural identity, it has an almost unquestionable authority among Zulu people. When Nomusa told her husband, "You're not respecting me as a wife," he knew what she meant, and he knew this was serious. He shouldn't be drinking away their money without sharing money with her, and he shouldn't be using his physical and social power to harm her.

Among white people, however, the moral code of respect did not necessarily have that same authority. Zulu people, like many historically disadvantaged people in the world, consider themselves to have an understanding of respect that exceeds that of the privileged people around them. That fact goes a long way toward explaining what is not working about work.

## Respect at the Intersection of Work and the Good Life

One numerical calculation I made based on my interviews was to count up the reasons people gave for leaving jobs. If the laziness myth were accurate, you would expect people to mention the strain of the workplace, the difficulty of tasks, or the desire for more time away from work. These types of answers rarely came up, and when they did, it was in the context of another reason: relationships. The single most common reason people gave for leaving jobs was relationships that were in some way not right. Of the thirty-nine people who told me they had quit a job, fifteen cited poor treatment by an employer, including five mentions of racism and one of sexual assault. Eight mentioned problems with their coworkers, including backstabbing, false accusations, and jealousy. Only three people cited low wages as a reason for leaving. Whenever pay was mentioned, people talked about it in the context of human valuation, like "I was not paid enough to put myself in that danger," or "only the old people will take that kind of pay, because . . . they don't have a relationship with the boss to speak up." People described having been treated on the job like a dog, a pig, a monkey, a baboon, or a machine. They were not being treated as human, and by definition, were not being respected.[27]

When I asked what people wanted at work, they also talked about respect. One young woman gave this short and to-the-point explanation of what she wanted in an employer: "I like the truth. I want someone who will respect me, and I will respect her. It will go well then." Others gave longer explanations of similar ideas. When I asked Duduzile to describe what a good workplace meant to her, she talked about the relationships between employees and bosses: "I need to respect that person and that person needs to respect me, because we need each other. . . . So it's the exchange. Because we *all* need each other." When workplaces work, people see each other, they share with each other, and they treat each other like valuable humans no matter what their position in the company.

In many cases, people tried work and found no respect there. Sometimes unemployment offered a better route to the respect people sought. One afternoon I stood around talking with some young men who were washing cars at the Mpophomeni taxi rank. Two of the guys shared some of their rap lyrics with me and talked at length about what music meant to them. One man said, "We get respect for this." One had attended some courses after high school, but neither had a paying job other than earning a little money washing cars. They both insisted, though, that the only job they wanted in life was rapping, even if it didn't pay anything. "I don't see myself working. Just rapping," one said. For him, rapping meant "being a messenger, and helping people." As rappers, they built relationships with people who greeted them "with hugs" and cared for them "like family." "You give back," one explained. "That's the way people respect you." Rapping offered a means to live according to a moral code of respect, performing human value and giving to others according to what they had. They were side-stepping work altogether in an alternative vision of the good life. As one of them put it, "Respect is better than money."

White people too often missed the subtleties of what the moral order of respect requires. Take promotions, for example. I heard many stories from white employers frustrated and befuddled when they promoted a Zulu employee to a higher-paying leadership role, and soon after, that promoted person quit. White employers used this as evidence that Zulu people were cognitively or morally impaired—in quitting a good job, they were being either irrational or lazy.

When Zulu people told stories of the same sorts of events—leaving jobs after being promoted—the point of the story came out very differently. A young woman who rode in the car with me one day said she had left a job at a restaurant near my home because of "personal reasons." When I asked her to elaborate, she said, "Because the others didn't like that they saw I was communicating with the boss." We talked at length about how sad she felt to have excelled in her job for six months, and then made the difficult choice to leave to preserve relationships with friends who had been her coworkers. People who told such stories brought them up not as exceptions to the norm, but with the emphasis that this was a frequent, regular problem. Often frictions happened when a young or recently hired person was promoted over their elders, which was common in part because young black Africans had grown up with better opportunities to learn English and gain higher education. The problem was not so much that a hierarchy existed at work, it was a problem of how that hierarchy was enacted. As Bullet explained, people don't have a problem respecting a manager who they consider qualified for the position, but tension arises when the qualifications for promotion are disputed. Bullet said the problems come up when people are hired under the assumption that everyone is a "general worker," that is, a person whose job description offers no particular qualifications. In practice, white employers often select general workers for managerial promotions for various reasons, such as innovativeness, fluency in English, or seeming to get along well with other managers. In jobs where employers have not made clear the qualifications for promotion, people who have been there longer than the one promoted will think, in Bullet's words, "'We all have qualifications, so what makes you better than me? I know this place inside and out.' . . . They feel like they should be manager, because in this case, qualification in years of service." The one who accepts the promotion now becomes disrespectful of those with longer terms of service who were not promoted. In response to the perceived disrespectful move, coworkers can make the life of that promoted person miserable, sometimes so much so that they quit.

It is no accident that people who have been systematically deprived of resources by a white or otherwise powerful elite often have a high regard for right relationships. A strong moral code of relationships is a survival tactic. George Lipsitz surmises that among black communities in the United States, solidarity among the black community "stems not so much from an abstract idealism as from necessity." But this intense need for relationships can have a downside. Lipsitz goes on, "Because it is difficult to move away from other members of their group, they struggle to turn the radical divisiveness created by overcrowding and competition for scarce resources into mutual recognition and respect."[28] Indeed, needing to rely closely on a community while competing for scarce resources has a drawback that came up often—jealousy.

## The Burden of Having

The flip side of having a network of people to support you on the day you lose your job is that you also have people to support on the day you get a job. Think about what happens when only 43 percent of working-aged adults have jobs, as was the case in South Africa by 2018.[29] Those adults were financially supporting all the other 57 percent of adults plus the elderly and children. That's a heavy load to bear.

Employed people often told me that payday was the most stressful time of the month. "Each and every month at payday," one twenty-something-year-old factory employee said, "my head become big." He gestured to demonstrate a headache as he listed off expenses he would try to cover—groceries, clothes for his child, school fees, and doctors. "I end up with R250 in my pocket." Others would consider ending up with anything at all in their pockets to be doing well. A young woman in Mpophomeni named Simphiwe listed the people she supported: eight people, including friends, old lovers, nieces and nephews, siblings, and school friends. Simphiwe was twenty-four years old, single and childless. She earned about thirty-eight dollars a week stocking grocery store shelves. If she spread her earnings evenly across those she supported, she would have about one dollar per day per person. Later that year she quit one grocery store job and took another grocery store job with less pay. Her reason was that the timing of paydays differed. The new job had payday every other week, and she thought spreading out the paydays would help her avoid some of the requests for money and allow her to put more into her own savings.

A police officer who had moved from Mpophomeni to Johannesburg explained that people who are trying to move up the social ladder face intense pressure to help those with less, while also feeling pressured to act like they fit in with the next level up. In Johannesburg when he went out with coworkers, this police officer would buy expensive whiskey or cognac to share. Back at home, he had to give gifts to people, but he could not be as generous with everyone. "If you are very soft, then you're gonna be a target; everybody will walk on top of you. Sometimes you must put your foot down." With pressures from above and below, it's no wonder that people with lucrative salaries in South Africa are just as likely as unemployed people to be deeply in debt.[30]

Just having a job does not predict how satisfied people are. Another research study in South Africa found that employment was a less accurate indicator of a person's perceived happiness than the employment level of one's surrounding community.[31] Another study in South Africa found that employed people were actually more likely than unemployed people to view their households as poor.[32] Still other research has found that even in farming and domestic work—jobs that saw significant increases in minimum wages in the decades after apartheid ended—increased pay often came with a decrease in people's perceptions of their own well-being.[33] When obligations to others outweigh one's ability to share, employment becomes a burden. Thus, as rising inequality and unemployment stretch people's circles of dependents ever wider, going from unemployed to employed can bring people more strain than satisfaction.

Many people in low-wage work talked about their struggles trying to help meet the needs of dependents with even less than they had. When you're the one without a job, they said, you want to get a job to "have pocket money" or "be independent." Once you get a job, though, you signal to relatives that your role has changed. Now you have new responsibilities to provide for others. These responsibilities can leave you with a net loss, leaving you less pocket money at the end of the month than when another relative provided for your basic needs. For young people, this shift to becoming a breadwinner was especially burdensome. If you didn't have work, relatives might still consider it socially acceptable for you to get by on the provision of others, but if you did have work, your role became giving back to others. There is a minimal threshold in wages below which you may be unable to adequately meet the cultural expectations associated with employment at your life stage.[34] Below such a threshold, it may be economically preferable to be unemployed—signaling to your relatives that you are not the person to ask for help—rather than have people expect you to help them from your impossibly low wages. To outsiders, the choices that result from this scenario can look like laziness. It could seem like some people prefer to depend on others rather than work. But calling that situation laziness overlooks the rationale that when there are not enough jobs to go around and job benefits are extremely low, getting a job is not always in an individual's best interest. Sometimes prioritizing right relationships with people around you meant turning down jobs that would not make right relationships possible. The pressure to share has shaped spending habits and migration patterns across the society. On paydays and government welfare payout days, people often spent nearly all their money and paid back as many debts as possible in the first day or two, leaving them with the excuse of being broke if people requested money the rest of the month. Big expenditures with regular automatic payments, like cars and furniture on credit, similarly locked away money from the requests of others. People admitted, often with a sense of regret, that moving away from relatives also made it easier to turn down their requests. This was one more factor pulling "haves" further from "have-nots" and perpetuating the image of the township as a place where no one worked.

When people talked about how much to share with relatives and who should qualify as a dependent, the debates got fierce. In one job-readiness training session I observed, a trainer asked thirty-two young unemployed people, "Will you give away your first paycheck?" Participants stood up and walked to different signs posted in the room to vote their responses. Only one person stood alone at the sign that said "no." Four people stood at "maybe." Twenty-seven crowded together by "yes." A heated debate ensued. The twenty-seven slung moral accusations at the five who dared question these practices. They described obligations to give not just some, but all of their first paycheck to parents, churches, or offerings for ancestors. They said without the support and guidance of those people, they would not have been able to get and keep a job, and they needed to start their working lives by giving back.[35]

I first stumbled into a debate of this sort when I worked with the microfinance organization. I was leading an activity in which young adults were asked to list all the steps it would take for one member of their group to achieve a goal—in his case, becoming a carpenter in Johannesburg. They listed things like getting training, finding someone to stay with in Johannesburg, and buying tools. Then one woman burst out loudly, "But he has to remember where he came from!" I asked them to explain. They said to "remember where you came from"—in Zulu, the often-used phrase "khumbula ekhaya"—meant to give back to the people who supported you. People around the meeting table nodded and agreed that this was an essential piece of achieving his dream, and in fact it was probably the hardest. Some people insisted this would prevent the aspiring carpenter from ever achieving his dream. His relatives in their rural area would expect too much of him if he moved to a big city where they imagined wages to be high and life to be easy. In a new self-owned business, they predicted, he could never earn enough to support all the rural relatives who would expect his help.

## Is Respect Achievable?

That brings us to an intriguing thought: If people define the good life as having and giving respect, is that life achievable? Answering this question requires considering at least two possible ways that the good life, defined by respect, could be achieved—at the microlevel of an individual who calls their life good, or at the macroscale of influencing all of society for good.

Individuals who described themselves as currently living the good life often tied that good life to good relationships. Multiple people described work experiences that they genuinely liked, and most often those experiences included employers who followed relational moral codes of sharing and respect that went beyond the requisites of their contractual relationship. One man raved about an employer who entrusted him with duties he did not know he was capable of, overall "believing in" him. This had practical ramifications for the responsibilities and resources he acquired: the employer entrusted him to travel widely at work, and she paid for his medical bills beyond what was contractually required. People spoke of various companies where they experienced and appreciated respect. I'll provide more detail in chapter 6.

People also described situations in which they experienced respectful rela-tionships outside of work. For a country with skyrocketing unemployment rates, it should come as good news that this kind of good life does not wholly depend on whether someone has employment. When I met Duduzile, she had recently quit a job for reasons that included disrespect from coworkers. When I asked whether she was living the good life right now, she answered with an unequivocal "yes." Despite becoming unemployed, living in an impoverished neighborhood where she only had running water for a few hours in the middle of the night, being HIV positive, never having children, and caring for her aging mother, she had good relationships.[36] She cared for her neighbor's children, helped pay for a friend's school fees, mended clothes for neighbors, and sometimes received pay for her help. What they had—and what she and others told me they protected and defended for their communities and future generations—was respect.

At the microlevel of interpersonal relationships, then, respect offered one nar-rative of the good life that at least some marginalized people used to describe their actual arrival at the good life. But what about at the macrolevel of changing entire structures and systems that cause marginalization? Does the aim of finding respect within unequal interpersonal relationships have a multiplying effect of changing wider systems, or might it distract people from larger goals of changing the causes and sources of inequalities?

My evidence here is insufficient to make any firm conclusion, but I can say that people at least envisioned respect as a way to change systems beyond just one-on-one relationships. People named experiences of respect that they had in low-wage, low-skill jobs. One woman summarized the ideal relationship between employers and employees, "Nizwana," a word that translates as people both "understanding each other" and "feeling for each other." Nizwana meant recognizing each other's humanity. She didn't name a company she had worked for where she had had this experience, but the word gave her a name for the kind of workplace she wished for. Respect named a quality of social structure that people sought in workplaces and in the broader society.

When I returned to visit in August 2017, two years after Nomusa and I met, she had just been diagnosed with leukemia. While her forty-year-old body appeared as healthy as ever, she was making preparations for her sister to care for her children when she no longer could. In the midst of these heavy conversations, I figured I should at least ask again the question that had originally brought me to meet her—What was her work situation like? She said that she had recently been hired for a job at a nearby factory, but she heard rumors that the white boss had raped Zulu women. Besides, to start work on time she had to walk to a bus stop in the early morning darkness. One morning when she was walking alone, someone mugged her and stole her cell phone. She and her husband agreed the job wasn't worth it, so she quit. She had never revived her shop, but she and her husband were renting out two rooms in their house. They had settled into a plan to live together, sleeping in separate beds, with the money for one room's rent going to her and the other to him. For a while anyway, their relationship seemed to be working.

I began my research set on writing about what people looked for in work and why it was so hard to find it. My relationship with Nomusa taught me something that does not come across in a typical research interview about unemployment, especially when a researcher shows up, asks a few questions, and moves on to the next interview. Nomusa taught me to see how work fits as only one small piece in a much larger picture of what it means to seek the good life. When I drove away after visiting Nomusa on my last visit in 2017, thinking about her stolen cell phone, her precarious marriage, and her leukemia, the thought struck me, "Work is the last thing she's worrying about now."

Nomusa was worrying, as she had all her life, about relationships. Her life included standing up against abuse, caring for and being cared for by siblings, negotiating custody for children, managing the goodwill of employers, and balancing strictness and leniency with customers. She maintained relationships with her deceased relatives, with neighbors who might use malevolent spirits against her, and with the God of Christian churches. I hated thinking that Nomusa could easily be further mistreated by her husband, and yet her ways of protecting her well-being were impressive. She made the decision to stay with him knowing she had the support of social workers, police officers, friends, and relatives. Importantly, she also had a moral code to stand by and a socially acceptable means to use it. By demanding that people follow that moral code of respect, she found ways to survive and even thrive in the difficult inequalities in which she lived. She hung on to a strong sense of respect and had the courage to claim it.

Likewise, when it comes to fair treatment at work, people seek out and create resources and systems that they can use to command respect—the unions, the government labor mediation commission, laws, and lawyers that parallel the social workers and safe houses Nomusa used. When people insisted on respect in the workplace, they were not accepting exploitation. Quite the opposite—they chose a particular way of dealing with exploitation and oppression. Sometimes resistance to oppression means actually removing powerful people who refuse to practice respect from their social position, as with the ending of apartheid and the more recent removal of President Jacob Zuma from office. Other times it means calling people in power to account within their position by insisting, *I matter. See me. I am human as you are human. You need to help where you can, just as I need to help where I can.* Nomusa was rarely able to change her social position—in 2017 she was still a wife in a patriarchal society, still unemployed.

Yet she harnessed the moral code of respect in ways that did get people to relinquish certain powers over her—the power to define her as less than human, the power to hoard wealth, the power to become unresponsive to the needs of others. In a country and a world where inequality keeps widening and unemployment rates keep rising, it's worth watching how people also use this moral code of respect to create the systems that shape societies.

# "HUSTLING IS WHEN YOU TRY TO MAKE A GOOD LIFE"

## The Hustling Narrative

One afternoon as I stood outside the Mpophomeni library eating a sandwich before heading back inside to catch up on field notes, a young man with spiky dreadlocks, a wildly patterned shirt, and a bright smile leaned up against the brick library wall and introduced himself. He told me to call him by the name his friends used, a name he had chosen for himself: Teeza. When Teeza heard that I had come from the United States, he asked if he could come back to America with me in a suitcase.

Like many anthropologists, I found this kind of conversation a little awkward—I was supposed to be there learning about *his* place after all, not promoting the oh-so-prevalent idea that America is the best place in the world. I tried to shift the conversation by asking what he would do if he were in America.

He casually glossed over some previous jobs, saying he had done "all kinds of things," and then said that what he would really do in America was fashion. Maybe reading some skepticism on my face, he insisted, no really, he would make it there one day. If I didn't believe him, he said, I should come see his fashion design company, Black Teardrop.

Whether it was my misunderstanding or because he misled me, during that conversation at the library I got the impression that Teeza owned and managed Black Teardrop. In the months that followed, I would never see Teeza do more actual clothing production than cut out a piece of fabric and pick up a few sewing machine parts that had fallen on the floor. What Teeza did do for the business—and I immediately became a case in point—was promotion. He was the company's image-manager extraordinaire. A half hour after we met, Teeza was showing me around the little fashion design studio and introducing me to the real mastermind behind the start-up business, a young woman called Sma.[1] I sat on a low couch along one wall of the small cement building while Sma sewed a pair of pants out of bright patterned cloth. The walls and floor were painted in sunny yellow and turquoise with large letters spelling "Black Tear-drop," plus other words and images filling the walls in graffiti-style spray paint. Teeza perched himself on a table, just beneath a word in big red letters, "Fashion." In the many conversations with Teeza and Sma that would follow, they used a word that I came to think of as a title for the ways they mixed entrepreneurship with seemingly insurmountable challenges to fashion a good life: hustling.

Our conversation alternated between sober thoughts about township life and their playful teasing of each other and me. Sma told the story of how she dropped out of electrical engineering school to begin this business. "I was scared," she said, "afraid I would never be someone that I want to be. I was crying every day." Now six years later their shop had three sewing machines (in various states of disrepair), and people across the township were wearing their clothes. More than that, the building had become a sort of youth center where young people hung out, brainstormed ideas, and found empathetic friends. "Everyone who comes here tells their story. They cry, and we come up with solutions," Sma said. Then, as if embarrassed by the serious direction of our conversation, she looked at me with a mock pouting face, "Even you, you look like you're going to cry a tear." Teeza burst out laughing.

When I asked about Teeza's role in the company, he said he found customers, promoted the company outside the township, and served as a fashion model. He wore the clothes Sma made with confidence. On a typical day, I would find him striding through the township in a sharp-shouldered blazer over a black T-shirt with brightly patterned drop-crotch pants and a pair of sunglasses perched on his short dreadlocks.

On the surface, Teeza and Sma seemed to be living the entrepreneurial dream that had become the obsession of the South African media and government. The South African government was pouring big money into promoting entrepreneurship. Government websites boasted that the government devoted over a billion rand to business development from 2013 to 2014, and its "National Development Plan has identified [business] incubation as key to the development of a vibrant and growing small enterprise sector."[2] As I mentioned in the introduction, I came to South Africa for the first time in 2006 riding on this wave. My husband and I were hired as codirectors of a pilot project that was designed to help young people in rural areas start businesses. Our organization's advisory board included Muhammad Yunus, the founder of Bangladesh's Grameen Development Bank, one of the first and most publicized large-scale microfinance organizations in the world. We heard the news soon after we arrived in South Africa that he had won a Nobel Peace Prize. His books, one of which I read as a MBA graduate student, promote small loans for small business entrepreneurs as a one-size-fits-all solution to poverty.[3] By 2014 much of the scholarship on microenterprise was pointing out the shortcomings and potential harms of all this global hype and investment in entrepreneurship, but in practice, the government and many nonprofit organizations in this part of South Africa were still pinning their hopes on small business development as a solution to poverty and unemployment.

The South African media had also readily taken up the cause of promoting entrepreneurship among the poor. One could scarcely open a South African newspaper without finding a story of a successful small business, a government speech about small business funding, or an editorial extolling the importance of an entrepreneurial mindset among youth. Serial television shows included interviews of business owners and reality TV–style dramas of new start-up businesses. Among the nightly soap opera–style serial dramas—the most commonly watched and discussed programming in the township—every episode I sampled over a ten-day study included a character owning or managing a business.

Often the government and media messaging about entrepreneurship used one of two strategies to promote entrepreneurship. Each strategy was based on questionable assumptions about unemployed people. First, promotional material extolled the benefits of entrepreneurship. This strategy implicitly assumed that unemployed people were either ignorant of the benefits of entrepreneurship or too enamored with leisure to see how entrepreneurship could benefit them. Second, promotions promised skills and resources to help people start businesses. This strategy was based on the assumption that to run a business, unemployed people only lacked a few basic skills and a little money. With the assistance of the government or another organization, anyone could run a business. Infused with the narrative of hard work curing all social ills, these pro-entrepreneurial messages implied that anyone could work their way out of poverty with a little business ingenuity, start-up money, well-targeted skills training, and the all-important work ethic.

In some ways, Teeza and Sma seemed to be living the pro-entrepreneurial dream. But in the coming months as I visited their colorful sewing shop, I heard stories like those I had heard in my previous work with a microfinance organization—accounts of the challenges that black small business owners faced in South Africa that could not be overcome with a little investment capital or a little skills training.

And there were also aspects of the Black Teardrop business that lined up with criticisms I had heard mingled with the same pro-entrepreneurship messages that would have applauded their hard work. I had heard many people, both black and white, complain about the unemployed youth who spent what little money they had on the right clothes, the right shoes, the right hair, the right music, and the right image.[4] The entrepreneurship and job-readiness training programs I visited included training sessions on how to spend less money, which included avoiding expensive fashions. "They need to learn to save," one trainer told me. "They have to develop a mindset of keeping money rather than spending it. They're not looking to the future." Teeza and Sma were running a business, but their business was based on selling a fashionable image to the people who were—in the pro-entrepreneurship narrative—supposed to save money for more necessary purchases. Business and personal image weren't supposed to mix.

These complaints were especially common among older black South Africans talking about the younger generation. In one conversation, an older black man sat on a couch at a mutual friend's house expressing his deep frustration as he talked about his son. He had built up a taxi business over his lifetime and recently had given his son a taxi to start making his own living. Now the son was racking up more debt than earnings. "He is eating all the money," the elderly man complained. "He gives rides to all his friends. He buys everyone beer." The son had bought a R15,000 sound system for the taxi. "But he's very lazy," the father complained. His son, like Teeza and Sma, struggled on a path to the good life involving self-fashioning and struggle, but to this father, something about that style of business looked like laziness and trouble.

In this chapter, I focus disproportionately—as has the popular discourse on the dangers of unemployed youth—on young black men, though I also include examples from women like Sma who shared similar narratives. This was the group that everyone else seemed quickest to condemn. At the time of my research, statistics showed that as many as 52 percent of the youth had no work or were not even seeking work.[5] For white or older people, the perception that they were surrounded by unemployed black youth mingled with images of dangerous idle black men, gangsters, and drug addicts to stoke a good deal of fear. Young people were seen as "throwing their lives away" through substance abuse, fights, unprotected sex, or other behaviors that seemed to place a low value on their own or others' lives. Assumptions that they were inherently dangerous—to themselves and others—produced patterns of social separation that furthered the cycle of unemployment and inequality.[6] Suspicion also rendered invisible the narratives of a good life this population lived by. In the dominant pro-entrepreneurial narrative, these youth were either entrepreneurs (good) or wasters of time and money (bad). The first group was expected to succeed, the second wasn't.

These people, though, lived by a narrative that diverged from the dominant pro-entrepreneurship narrative in significant ways. Yes, they used entrepreneurship as a means of self-actualization and earning an income, but the ends and the means of the narrative differed significantly from a late-neoliberal entre-preneurial narrative. Foremost in their conception of the good life was the real-ity that the journey would not be easy. In their conversations about their path to the good life, they emphasized that they would most certainly face obstacles that were inequitably distributed along racialized lines. They also did not take for granted that the journey would be linear. Some spoke of paths to the good life that were cyclical, temporary, or sporadically unpredictable. Their views of morality did not emphasize the values of saving and restrained consumption that Protestant Europeans had long promulgated. Instead, they valued uphold-ing an image of success even within their struggle, fashioning that image for themselves and for others as a means of retaining dignity and direction. And their lives revealed that there are many kinds of entrepreneurship—some that do not appeal to young people, some that appeal but are unattainable, and some others that are nearly impossible to escape. Compared to the conceptions of entrepre-neurs that dominated the media and entrepreneurial trainings, their lives were tougher, their obstacles rougher, and their choices geared toward bridging the gap between hope and uncertainty.

One question about these young people that others have been quick to ask—and perhaps too quick answer—is whether their narrative was working—Did it lead to success? People who criticized the lifestyle of people like Teeza often concluded that these young people were making choices that caused their own demise. In subtle and loud ways, society has accused them of being incapable of planning, unconcerned about preserving their lives, or a bane to society. In the years since I had met the people in this book, I saw some of them move closer to the good life they wanted while others seemed to drift further away. Yet a central question of this chapter is whether these examples mean their narrative itself is failing. Or is it possible that even if people do not often succeed in fol-lowing their route to the success they aim for, the narrative succeeds in another way? Narratives, after all, are not like trains that people can hop on and all travel together to the same destination. Narratives are ways of making meaning out of circumstances.

In recent years, black theorists have wrestled with questions of how to live and think amid the dominant narratives that have for centuries failed to describe—and allowed colonizers to disguise—the realities of black experiences. A narrative that dominates Western thought, particularly in the United States, is a redemp-tive narrative that foresees good coming out of any suffering. As Frank Wilderson has pointed out, the possibility that the history of American slavery might never follow a redemptive narrative is "terrifying" to liberals because it implies that there could be "suffering for which there is no imaginable strategy for redress—no narrative of redemption."[7] He goes so far as to suggest that, for black people in the world, the violence that characterizes black life is so unrelenting as to "make narrative inaccessible to Blacks," leaving black people in what Hortense Spillers calls "historical stillness."[8]

The people presented in this chapter do not describe their lives according to a narrative of redemption, but neither do they give up on narratives altogether. In contrast to Wilderson, I do not see an absence of narratives that make sense of black experiences, but rather, a creative profusion of narratives that are underrecognized within white discourse. In addition to the narratives described in these chapters, I heard South Africans describe the good life like a stoplight that exerts its own intransigent power to alternately prevent or allow various groups to halt or proceed. Others described the good life using a Zulu saying, "isondo iyajikajika," "the wheel turns and turns," bringing people up and down in cycles of inequality. Such metaphors subvert the naive optimism of the Western redemptive narrative. People go on making meaning in their lives by finding narratives rooted directly in the tension of struggles that do not necessarily have happy endings. One of the clearest descriptions of that tension comes from Derrick Bell, a black American essayist who explores how people can simultaneously recognize the permanence of racism and continue the struggle against it. He writes: "Black people will never gain full equality in [the United States]. Even those herculean efforts we hail as successful will produce no more than temporary 'peaks of progress,' short-lived victories that slide into irrelevance as racial patterns adapt in ways that maintain white dominance. This is a hard-to-accept fact that all history verifies. We must acknowledge it, not as a sign of submission, but as an act of ultimate defiance."[9]

In the midst of struggles for unachievable success, people still pursue meaning and still create narratives. There are many forms of narrative, and some are paradoxical or inconclusive. The narrative in this chapter—like the one Bell suggests black people have engaged in since slavery—involves "carving out a humanity for oneself with absolutely nothing to help—save imagination, will, and unbelievable strength and courage. Beating the odds while firmly believing in, knowing as only they could know, the fact that all those odds are stacked against them."[10]

## A Hustler Is Someone Who Tries

As I sat in the fashion design studio one day, Teeza mentioned that he was getting pressured by his parents and his baby's mom to provide for his child. "So I become the hustler," he said.

"You guys use this word hustler all the time," I said. "What does it mean to be a hustler?"

Sma answered first. "Like what we doing. That's hustling. A hustler is someone who . . ."

Teeza interrupted with a series of broken sentences. "Tries to make change for a living. Tries to make a good life for her or him. When I say I want to be better, I want to produce myself to another level, I want to like, create my own image, myself, to me. That I found everything that I want to. I have to work hard, I have to."

Sma went on. "A hustler is a person who has his own business, like he's hustling, until I get whatever I want."

I couldn't tell whether they saw hustling as something they aspired to or hated. "Is it a proud thing?" I asked. "Are you happy when you're hustling or is it like you want to stop and be done with that part of your life?"

"When you hustling, it's when the business is small or the business is growing," Sma said. When you're "done hustling," she said, "you become a businessman or woman. But when your business is too small you're hustling. A hustler is working too much!" She shook her head and gestured at the sewing machine in front of her. She was talking about herself in the present, but also about what she had to believe was coming in the future. "I hustle until I get whatever I want."

Teeza said he wanted to come back to my question about whether it feels good to be a hustler. It depends on age, he explained. "I tell myself that when I'm 48 I want to be chill at home. Yeah, feeling good. Not do anything, spending my money that I hustled." Hustling, apparently, was OK for a while, but it was supposed to end as you grew older.

I tried another clarifying question: Is working a formal job in town considered hustling?

"No you have to do it yourself," Teeza said.

"You do something for yourself." Sma agreed. "A hustler is a person who has his own business."

I started to notice this word "hustling" everywhere. It came up in the lyrics of popular rap songs that played on the radio and television, both by South African and American artists.[11] When I asked if the word had Zulu equivalents, Sma and Teeza taught me similar slang Zulu words—*ukushizila* and *ukupanda*. They said it could also be said simply with the common Zulu word *ukuzama*, "to try." A friend who was in the fashion design shop at the time interjected, "Hustling is like *angisebenzi, ngiyazama*," that is, "I'm not working, I'm trying."

Their explanation of hustling offered clues that could begin to answer the questions many critical voices have asked of South African young people who live outside of formal employment: Why do they seem to live in the present, spend money on themselves, and avoid certain kinds of employment and entrepreneurship? Hustling requires operating on the fringes of social acceptance, and that makes it all the more important to cultivate the opinions of others—in Teeza's words, to "create my own image" and "produce myself to a higher level." Hustling is to press on in a struggle that might not have an end, but which could, for at least a few lucky ones, someday yield the reward of "being chill." To hustle is "to try"—it is a way of living without guaranteed success.  *retirement*

## Invisible Entrepreneurs

For years I had heard everywhere from academic studies to conversations over tea that South Africa had an entrepreneurship problem—the country had too few entrepreneurs, and too few of them were black South Africans.[12] But as I discussed in chapter 1, the very perception that black South Africans were lazy could shape both the likelihood of their starting businesses and other people's capacity to see and recognize businesses that did exist. Were Teeza and Sma unique in seeing their small business start-up as a means of achieving the good life?

Informal businesses are, by the very definition generally used, not registered, so there are no government registries or easy survey methods to find them.[13] Many come and go seasonally according to monthly payday cycles and household cash flows. Often, registering a business means little more than paying a fee, but those who pay the fee are not necessarily much different from those who don't. For most black-run small businesses, registering had little benefit and significant costs and risks. Several Howick business owners complained that it cost about ten dollars a month to sell near the taxi rank, but people found ways to avoid paying. Government bureaucracy had a reputation for being slow and confusing. For people who have not historically been treated favorably by authorities, it makes sense to stay out of the government's way. Going unregistered might not be legal, but to most people it did not seem exactly illegal either. To the extent that the white-dominated legal system has often turned a blind eye to activities that do not directly affect whites, the black townships turn a blind eye to white-dominated legal systems.

I did a brief in-person survey of the businesses in a six-block radius near the Howick taxi rank where most of the informal businesses in Howick operated. Every morning, venders arrived with shopping carts, duffel bags, and pickup trucks to spread their wares on the sidewalks or in stalls built by the city. Others walked along the streets showing off their goods. The sidewalks lined rows of adjacent one-room cinder-block shops, offering a more permanent vending space for slightly more lucrative businesses like hardware stores, tailor shops, hair salons, and appliance stores. There were a few chain retailers in the area—two grocery stores and a couple of discount clothing stores—but most businesses were run by locals. Out of seventy-four businesses I counted in this six-block radius in the middle of one month, I found only fourteen where the owners, as well as any employees, were entirely Zulu South African.[14] Most small businesses in Howick's informal business district were run or staffed by Indian South Africans and immigrants from other African nations. Foreigners from elsewhere in Africa, often driven by political violence or economic crises, have tended to arrive in South Africa with previous experience, social networks, and a certain desperation to run small businesses.[15] In several conversations when I asked people to direct me to Howick businesses run by Zulu people, Zulu and non-Zulu respondents could only think of the three Zulu funeral parlors in town, even though there were at least eleven other Zulu-owned businesses in the area. So if businesses in that part of town were an accurate indication of small businesses, Zulu South Africans were indeed underrepresented.

The obvious images of market stalls and ambulatory venders in that neighborhood of Howick were not the only evidence one could find of entrepreneurship, though, if one took the time to look. In Mpophomeni, there were small businesses operating in homes and less obvious commercial areas on every block. Tuck shops like Nomusa's were well-known to neighbors, and sometimes could be spotted by strangers if the owners invested in barred windows through which to pass money and goods, but more often they looked no different from other homes. Like Teeza and Sma's unmarked cement-block building hidden out of sight from the road, workshops and studios of carpenters, artists, and musicians were scattered across the township but almost never had visible signage. Other businesses like washing cars, braiding hair, or selling from a stash of secondhand clothing in a closet required no regular hours and left no visible trace when not actively serving a customer. Even asking people directly whether they have run a business will not necessarily produce an accurate count. I regularly had the experience of people denying in interviews that they had ever run a business, and then learning later that they had in the past or even currently ran some kind of business, but for reasons I'll come back to later in this chapter, they didn't think of that activity as a business.

Recent studies show that because of this invisibility of businesses, scholars have tended to underestimate the number of black South Africans involved in informal sector entrepreneurship. A 2018 study found that one in six working South Africans had jobs in the informal sector.[16] Another study found that in townships, only 24 percent of informal businesses were located in the main commercial thoroughfares of townships. The rest were based in homes and residential areas, making them largely invisible to outside observers.[17] In a country where so much criticism and effort has gone into promoting entrepreneurship, much of the entrepreneurship that already exists is being overlooked.

The struggles entrepreneurs faced were also often invisible in the dominant messaging about entrepreneurship. In particular, the history of social structures that have made it harder for black people than people of other races to run businesses was largely unaddressed in the trainings and media I observed. Under apartheid, black people were forbidden from running most types of businesses. Still, they found ways to run certain businesses, often thwarting legal restrictions. When white people refused to provide public transport for black employees, for example, black ride-sharing businesses sprang up, and systems of minibus taxis developed into cartel-like organizations. Taxi owners fiercely defended their routes through carefully manipulated power structures. Indian people, however, faced fewer restrictions than black people on running businesses under apartheid, and they were often less reluctant than white people to open businesses in black neighborhoods. Thus, many Indian business owners found a niche selling in black networks while developing supply networks that extended among white and Indian South Africans and internationally. These social networks and supply chain access are invaluable, and no amount of training can offer black people a shortcut into the advantages of generations of trust-building within business networks that formed along racial lines. Today, new entrepreneurs compete with international companies that can leverage wholesale discounts, credit, generations of experiential learning, and other advantages of scale that simply are not available to most new black entrepreneurs.

Having heard multiple complaints from township residents about the ineffectiveness of government entrepreneurship-development programs, I decided as an experiment to visit one of the government offices for entrepreneurship services to ask some questions on behalf of a carpentry business in Mpophomeni run by a man named Mandisa and his two employees. Mandisa had told me that he struggled with cash-flow problems. Every month he had different projects, paying at different times, often requiring insistent negotiations to get customers to pay their bills. He was further constrained by a lack of capital to increase his stock and buy more tools. Much government funding for entrepreneurship development is funneled through the government's Small Enterprise Development Agency, SEDA, so I followed SEDA's website to their nearest office in Pietermaritzburg in search of possibilities for Mandisa.

I drove the forty minutes from Mpophomeni to the office only to find that it had relocated across town. Having the convenience of a car and a GPS, neither of which Mandisa had, I then drove the several miles back across town to the new office. There, I walked around a building twice before choosing an unmarked entrance where someone at a desk, also without any sign, directed me to a room on the second floor. Having finally arrived at the SEDA office, I explained that my friend Mandisa was interested in what the office could do for his business.

SEDA would need to "do a full assessment," she said, and if they found that he needed any "service providers" (which she did not explain, but which, from her handouts, I inferred meant companies providing marketing and other business services), SEDA could contact their service providers to get a quote. SEDA would then pay 90 percent of the lowest quote.

"How long does that process usually take?" I asked.

"No, you can't say how long it would take, because it's a long process," she replied. "He would make an appointment, and we have tools to assess his business. And then there's the quotes. And also sometimes the people doing their quotes don't have the proper documents for what SEDA needs."

She said that first he would need to register his company. I asked how. She pointed to an address on a page near the end of one of the dozen brochures she had handed me. "It can be done online," she said, "but it can be challenging," so they have a consultant who helps, but the consultant is not in Pietermaritzburg. Nor did Mandisa have internet access at home. I could not envision Mandisa or anyone else hurdling all the bureaucratic obstacles to get any benefits from SEDA.

Closer to Mpophomeni, youths could visit the municipal Youth Development Office in Howick. There, they could receive free job counseling, computer access, and application assistance for higher education and scholarships. On the multiple occasions I visited the office, I found between two and eight people using computers or waiting for appointments. Had Mandisa been looking for advice writing a résumé or filling out a university application, they might have helped, but they did not offer help for small businesses.

Many private companies also offered entrepreneurship assistance, in part because government tax structuring offered strong incentives for private businesses to spend corporate social responsibility funds on promoting job creation. In an office not far from Mpophomeni, I met with a manager for an entrepreneurship development project funded by Mondi, one of the largest forestry companies in the country. Mondi had contributed R70 million to match government funds to create new jobs through small enterprises, and the manager explained their mentoring process for black South Africans in businesses that would create new jobs. However, because Mandisa's business was not registered and because he had only two steady employees with no intention of adding more, his business would likely not qualify for assistance.

## The Business of Struggle

Hustlers, by Teeza's definition, are people who run their own businesses in order to "do something for yourself" because "you have to." In our first conversation about their business, Teeza and Sma talked at length about the many challenges they faced as business owners—people not paying them for commissioned work, the government breaking promises, family members expecting free services, and backbiting among people working with them. Teeza summed up the list of challenges: "You know, we hustle. I'm doing this, I'm doing that. Our people they bring us down. That's challenging." It was as if challenges and hustling merged into a single idea. The work of hustling was not just a means to earn money; it was a way to perform a ceaseless struggle amid adversity. Hustling told other people—and, just as importantly, it reminded the hustler—that he was *struggling*. Hustling demonstrated that you were "keeping up the struggle," moving forward, and doing so not out of resignation but because you still had pride. You had not given up. You were fighting hard in a hard world where forces were always stacked against you.

In the hustling narrative, struggling itself had value. To understand what struggling means to people in groups that have been historically disadvantaged, it's useful to look at another setting where the word "hustling" comes up often: among underemployed young urban populations in the United States. Katherine Newman, who studied low-wage employees in New York City, offers insights that apply in both that setting and South Africa.[18] As they struggled to make ends meet, she points out, black youth in the United States were not rejecting dominant narratives about hard work. In fact, they were doing the opposite: they followed a localized and even intensified version of the middle-class value of hard work. That is, people of stigmatized groups took the dominant messages about needing to work hard and fit those messages into the context of their class and racial subjectivity. They grew up hearing messages that they were less likely to succeed, and they formed an identity as a people who absolutely must struggle, working even harder than dominant groups. She summarized their perspective: "Forces of inequality, racism, and birthright have interfered with pure merit and help to explain why some people are living the good life and others must struggle."[19] They develop an image, a "public demeanor" that "signals control," in a world where they know their control is precarious.[20] In South Africa as in New York City, hustling differs from the dominant entrepreneurial messaging in that it does not assume that the people who succeed correspond to the people who work hardest. Instead, hustling acknowledges that some people will have to work harder. They'll have to work harder to succeed, and also harder to keep believing that they have any control at all.[21]

The idea of a constant struggle ran deep among black South Africans. In the all-pervasive Zulu greeting, one person asks another, "How are you?" (*unjani?*). Common responses include "I am trying" (*ngiyazama*), and the more passively constructed, "Things are being tried," with the implication that things are not going too well (*kuyazameka*). Other answers include, "I am developing gradually" (*ngiyathuthuka*), "I am walking along slowly" (*ngiyatotoba*), or simply, "I am alive" (*ngiyaphila*). In these daily greetings, people remind themselves and others that they have not given up—they are alive and struggling.

Reminders of the continued struggle also came up often in young people's art and conversation. Every Friday, Teeza invited dozens of young people from the township to attend the music session gatherings that Bullet also attended. The first time I joined them we met in the fashion design studio. People took turns freestyling improvised lyrics or performing songs they'd been working on. Someone brought a guitar, others played beats on their phones, and someone grabbed the top half of a female mannequin from a sewing table to slap beats on her plastic chest. Everyone attending was expected to contribute something—a spoken word poem, a song, or a story—and Teeza insisted, to everyone's delight, that I also take an occasional turn. Eventually, we moved into a meeting room in the library and joined up with a library youth writing group. Teeza moderated their Facebook group, and at the start of 2016, he posted the kind of motivational phrase he often worked into his banter between these Friday performances: "Let us be one thing and see what we will Become with our Talents—2016, Our Year." In the narrative Teeza drilled into the group every week, their *becoming* would happen if they would keep on *being* in the present. At one Friday music gathering, a young man from Mpophomeni sang passionately, "You only have one life, one heart, one soul to love what you do. So give it all. Give it all." Later, Teeza recited a poem he had titled "The kind of man that I am." In it he emphasized his perseverance: "Always trying. I make positive days into action." Once Teeza told me about a peer who had worked odd jobs for only R50 a day. "He's like gold, because he has experienced bad things," Teeza said of his friend. "You have to have the bad before you have the good. You can't tell me you good if you never ever go through that life experience."

In another conversation, Teeza and Sma talked about wanting to grow their business. They said one reason they wanted the business to succeed was so that people outside Mpophomeni would see what they had been through. Sma said, "I want people to know what life here is. I want people to *know*."

"And what do you want them to know?" I asked.

Sma answered: "Our lives, our stories, how we struggled. Yeah, everything. The problems."

For Sma, Teeza, and other young black business owners, running a business was one way to show the world that they were struggling. That never-giving-up lifestyle could itself be a kind of call for respect and dignity. As Teeza said, "You get your respect for hustling." But not every kind of business offered young people the same amount of dignity. Hustlers avoided certain forms of entrepreneurship but aspired to others. To understand why, I teased apart differing ways that entrepreneurship entered into young people's lives.

## Granny Businesses

Some forms of business, in the eyes of many young people, sent a message of desperation and lost pride. As the anthropologist Daniel Mains points out, publicly visible low-status jobs carry the added shame of having to be seen by friends. Such jobs were often "undesirable not because workers received low payment for demanding work," but because of "the fear of what others might think or say."[22] Growing and selling vegetables was one such business. As one person put it, growing vegetables was grannies' work.

Occupations anywhere in the world tend to be socially constructed to have gender and age expectations governing who can or should do this work. In the United States, for example, a pizza delivery driver older than forty years old or a male nurse are likely to bump into surprised—if not outright disapproving—responses because society trains people to think that these jobs are for someone else. In conversations in South Africa, people singled out selling baked goods, growing vegetables at home, and raising chickens as activities for older women. Many young men and women spoke highly of their female elders who did such work, but then offered qualifications like "I'm not the gardening type" or "That's what old women do." For young people, setting up a vegetable stand may have represented something they could do later in life or something they hoped to avoid all together in lieu of lucrative opportunities more fitting to their educational attainments. Either way, it did not fit the common picture of an appropriate step for their social stage or, for men, their gender.

The supposed failure of young people to take up gardening was a common complaint among older black South Africans and white South Africans. When I went shopping, I often made a point to visit a shopkeeper named Minah, a cheerful grandmother about a foot shorter than me with short, neatly curled hair. One day, as I sat on a plastic stool beside her table of neatly folded school uniforms, aprons, and women's clothing, she asked rhetorically, "Who will run the business for me if I'm sick?" She shook her head. She had tried paying young people to watch the shop, but "they take the money; they say they didn't sell anything, but they're selling for themselves. It's impossible to find someone." I often heard similar complaints from other business owners about the shortage of young Zulu joining them.

Within Mpophomeni, there was only one vegetable stand along the main thoroughfare, built out of wooden beams and tables just in front of the stretch of gardens where they raised vegetables. I usually saw three older people, two women and a man, selling at the booth. They also said that young people were not interested in helping grow or even buy vegetables. Young people would rather buy things at the grocery stores in town, they said. People I spoke with who were running projects doing gardening training and small business development training expressed similar frustrations. Their encouraging rhetoric promised that anyone could raise food with just a little money for seeds, some hard work, and compost (which, notably, was difficult to gather in settings where dogs, goats, and chickens ate the few kitchen scraps people had). I met young people employed as trainers in these programs, and even several of the trainers admitted they would not have their own gardens. Young people, especially men, rarely broke gender, age, and social position expectations to raise or sell produce.

Social constructions associated gardening with older women, but social constructions of other kinds of self-owned businesses can also deter people. I stumbled upon one such deterrence in a short conversation I had with a young Zulu woman selling cigarettes, candies, and calls on a public phone (a common microbusiness option where cell phones are still prohibitively expensive and frequently unreliable). I asked, "Why do you think there aren't more Zulu women with businesses like yours?" I assumed that my question would come across as commending her for something that few young people tried, but she seemed to take it almost as criticism. "I guess because we don't have pride," she answered with a shrug and a tone of sadness. She explained that if she had pride, she would not be out on the street like this—she should be home with her children. She said she was there selling because, she supposed, she was desperate.

Her words, "we don't have pride," struck at the heart of the controversy surrounding hustlers. Black South Africans held strongly opposed opinions about pride and its role in achieving a good life. Young people tended to say that keeping pride was the most important thing a person could do; elders said young people were failing because they had too much pride. According to the woman selling cigarettes, who was probably in her late twenties or thirties, she became an entrepreneur when she had too little pride. To her, having pride was essential to a good life, and the kind of entrepreneurship she did signaled a loss of pride to the point of disgrace. Better to stay clear of business than to run a kind of business which indicated that you had lost your pride. That loss would mean breaking your performance and understanding of yourself as a person who was becoming something better.

To the nonhustler, though, avoiding entrepreneurship or formal employment communicated an overabundance of pride. A middle-aged Zulu woman once told me that the cause of the nation's high unemployment rate was that youth "are just proud, too proud to want/seek work" ("uyaqhenya nje, ukufuna umsebenzi"). Another middle-aged woman complained about her own town-ship, "I think people here have too much pride." These moral critiques shaped the ways young people understood themselves. One young woman said she learned from her grandmother that in previous generations, people used to help each other more, growing and sharing cabbages and going out together to herd cattle. Summarizing her grandmother's point of view, she said, "Before, no one was hav-ing a pride. Now we only think for myself. It's a new generation. You've got pride." Even knowing this, she did not have a garden.

The complaints by elders about the excessive pride of youth resounded in the township, even as people heard the opposite message from their peers. A woman in her twenties who sat at a very visible small business on the main street of Mpophomeni lamented that she was one of the few people her age who would do this kind of work. An uncle who owned the business offered her decent pay for the work, but she did not want people to see it as her job. "The reason more people don't do business is pride," she said. "People have too much pride here." She described the ways people insulted her, asking why she worked at a fruit stand when she had graduated from high school. For a young person, particularly one who had the skills, education, and hope for a future outside the township, involvement in entrepreneurial activities required careful maintenance of a pre-carious pride. Maybe for her the pay made that risk of lost pride worth it; maybe she had other ways of communicating that she still had pride; or perhaps she relied on other narratives in which having pride played a lesser role in having a good life. What she and other young people showed in their actions and expla-nations of entrepreneurship, though, was that when a young, decently skilled person ran a certain kind of business, at least some of their peers would see it as a loss of pride. That could be a high price to pay.

## Soapie Businesses

At the other end of the spectrum, certain kinds of business signaled high-class city life and an abundance of dignity. I came to think of these businesses as "soapie businesses" because they reminded me of the ways businesses appeared on the popular nightly South African soap operas. In soap operas, business life was intermingled with exquisitely dressed women, expensive liquor, Johannes-burg offices, and millions of rand flowing through ventures cloaked with mystery and intrigue. The soapies rarely showed what products those businesses sold or what business people did all day.

Idealized future businesses with little detail showed up in many interviews. People in low-wage, low-dignity jobs (the focus of the next chapter) often talked about owning businesses, and I was surprised by the number of people who saw their jobs as a means to get the capital for a distant-future business. Of the seventy-seven people I spoke with about work, twenty-five mentioned plans for some form of entrepreneurship.[23] Of these, about half did not give a clear statement of what kind of business they would have. When someone talked about future plans for a good life, they often mapped out a trajectory like this: Get a job that pays enough to meet my basic needs; build a house for my parents to show gratitude for their investment; find a spouse and get married (for a man, this included giving a gift to the bride's family—*ilobola*—worth several thousand dollars). And then, somewhere near retirement, "I'll have my business." In this image, business ownership was a late life-stage event or a vehicle for holding wealth, comparable perhaps to Western ways of thinking about cashing out a retirement fund or buying a second home. It was also reminiscent of the African practice of building up a herd of cattle as a way of storing wealth.[24]

Even in Mpophomeni, people knew of business elites who fit the late-in-life successful business-owner profile. They were not necessarily the millionaires of soap operas, but class is a relative category, and in township settings, these were "big men." Among those who were men, many were literally big with a round belly (isiZulu has a word for it—*umkhaba*) that signified wealth, status, and eldership. They owned businesses such as taxi companies, larger township stores, funeral parlors, or combinations of these. Many were the "tenderpreneurs" of the New South Africa—securing "tenders," or government contracts.[25] These entrepreneurs were masters at moving capital and cultivating the connections necessary to work with government and big business. Their lives were stressful, but from the outside, having that kind of business could appear pretty relaxed. In the imagination fed by television and promoted in township discourse, their lives were sweet: make a few phone calls, check on a few people and tell them what to do, stand in the shade talking with buddies, and buy high-end drinks at the end of the day. They lived the lifestyle Teeza alluded to in his plan to someday finish hustling and become a "businessman or businesswoman" who can "chill at home. Yeah, feeling good. Not do anything, spending my money that I hustled." He believed hustling now put a person on a route that could, if the hustler succeeded, end in that place.

## Survivalist Improvisation

In between the granny gardening businesses that signaled resignation, and the soapie businesses that signaled the success of a later life stage, a buzz of entrepreneurship happened. This was the realm of the hustler. In this category of business, a hustler signaled that they had not achieved their aim yet, but they were trying. These were day-by-day piece jobs, errands, brokered deals, and quick sales that moved cash around the township. James Ferguson fittingly called this work "survivalist improvisation," a term that conveys both the art and the high stakes of their endeavors.[26]

Methods of survivalist improvisation often fell into a category that people called "helping" (*ukusiza*). Helping included everyday interactions like watching a friend's children, picking up groceries for someone on a trip to town, digging up a garden, building a fence, braiding hair, or washing a car. People helping often did not request a set fee ahead of time, but gave under shared cultural expectations of reciprocity. What money people received in return depended in part on who had greater resources, according to the expectations described in the last chapter that respect for someone with *more*, calls for greater redistribution for one with *less*. Part of a hustler's work, then, involved influencing people's malleable willingness to reciprocate.

One of the most adept survivalist improvisationalists I met was a young man named Mtoko. A foreign volunteer at a nonprofit organization in Mpophomeni introduced me to Mtoko when I told her I was looking for people to interview. Like many nonprofit leaders, she took note of people who seemed to exemplify a good work ethic. "He's a really promising young man," she said as she walked me directly to his house. She said he was one of several guys who would stop by at their office asking for work, but unlike most of them, he would take any job she had, even grunt work and jobs she could pay for only in donated baked goods.

Mtoko spoke highly of her organization, too. She had been encouraging him to join the job readiness course. "Hopefully that comes through," he said. "I have to study. And maybe I'll become something, stand up for my family. I will have to find a way forward."

Mtoko was twenty-two years old and living alone in what had been his grandmother's house. He said he did not know his father, and his mother and grandmother died before he finished high school. His girlfriend, Thandi, lived nearby with her mother, and I would often find her at his home with their daughter, who was one month old when we met.

When I asked about his work experience, Mtoko never called himself an entrepreneur or said he had run a business. But over time I learned that he was always finding opportunities to bring home money. For a while his family rented out a public phone, but an uncle sold it off when he needed money. Another time Mtoko and a friend owned a fryer for selling fresh chips on a township corner. Again something went wrong—the relationship went bad and they sold the fryer. When I met him, Mtoko was helping out a few days a week at a neighbor's car wash. Other days he would borrow a friend's grass trimmer to cut grass around the township, or do garden work for older women. He explained the dynamics of getting paid for such help: "As you're working, you're wondering what you're going to get paid. You might be thinking this job deserves R300 or R400, but they ask you how much you want and then they just give you 50 rand. You ask what the previous guy got paid, and then you say, 'I'll try to do it better, to get 20 rand more.'" The day before this conversation, he had washed eight cars at his neighbor's car wash. He thought he would get R10 a car for a total of R80, but all the neighbor gave him was R50. He said there's not much you can do about that. "Some people just want their stuff done; they don't care about you."

Inherent in the hustling narrative is a sense that "the world doesn't care about you" and "there isn't much you can do about that." You're on your own to survive, and sometimes survival means getting pushed to the fringes of morality and legality. Money moved in the township through plenty of illegal and quasi-legal ventures, from selling bootlegged music to reselling stolen goods to loan sharking. I ran into one young man I recognized as a graduate from a job-readiness program and asked if he had found any success in the job hunt. He said no, but he said he and another friend from the job training program were "starting a business just to make a little something." I asked what kind. "Something like small time loan sharks." Loan sharks were notorious for regularly charging 50 percent interest per month—for every R100 they would ask for R150 back the next month, making 600 percent annual interest. I heard stories about loan sharks who confiscated people's ID cards, pin numbers, and bank cards. With the bank cards, they could take out anything in the account, and disputes arose over sharks who took out more than their original agreements. With their ID cards gone, borrowers could not take out the monthly grant money that, for many families, was their main source of income. The young man who admitted he was headed in this direction didn't sound proud of it—he sounded like he had run out of options.

Convincing oneself and others that one's hustle is legal—or legal enough—is itself a part of survivalist improvisation. In his autobiography, *Born a Crime*, the South African comedian Trevor Noah writes about a time in his life when he was, as he calls it, hustling. He describes a typical deal. He and a friend would buy a possibly stolen CD player from a crack addict with their money from bootlegged CDs and sell the CD player on credit to another buyer. Instead of cash for the CD player, they might exchange it for a pair of Nikes the guy got at his workplace with a "discount" (which might mean stealing), and then they could sell the Nikes to someone else for further profit. On one level, people knew a lot of it was illegal, but on another level, they did not have the luxury of caring. Trevor Noah explains:

> That's the hood. Someone's always buying, someone's always selling, and the hustle is about trying to be in the middle of that whole thing.

None of it was legal. Nobody knew where anything came from. . . . You don't ask. It's just, "Hey, look what I found" and "Cool, how much do you want?" That's the international code. . . . It's easy to be judgmental about crime when you live in a world wealthy enough to be removed from it. But the hood taught me that everyone has different notions of right and wrong, different definitions of what constitutes crime, and what level of crime they're willing to participate in. If a crackhead comes through and he's got a crate of Corn Flakes boxes he's stolen out of the back of a supermarket, the poor mom isn't thinking, I'm aiding and abetting a criminal by buying these Corn Flakes. No. She's thinking, My family needs food and this guy has Corn Flakes, so she buys the Corn Flakes.[27]

Noah's description also points to the interrelatedness of poverty and hustling. Without customers willing to buy discount-priced stolen goods and without hustlers willing to be middlemen who don't ask questions, people procuring those goods have no market. With such interconnectedness, any single person in the system can be convinced that he or she is not to blame for the illegality of the situation. Buyers, procurers, and middlemen come together each with their own forms of desperation in socioeconomic settings that have systematically deprived them of legal sources of income to create a setting where hustling quasi-legal deals thrives.

Hustling happens where legal alternatives are few. The South African scholar Bhekizizwe Peterson points out that, for many black South African youth, music offers "the one and only legal hustle available."[28] He calls young township musicians "masters of marginality."[29]

> Stuck in between an immediate past where, for many, very little meaningful education was possible, and a "transitional" present where the "fruits" of post-apartheid South Africa seem to be a rumour orchestrated by the upper classes, young blacks in the ghetto use the notion of hustling, "*ukupanda*" or "to make life" as their armour. In this regard black youth are doing no more or less than a significant proportion of township dwellers whose survival depends on mastering the intricate machinations of the informal (but highly organised) internal economy that marks township as 'colonies' of a sort within the mainstream economy and society. In the apartheid and post-apartheid periods, 'colony life' also opened up the possibility of modes of survival alternative to the respectable route of hard labour and low wages: above all, that range of informal dealing, semi-legal practices, rackets and small-time crime classically known in all ghetto life as hustling.[30]

The men and women who gathered for Teeza's Friday jam sessions seemed to know, too, that music offered a rare good option surrounded by many worse options. "We don't want to do things to cause trouble. All we want to do is make our things and be heard," one young man said. The comment was sandwiched between his story of losing a job when a jealous coworker framed him for stealing, and the story of a government office asking his group to perform for a campaign rally and then failing to pay them. "We want money as a crew, but not big money. Because this is what we do for a living," he said. Hustling meant improvisation—sometimes literally as a hip hop artist, and more often in the daily uncertainties of negotiating prices, taking advantage of sporadic opportunities, and carving out legitimacy on the margins of society.

## Fashioning an Image

Just as legal legitimacy was scarce, so too was legitimacy in terms of dignity. Much survivalist improvisation did not look or feel very dignified. Herein lies the tension that drives the hustler narrative. On the one hand, hustling requires keeping up a struggle in a tough setting. On the other, hustlers want to show the world that they are not consumed by the struggle. Those two aims are often at odds. To survive the struggle, hustlers often face options that can damage their public image and pride. Marco Di Nunzio describes this tension as he saw it among street hustlers in Arada, Ethiopia. They were "faced with the fact that their engagement with hustling and cheating, smartness, and toughness had not taken them anywhere other than the poor neighborhoods of inner city Addis Ababa"; they were "trying to be and become something other than their constraints while living an existence that is firmly embedded in experiences of subjugation and exclusion."[31]

This desire to protect an image of dignity in the midst of the struggle helps explain why young people were interested in purchasing goods that conveyed an image of success. As I mentioned earlier, elders and nonblack South Africans sometimes complained that young people spent money on stereos, shoes, hairstyles, and clothing rather than savings or home investments. When I asked what fashion meant to Sma, she stopped sewing and turned to face me with an intensity in her voice. "Fashion changes me, it changes life, it changes everything. With fashion, they don't see what's inside. Like me, I'm shy, but when I'm wearing certain clothes, fashion can make me look like I'm not shy."

"Fashion talks," Teeza interjected, then jumped to his feet. He took off in a soliloquy of mock ecstasy, accentuating rhythms with the hand motions of a spoken word artist:

TEEZA: For me what I see of fashion, oh, fashion is everything to me. Like my father, mother. I put nice clothes on my body, I feel good. 'Cause everybody greeting me, I'm like oh, I'm somebody. So when I lose hope, when I see people struggle, fashion is like that. It make me cool. It make money for me. Yeah, fashion is everything. I will die for it.

SMA: [Laughing] You'll *die* for fashion?

TEEZA: Yeah, I'll die for it! I love fashion. I'm so sick about it. And I want to succeed with fashion. To have my own clothes, my own label, every people buy it. Us all popular. Yeah, that's what I want to do. Have our own, whole, own, big, big, big property of our own! So everybody will see. That's what I want to do. That's what fashion means to me.

CHRISTINE: What about you Sma?

SMA: Eh, I don't know how to say it when it comes to fashion. Because I love fashion. But I love fashion, I love it. I like clothes. Yeah, I think if fashion was a person, ooh, I would be so good with fashion. I would be so in love with fashion! [Laughter] Serious. Because fashion is good.

CHRISTINE: [Clarifying] Good, or God?

SMA: Good! It's not God, but I love fashion! And if fashion was food, I would always eat it. I love fashion.

When I had known Teeza for nearly a year, I flew back to the United States for a job interview. As I sat on the plane ready to take off, a text arrived from Teeza, who had heard about my interview: "That job is yours. Just be a person of that job." This was the encouragement that ran through the hustling narrative: Be the person you want to become. By claiming a particular identity in the present, a hustler asserts that the "becoming" will happen. Hustling entails keeping up a performance—presenting an image one step beyond where you currently are in order to prove you're going somewhere.

By thinking of certain choices as "performance," a term anthropologists have often used to understand human behaviors in various cultural and class settings, we can ask the important question, What is the purpose of these performances?[32] Thinking of hustling as involving performance illuminates the ways that hustling involves proving one's morality, one's dignity, and the direction of one's hope.[33] The performances of hustlers were also a way to demonstrate class distinction. Consider for a moment how people know when someone is of an upper or lower class. They watch others' behavior—language, accent, vocabulary, and mannerisms—as well as their purchases—what clothing, phone, computer, music, reading material, and car they buy.[34] Humans are constantly watching each other's performance, whether or not they recognize it as a performance.

In middle-class settings, a key element in performances that indicate class is the kind of job someone has. "What's your job?" is one of the first questions typically asked in introductions between middle-class people. Career stands in for a lot of unknown information as a marker of social status, character, personal likes and dislikes, or personality. When that question—What's your job?—is taken out of the equation, other methods of performing class take on greater importance. As the anthropologist Sasha Newell described the contrast between West African young people's spending habits versus the dominant Western narrative saying that only those with high incomes should be allowed to spend extravagantly, "the causal role between consumption and success is reversed."[35] For the West Africans he described as well as many young South Africans, consumption is a way to experience success when success by other means seems impossibly out of reach. This use of consumption is far from unique to these young present-day Africans. At the end of the nineteenth century, the philosopher and economist Thorstein Veblen, in his book *The Theory of the Leisure Class*, used the phrase "conspicuous consumption" to describe purchases that were made for decidedly nonutilitarian reasons.[36] The purpose of conspicuous consumption is to demonstrate the kind of person one is or wants to become and to thereby gain higher social status. The hustling narrative uses the secret that Veblen discovered a century ago—You don't need to reveal the source or amount of your money to show the class distinction that comes with money. As in any performance that is done well, the line between performance and reality blurs. "Being one thing" in order to "become" something—whether through musical performance, choosing clothing styles, or buying expensive liquor—offered young people one way to perform class distinction.

Performance, though, is always open to interpretation, and can be seen by some observers as something other than reality. Onlookers can accuse a performer of faking it. Teeza once posted on Facebook an image that read, "I may not be perfect, but at least I am not fake." Before the meme he wrote, "That Me Right there." His good life depended on convincing himself and others that they were becoming what they were meant to be, even in a world that would often accuse them of faking it.

Here, again, lies the tension of hustling. Bullet reflected most profoundly on the strain between struggling and trying to retain dignity. "No street hustler wants to be a street hustler," he said, "except the people who are not street hustlers yet, they want it. But there's nothing glorifying or beautiful about it." He said having to lose their pride is what makes hustlers "so angry all the time."

I asked, "Then what is it that makes people want to be a hustler?" He responded:

> I think it's because they don't know the whole story. . . . When you want
> to be a street hustler you don't look at the person who's picking up the

metal at the dump. . . . To you they're just a bum that never made it. The street hustler to you is the homey still on the corner still rocking the high kicks, still getting the girls, a bad boy with attitude still drinks whenever he wants to drink, he got the money to do that, and he doesn't work. Where does he get this money from? That—you not knowing where the money comes from, when he doesn't work, is what makes you think, "This is what's up! He don't have to wake up early in the morning. He don't have to go nowhere! He's here all the time, yet he's better known than all those people who go to work, they're not balling like he is." So people look at him, they wonder, they admire, because they don't know. . . . Hustlers are the best actors in the world. Nobody's act is better than the street hustler. They play everything. They play everybody, but they don't see that they being played. They lying to themselves. That's what I hate.

Bullet saw through the image of pride that hustlers projected and the admiration others held for hustlers to see that hustling masks a desperate struggle for survival. Hustlers live between granny business and soapie businesses, negotiating another path, where dignity and survival are of utmost value but always scarce. For all the image of becoming successful they project, at least sometimes, "they being played." This returns us to the question of whether the hustling narrative works in the sense of producing the good life it promises.

## "I'm actually trapped here"

The hustler narrative is produced among lives that are—and will continue to be—difficult. Hustlers know life will require a long, tough struggle. They know they have been screwed over by history. They have every reason to distrust the linear progress metanarratives that have failed to bring employment to so many people in their surroundings, yet they have not given up on narratives altogether. Instead, as we have seen, they focus on being as a link to becoming, and struggling as their task for the present. As one university student from Mpophomeni said, success from the township is like a rose growing in concrete, an image from the rapper Tupac Shakur's song, "The Rose That Grew from Concrete."[37] The young man explained:

It's difficult, then, for a rose to grow in concrete. Because you know, like us, the situations we are under, if you want to be at the top, you have to work hard. Hard, hard, hard. You have to work harder than most people. But then if you see a rose blooming from concrete you would be shocked. Like how did this happen? But you shouldn't be asking that. Like if you see a young kid making it from the ghetto, you shouldn't be asking yourself how did this happen, because it's *supposed* to be happening. Our destiny is to be at the top. We're all destined to be—it's like dying. It's something that is certain. We all supposed to be successful.

Young people often began their responses to my questions about the good life with images of a someday hoped-for lifestyle—a big house outside their current township, a salaried job, a good car, a spouse properly married through the expensive Zulu marriage process, kids better off than their parents, and some element of ease (to "chill," as Teeza said). They looked forward to someday landing that life.

Yet sometimes they won't. For many, the days of being "chill" with a steady income would never come. What if there is no "rose" ending for many hustlers? Is the narrative itself a failure, a false hope misleading young people on a path to failure? Are young people wasting their money on nice shoes when they should be trying to store away money in savings accounts? Are they wasting opportunities by operating outside formal employment?

Perhaps. Perhaps the narrative fails them. Many of their critics would say as much. But another way to see it is this: if the hustler narrative fails to produce easy living, perhaps it's not a failure of the narrative so much as a proof of the narrative. Hustlers know that the struggle is going to be hard. They know that dignity will be hard to come by. In these ways their narrative is right and honest. It is a narrative forged in the hood and the township, and if nothing else, what it does for people is to demand hope and keep on demanding it. They were right about the tough odds the world gave them, and sometimes they lost to those odds.

Sometimes the desperation of hustling could cause people to lose their most elemental respect for human life. Bullet said hustlers were not just guys looking "baller," they included women picking through garbage for food, and "the man who's ready to just kill you" because that's the only way to survive. "He don't *want* to do that," he went on, adding that neither does the old lady want to pick through trash. "We all people, everybody got their pride. But most of the time you got to push it aside. And that's the worst, the lowest street hustler you can get."

Other times hustling produces the suffering of people in the hustler's own community. As Bullet emphasized, that's not what people want, it's where they end up.[38] Even when turning to harming themselves or others, hustlers use performance as a way to retain their dignity and purpose. Sometimes that performance works all too well. They spread the allure of criminality across the township. "We respect gangsters," Bullet explained with a tone of exasperation toward his peers. "They be like, 'That's the scum of the location, but that scum got a car!' The whole thing just becomes like a game. Like if you winning, good for you, but if you losing, too bad." In a sick twist, a gangster's nonchalance makes even addicted customers look up to him because his performed pride in defiance of moral codes is convincing. Hustlers have a power that invokes both awe and fear.[39] Shaping these interpretations is what makes self-fashioning performance all the more critical.

Another day Bullet described the feeling young people experience knowing their lives are breaking the moral code of their elders, but feeling that they have no option but to live as they do.

> It's like everybody just kind of has this idea that when you do wrong, you don't know that it's wrong. But you do know that it's wrong! And that's what makes it even worse. And harder. You know what I'm saying? It makes you more angry. When you gonna be doing something wrong, and everybody just keeps telling you how wrong it is, like [in a scolding tone], "Look at you, look at you, look at you." Like I don't see me! I do see myself! I do see what I'm doing. But don't you see that I'm actually trapped here? You know what I'm saying? It's like they see the wrong but they don't see why.

Bullet and his peers were "trapped here" both in a position of going against the morals upheld by their communities, and trapped on a path that very likely would not end in the good life they hoped for. Recall his words in the introduction, "It's either you gonna be a gangster and die, or be a gangster and maybe survive in the end."

When I asked some colleagues to read an earlier draft of this chapter in 2016, they asked if I could give an example of someone who hustled and survived in the end. I thought of Mr. Khumalo. When I met him in 2015, this older man had just opened a bar and restaurant in Mpophomeni. It was one of the most high-class eateries in the township with some of the most conspicuous new investment pouring into it.

I met Mr. Khumalo one night when my husband and I came to order a steak roasted on the grill outside at the back of the restaurant, and he invited me to return and talk more. Mr. Khumalo offered a tour of the building, pointing out that the automatic hand driers might be the first in the township. I returned one afternoon, and we sat on black, faux leather couches talking while his son prepped for customers at the bar. He told stories about racism—black employees kicked off of white people's properties, and a bank that denied him credit before giving credit to the white customers in line just behind him. He recounted experiences with government officials involving bureaucratic chaos, broken promises, and political backbiting. And he described the challenges of having money when so many others did not—trying to create jobs where so many people needed work, knowing others were gossiping about him, and losing a business associate who was murdered. Years earlier, Mr. Khumalo's house, car, and another business had been burned down in what he believed was an arson attack by jealous neighbors. Yet he still went back to trying to run businesses. He said he pressed on in part because he wanted his kids to learn to hustle in a difficult world. "I did train them to become business people because the only way that you can survive is to own your own thing. You don't have to depend on someone else. You've got hands, you've got brains, and eyes; everything is around you." He insisted he would stay strong despite any challenges.

As customers and employees surrounded him in his newly opened business, he was the picture of surviving by "owning his own thing," making it from the early days of hustling to the life of a "big man." His story was not finished, though. Two years later, I would find his life changed again, a story I'll save for the final chapter.

Like Mr. Khumalo, young people across South Africa were well-acquainted with reasons to give up trying. In Zulu-English dictionaries, the same Zulu word—*ukulwa*—is often translated as both "struggle" and "fight." When I asked one young man who was starting a new business who his heroes were, he paused and then answered, "That Indian guy. Muhammad?" After some clarification, I realized he was not referring to Muhammad Ali the boxer or to Muhammad the Muslim prophet, but Mahatma Gandhi. Gandhi was highly regarded in South Africa for inspiring the nonviolent protests that shaped the anti-apartheid struggle. I asked Siya why Gandhi, and he responded, "Because he was a fighter. The way he stopped eating. He was a rock. He was a fighter. Gandhi's my guy. Because I'm a fighter." I asked what he meant by a fighter. "I'm changing my life. Finding work, whatever work, then growing myself."

The hustling narrative offers a call to fight. After one Zulu church service, I talked with a sharply dressed young man who had delivered a message during the service encouraging young people to work hard and not give up hope in their career paths. As we talked, he told me about his own experience landing a job with the government. "I can't run away from the fact that there are obstacles," he said, describing what got him to his current job. "Challenges are there to prune us, shape us. Challenges are not there to kill us or ruin our future. In this world nothing comes easy, you have to fight, fight, fight." Even as he saw himself as the victor of his own individual fight, he interspersed the conversation with phrases like "luckily enough," "blessed," and "with God's help" which conveyed the chance, luck, and circumstances beyond his power that resulted in his rare success in a world of challenges. Others were not so lucky, but for him, the fight had paid off.[40]

Hustlers know their path could end in poverty, disgrace, addiction, jail, or early death. The hustling narrative gives meaning and direction to life within this reality. As hustlers perform their identities one step ahead of their present reality and demonstrate their perseverance, they embrace a paradox between agency and constraint. To hustle is to claim one's agency to keep struggling and hoping. It is also to know that social constraints are real, and all too often the hustle ends in death.

## Postscript: "Every day you fight"

In one conversation with Mtoko, I mentioned Siya's words about being a fighter. Yes, Mtoko said, it's just like that. "Every day, you have to fight just to wake up." We were walking from a neighbor's house to Mtoko's house, and he paused at the gate of his home to face me. "It's like everyone has something inside they're fighting, and they take that out on everyone else." He paused a moment and asked, "I told you I was in jail?" He had not. He stared into the distance and told his story. He and a friend who was "all about bad" got a fake gun that was convincing enough, and they would rob people around Mpophomeni in the dark. It worked, he said, until one person fought his way free and called the police. Mtoko did seven months of jail time. After that, he said, he just wanted to turn his life around.

In the months that followed that conversation, Mtoko seemed to be losing the fight. In quiet conversations filled with gaps and innuendos, I learned from neighbors that he'd been caught stealing and was punished by the Forum, the township's informal security force that intervened in anything from gang violence to domestic abuse. "He's lucky to be alive," one woman said quietly when we were alone. He had been dragged by a rope behind a car. Mtoko had been one of the first people to tell me about the Forum. People generally agreed that the Forum, certainly not the police, were responsible for the relatively low crime rate that Mpophomeni enjoyed, but it came at the controversial cost of rule by force—"canes and chains," as Mtoko put it. There were stories of people killed by the Forum. Often the Forum punished through humiliation. Mtoko told me about one guy who had to hop like a frog for kilometers, another who had to carry the television he had stolen above his head while singing at the top of his lungs. Mtoko said it always worked. "To embarrass someone, it's like killing you. Even if it doesn't kill you, it kills the pride. We're scared of being embarrassed."

One day when I was visiting, Mtoko was optimistic about a job opening he'd heard about at a grocery store in Pietermaritzburg. "I'll work there just until I can save up the thousand rand for my business." He needed R16, about $1.60, for transport to the city, but he sounded confident that he could get the money and move in with a friend in the city. I left him walking to a neighbor's house to borrow a phone to make plans. He said goodbye as if I wouldn't see him for some time. Two weeks later, I found him at home. He said quickly, before changing the subject, that he never got the transport money and he couldn't contact the friend.

Often my knock on Mtoko's door would wake him from sleep. Sometimes I could hear the television or radio playing inside but no one answered. "A lot of times I just end up sleeping," he admitted when I asked him once to describe a typical day. He seemed to be fighting an endless cold. His arms were thin, and his eyes were bloodshot. More than once I recognized he was high when we talked, and I wondered if what he used was just marijuana. The drug to worry about, people said, was *wunga* (also spelled *whoonga*). For as little as R5, about US fifty cents, someone could buy a straw filled with the powder; many addicts did five or more straws a day. Mpophomeni residents said that the drive for drug money led to most of the petty crime in the township. According to several South Africans I talked to, wunga was concocted by amateur drug producers who tried adding all sorts of ingredients, ranging from illegal narcotics to the fluid from refrigerators. One famous recipe was said to include rat poison and the antiretroviral medicines for treating HIV. This ingredient base is considered by some scholars to be an urban legend, but the ARV-plus-poison story offered a powerful expression of the fear and mystery surrounding wunga.[41] "Think about what rat poison does," one woman explained. "Wunga eats your insides. It eats up your brain. Nobody lives long on wunga." I knew of more than one person who had attempted suicide with rat poison. There was a poignant irony in the common perception that by combining one of the township's most common suicide weapons with one of its most lifesaving medicines, drug pushers had created a highly addictive drug that offered a few minutes of bliss in exchange for an ever-shortening life span.

Months passed and no one answered when I knocked on Mtoko's door. A neighbor said he had left on a bus with a suitcase, but no one could tell me where he was headed. At Christmas I spotted his door open and found him at home with a dozen family members visiting. He avoided explaining where he had been, saying he was doing OK, trying things here and there. Another week later, he was gone again. A neighbor said his family had taken him to a treatment center for drug addiction. His girlfriend went to live elsewhere, and the job-readiness training program began and ended without Mtoko attending. A neighbor said they spotted him in Pietermaritzburg, strung out on drugs. I never saw him again, and neither did the neighbor. Two years later, a neighbor confirmed he had died somewhere on the streets of Pietermaritzburg. "It's like he disappeared from the face of the earth," she said.

# "I'M JUST A LABORER"

## The Laborer Narrative

Every now and then a person who grows up in poverty wins the lottery of life and lands their dream job. They go off to work feeling like their work matters, and when they come home, they aren't ashamed to tell their friends and family what they do during the day. You'll meet one of those people in the next chapter—a man who grew up near Mpophomeni, who now manages a team of engineers building water systems that bring clean water to thousands of South Africans.

For most people who grow up in the township, though, dream jobs don't happen. More often their lives are like that of Thami (pronounced Tommy), a young woman who worked at the chicken farm near Howick owned by Scott, the farmer introduced in chapter 2. When I went to visit the farm, Scott selected her as my guide for the day, saying, "Thami is a bright young woman. It's a shame she's being wasted in a chicken farm."

As we have seen, one way to cope with difficult circumstances is to find a narrative of the good life that makes sense of those challenges. We saw one such narrative in which people demanded respect, regardless of their power, income, or social status. In a second way of making sense of the good life, people made themselves out to be hustlers, people who struggle on despite knowing that life does not give them fair odds. For workers like Thami, in low-wage, unfulfilling, and seemingly dead-end jobs, what does work have to do with the good life? In this chapter, we'll look at another narrative people turn to when the answer to that question is "not much."

Thami began working at the farm when her sister got pregnant and suggested to Scott that Thami come and take her place. They grew up in a rural area over an hour away, where work opportunities were even scarcer, so Thami took the job even though at first the job worried her. When she was little, she said, she was afraid of chickens. Besides, the work was physically and mentally demanding and she was afraid of doing something wrong. She said it's not hard now because she's doing the same thing every day. Thami never complained to me about the job, but when I asked where she wanted to be in five years, the first thing she listed was having a different job with better money. I asked if she might be promoted at the chicken farm, but she could not think of how. She hoped instead to be a nurse.

On the day I shadowed her, Thami led me first to one of six chicken sheds to "shower in," as workers did every morning to prevent the spread of potential diseases. She handed me shower gel and an old plastic sack for scrubbing as we shifted places in the concrete enclosure. We put on freshly washed red uniforms and hairnets. Then she pried open the interior door of one of the farm's six chicken sheds, gently pushing chickens out of the way as we stepped inside. A smell of manure, sour but not overpowering, met us. Thami explained that the building was well ventilated, and they lessened the smell by keeping everything dry, raking and adding new wood shavings often. The lights were kept dim to keep the juvenile birds from pecking at each other, and it took my eyes a minute to adjust.

The ground was an ocean of white birds, thousands of them. They had space to move and seemed content, flapping their wings and scratching in the wood shavings. There was a steady sound of squawks, and beneath that a sound like the drumming of rain on a roof. After some time, I realized it was the sound of thousands of beaks pecking at plastic feeders. These were meat birds, bred to do little more than eat and grow, but if they ate without restraint, their bodies would never produce eggs. This farm's purpose was to maintain the controlled environment where meat birds would lay eggs, so the birds pecked at empty feeders waiting hungrily for their carefully calculated daily rations. When they reached sufficient maturity, the birds would be transferred to egg-laying buildings, open to bright sunlight to encourage laying, where they could roam between rows of stacked nesting boxes. Workers collected eggs from the nesting boxes, sorted them, and loaded them onto trucks that delivered the eggs to hatcheries at other farms. There they hatched into chicks bred to grow plump in just a few weeks for maximum profit in egg-to-supermarket turnover time.

Thami's main duty was weighing chickens, and she was the only one assigned solely to this responsibility. Working with another woman named Slindile who oversaw the shed of juvenile birds, Thami taught me their expertise—how to swipe your hand under the bird to grab the feet, hold on tight while the bird flaps wildly and then settles to rest with its head hanging down. While I cautiously picked up one chicken at a time, Thami and Slindile picked up chickens with one hand and held them three, four, or five at a time. They hung each bird upside down from a scale, gently wrapping its feet in a soft string. The bird would rest still and the scale would register its weight into its digital memory. Thami showed me buttons on the scale: one that started the scale for the day and one that showed the count of chickens weighed and the average weight. She followed charts specific to the chicken breed to know the precise measurements aimed for, sorting birds into groups that would receive more or less food in the coming week. At the end of the afternoon, she would bring the scales to Scott, who would print off charts showing how many birds were below or above weight, the trajectories of their growth, and numbers of culled birds.

When we finished weighing several hundred birds in that shed, Thami gave me a quick tour of a room with controls for feed, temperature, and other dials she could not identify. The boss touches them, she said. When I asked if she uses them, she said in English, "I can't, but maybe you can," as if something about who I was qualified me to understand these controls despite being a first-time visitor to the farm.

When I asked what job duty Thami liked best, she said weighing, because "I just do the job. I report to the boss, and it is done." She mentioned compassionately that Slindile's job was not nearly so nice. Slindile managed an entire shed herself, which meant she would spend most of her time in a darkened shed alone. She was very good at what she did, Thami said. Slindile could tell "if a bird is sick, and what a bird needs. She has worked here seven years." Then she added, "She is very lonely." I could imagine so, thinking of Slindile's strange life in the dark, alone most of her days with six thousand birds.

We went next to a shed for the adult egg-laying birds, with its open windows and bright daylight. As Thami continued weighing birds, she left me with Philisiwe, a young woman who taught me to sort eggs into crates. In the time it took to pick up an egg, Philisiwe and the two women with her could gauge its size, shape, and cleanliness, then place it among rejects, too small, jumbo, cracked, "floor" (meaning dirty), or the good ones for hatching. Machines existed to do this work in other companies, but the women seemed to enjoy it as an easier part of their day, being rewarded periodically by a trip to the cool refrigerator room to deliver full boxes. Philisiwe showed me how she and her two coworkers filled food trays, picked up eggs, labeled boxes, and refilled the nesting boxes with sawdust. Most of these jobs were physically demanding—filling buckets from feed sacks, moving hundreds of pounds of new wood shavings that made us both sneeze. By noon the temperature had reached 100 degrees Fahrenheit outside, and while the sheds had fans and long open windows to catch breezes, everyone talked about the heat. The oldest woman in the group conveniently assigned herself to an hour in the refrigerated room organizing and labeling boxes of eggs.

At the end of the day, Thami wanted to show me what she called the farm's most modern shed. She explained that it was the nicest shed to work in. "It's easiest. You don't have to weigh and carry feed, because it has automated feeders for both hens and roosters. All you have to do here is sort eggs," she said. "Everyone wants to work in that shed." She had taken me out of the way to see the shed as if to show off how modern the company was. That shed, she told me, only needs three people to work there instead of four. She seemed not to calculate that these machines making their work easier also meant one fewer person hired, a person who could have been her own unemployed sister.

At night, Thami walked a quarter mile up a winding country lane, past sheep, calves, green pastures, and a little winding stream. Like many of the workers, Thami spent most of her life at the housing provided on the farm, leaving only a couple of weekends a month to visit her mother and preschool-aged son who lived a couple of hours away. At the farm she shared a house with three relatives who had also moved there for work. Their green-painted mud house, nestled among a dozen or so similar homes in various colors, was spacious, with a separate bedroom for each adult and more furniture than many homes in Mpophomeni. She opened a large refrigerator to hand me one of the frozen treats her cousin sold as an extra income source. I asked if Thami had any hobbies. She said she liked netball, but it could not happen here—everyone gets too tired from work, there are no nets, and the employees don't go on break all together on the same weekends. For dinner that night Thami would cook corn porridge ("usually with meat," she told me with a smile that said "not always"). After dinner she would turn on the television to watch the nightly soap operas with her cousin, and head to bed in time to wake up the next morning at six o'clock.

Of course, people who grow up in lower-income neighborhoods like Thami's are not the only ones who don't get their dream jobs. Scott, the owner of the chicken farm where Thami worked, never wanted to run a chicken farm either. He got into poultry because he heard that selling eggs would solve the cash flow problems farmers run into raising crops, hogs, or cattle. "It wasn't really my passion," he told me. "But I had to realize that I had to do what was necessary, not just what I loved." Scott grew up in the United Kingdom and moved to South Africa as a young man. In both settings, messages abounded saying white people can grow up to do virtually anything, so long as they put their minds to it and have the patience to move from school to school and job to job until they succeed. These messages urge young people to discover who they truly are and make work an expression of their inner purpose and passion. Don't just take any job, the advice goes, find a job that means something to you, and better yet, a job that means something to the world. Your job is where you make yourself valuable and make your mark on the world.

For over a century in South Africa, those messages to dream big and express yourself through work were reserved for white people. With the end of apartheid, shifts in social structures also accompanied shifts in the messaging about work for black South Africans. Thami grew up in the Born Free generation of children who were raised while the seemingly miraculous end to apartheid unfolded. They heard messages that the future was full of opportunity for white and black South Africans alike. Now, two decades after the end of apartheid, the messages taught to Scott and Thami might be similar, but the social constraints they faced still were not. As a white owner of a relatively small South African farm, Scott faced market constraints that forced him to rule out raising cattle, sheep, or pigs, but he still had options that Thami never had. He had trusting relatives and friends who could offer loans, jobs, advice, and business connections. For Scott, the odds of finding a world-changing, passion-driven, self-expressing job were slim, but for Thami, they were microscopic.

Thami's experience says a lot about what people do when, despite the common well-meaning optimistic advice to the contrary, they find themselves unable to get dream-fulfilling jobs. Notice a couple of things Thami said about her work. First, she appreciated that her responsibilities were limited. She told me that weighing chickens was her favorite part of the job, not because it fulfilled some great purpose, but because "I just do the job. I report to the boss, and it is done." When she walked past the computerized controls for the chicken shed, she described herself as someone who could not touch those controls, in contrast to someone like me who maybe could. Second, she distanced her work from her goals. When I asked if she could get promoted, she said no. Instead, she said she wanted to work as a nurse, a very different kind of job. In these comments, Thami was making herself out to be someone outside of the work. She limited her responsibility and refused to be wholly identified with her job.

Some of what was happening when Thami made these comments was undoubtedly due to the hegemonic narratives of black disempowerment that she grew up with. Recall Duduzile saying that white people have cleverness and black people have strength. Thami's assumption that I—a white person who showed up with a researcher's notebook and walked into her boss's office—might be able to touch a set of controls that she could not, fit into that hegemony.

But Thami's comments did more than just repeat an unexamined hegemony. In fact, remarks like hers drove employers crazy. Employers wanted their employees to be committed to their jobs. Yet employees kept on holding themselves back, even in direct contradiction to what they were told at work trainings, at school, and in much of the dominant advice on how to improve your life. Thami's statements were a form of resistance against her employer, and they were useful to her in ways that employers and trainers tended to overlook. In a narrative that showed up among many low-wage laborers in less-than-hoped-for jobs, people were saying to themselves, their communities, and their bosses, that their jobs would not define them. Their jobs meant little to them and had no hold on them.

## Just a Laborer

Driving down the curving country road from my home to Howick, I often picked up hitchhikers.[1] Minibus taxis came down the main road out of Howick only two or three times a day and never down my side road, so hitchhiking was a normal means of transportation for the many people without vehicles. As I drove I would chat with people in whatever language seemed comfortable, and usually the topic of work came up. Often, as I asked the people who worked on farms along our dusty country road whether they had a job, they would respond, "I'm just a laborer." This phrase caught my attention both because it came up so often, and because people used those words in English—"just a laborer"—even in the middle of Zulu sentences.[2] I once asked a couple of hitchhikers, "What is a laborer? What does a laborer do?" Despite my efforts in both English and Zulu, they seemed confused, even possibly frustrated that I would ask such a question. It was as if my question did not make sense.

This made me want an answer all the more, so I asked someone I had visited many times already, a man named Muzi. He was an accomplished painter I had met at a training for business entrepreneurs, and I stopped by his home or painting studio to talk with him every few weeks. When I asked him what "laborer" meant, he explained, "It's a person who's just working without skill." He laughed at the bluntness of his own answer, then tried to clarify by referring to a painting he had shown me the first time we met. He had first shown it to me when I asked if he ever painted just for his own sake, not to make money, but to communicate about something important to him. This was an oil painting, making it more expensive and time consuming to paint than his usual acrylic paintings, and it was very different from the idyllic township street scenes he was painting at the time for tourists. His inspiration for the painting, he said, was the Marikana platinum mine strikes of 2012. The strikes spreading across the country at the time involved over 75,000 miners, including 17,000 who lost their jobs and at least 34 who were killed by the police.[3] In the end, mining companies granted only 10–22 percent wage increases rather than the 300 percent that miners had called for. "I saw a lot of exploitation," Muzi said when I asked what compelled him to make the painting. "Guys working hard, getting paid peanuts. I was angry." In the foreground of Muzi's painting, a muscled young man with piercing eyes bends forward as he grasps a shovel. Smaller figures behind the man bend under loads on their backs or swing picks and shovels beneath a turbulent orange background. These, he said, were laborers. "For me," Muzi added, "I hate being a laborer."

I also asked Duduzile what "laborer" meant. She explained, "A laborer is, 'I'm just doing the work I'm asked to do and I know that I can start at this time and end at this time. I don't have any input or suggestion. It's just to treat myself that I'm just the laborer, and if there's anything going wrong, I'm just the laborer." At this point she paused to think out loud if there were some word for a laborer's opposite, something "more" than a laborer. Maybe someone, she said, "who can negotiate with the employer, who can have some input into things," who would

**FIGURE 6.1**  Painting titled *Cheap Labour*, by Muzi Ndlela. Used by permission of artist.

put in <u>extra effort</u> whenever it was necessary, saying, "I can give myself if there's a need for an extra mile."

Muzi's and Duduzile's answers helped me understand why my question—What does a laborer do?—did not make sense to my hitchhikers. It does not matter what a laborer does—the very point of the word "laborer" is to say that job duties are irrelevant. A laborer is "working without skill," "just doing the work," not doing things that people aspire to do. A laborer might be a farmhand, factory worker, gardener, or cleaner. Their work might be temporary or permanent, formal or informal, indoor or outdoor. What made someone "just a laborer" had little to do with their job duties; instead, it had to do with their relationship to the work. A laborer does not have input or negotiating ability, but they also lack something else: responsibility. That lack turns out to be very useful, and partly explains why people actually made themselves out to be just laborers, despite, as Muzi admitted, the fact that people hate being a laborer. As Duduzile put it, laborers say, "I treat myself that I'm just the laborer," meaning that a laborer actually participates in giving themselves that meaning. Why? Because a laborer can end the job at a certain time, not caring if something goes wrong, free from the responsibility to go the extra mile.

Treating oneself as just a laborer is a way of demanding a certain bargain. It's saying, I'm in a job that does not offer dignity or a good life, and I will not offer my life to the job either. Before we return to the question of why workers make that bargain, let's consider how this narrative fits—or doesn't fit—with the prevailing advice about how to merge a career with the good life.

## Training Good Workers

In South Africa in 2014, copious organizations existed specifically to train unemployed people in how to get jobs. Within a thirty-kilometer radius around Mpophomeni alone, there were at least twelve organizations that offered services preparing unemployed people for work. They included a farmer-mentoring organization, an entrepreneurship class, a consulting firm for business owners dissatisfied with their employee retention, a gardening project, a government employment agency, a philanthropic entrepreneurship program started by a large international company, and even a youth golfing program with a work ethics training curriculum. I met with project leaders, trainers, and trainees at these twelve organizations and attended over fifty hours of various trainings. As trainees in these programs learned such skills as how to write a résumé, how to respond to interview questions, how to choose clothing for an interview, and how to ask for a recommendation letter, they were also bombarded with messages saying never, ever be "just a laborer."

I visited a white woman named Terry who had led some of the training sessions in a series of workshops designed to prepare unemployed people to find work. Business owners also hired her to give workplace trainings that taught workers how to think of themselves as team players contributing to the business's mission. Such a mindset would make them more valuable to employers, and that, she promised, would also bring them successful careers. Terry explained her role as "trying to get people out of the money-only idea of work" by showing them that their work was part of something bigger and more important than just wages. Teaching this message, she said, was difficult. Many of the people she trained did not think that way about work. "Most work to survive, they're not looking to the future. The job means nothing but survival."

I had met people whose ideas of work lined up with Terry's description. Here's a portion of one translated conversation with a mother and her nineteen-year-old daughter:

> CHRISTINE: [Addressing the mom] Which of your three previous jobs were your favorite jobs?
>
> MOM: It doesn't matter where I work, only that it gives me money. A lot of money. I don't choose this job or that job, it only matters if a job gives you money.
>
> CHRISTINE: Tell me about what you don't like at jobs.
>
> MOM: What I don't like, I don't like jobs that don't pay much money. I want a job that helps my kids at home. It gets them food.
>
> CHRISTINE: [Speaking to the daughter] What do you think? If you had a good job, tell me about what you think is a good job.
>
> DAUGHTER: I have never worked. I applied for one but they never responded. Now I just stay at home.
>
> CHRISTINE: What would you like to do? Would you like to study, get a scholarship, get a certain job?
>
> DAUGHTER: I would like to get a job. I would like to earn money.
>
> CHRISTINE: And what job would you choose?
>
> DAUGHTER: Any kind.

For this mom and daughter, choosing work for reasons beyond urgent pay was a luxury they could not afford.

Frequently, strangers approached me asking for jobs, and I often heard a similar refrain about what work they wanted: *Anything. Any job, so long as it pays.*

Terry was quick to admit that white South Africans like her had designed the system that produced this "money-only idea of work" that she was now trying to reverse. "How do you expect them to think when they've been told everything? If your family has only been a servant, what do you expect their thought process to be?" A typical white family, she said, sits down to dinner and the adults talk about their jobs. "What do servants talk about?" Terry asked rhetorically. At this point a Zulu woman who had been typing on a computer on the other side of the room cut in with a response: "Family. Not the job."

Other organizations were also trying to train people to think of themselves as more than servants and their work as more than a way to get paid. A handbook used by an organization in Mpophomeni and other organizations nationwide offered the following advice:

> It is good to consider taking a job for less pay or even a job you don't like because working brings: dignity and respect; it gives purpose and meaning to wake up to each day; it compels contact and shared experience with other people; it presents us with goals and purpose; it gives a little money that can feed and give shelter. . . . Sometimes we do things because others are doing them. Your vision has to be yours. You have to own it. . . . A lot of people give up their dreams of studying because they have limited resources. However, with wisdom, perseverance, and hard work, ANYONE can study.

According to these trainings, the primary reasons for having a job were to find dignity and a sense of purpose and to formulate new goals. Earning "a little money" was a kind of side effect, worth sacrificing on behalf of these more self-determinative aims. The path to attaining a job also required having a vision and staying true to oneself. The manual included a seven-step plan for "career decision making":

Step One: Find out about yourself, your capabilities, and what you want to contribute.
Step Two: Find out about what work is needed, what opportunities exist.
Step Three: Find career paths that best bring together who you are and what work needs to be done.
Step Four: Choose a career path to follow.
Step Five: Make an action plan for steps along the path.
Step Six: Implement the action plan.
Step Seven: Monitor your progress and revise the plan, or start again in a new direction.

The key to finding a job—and, presumably, to attaining the good life—was to figure out what career would fit the unique person that you are. Then make a plan, be a devoted employee, and keep moving forward to better things, always believing that your work has a greater purpose.

Trainees nodded their heads as they heard such advice in the workshops, but it was unclear how much difference it made in the face of real-world constraints. For at least one graduate of these trainings, a man named Sbu, the career decision-making plan seemed to have little to do with what happened after he finished the training. I ran into Sbu while we lingered at the back of a theater in Mpophomeni waiting for a hip hop event to start.

"I found a job," he told me when I asked how he was doing.

I had a vague memory of Sbu and another guy cracking jokes on the first morning of the training. Now that confidence was gone as he slouched in front of me, awkwardly glancing from the floor into the distance and back to the floor. In front of us a crowd of rowdy preteens and teens were bouncing in their seats and climbing on the stage to practice rapping into their cell phones held as mock microphones in their fists. The event organizers came to shoo them off the stage before disappearing to finish preparations for the event.

"That's great," I responded with enthusiasm. "Where's the job?" I noticed Sbu had not volunteered this information. People rarely did. If I wanted to know the name of the company or the kind of work they did, I would generally have to ask.

Sbu responded with one word, Sunshine, the name (a pseudonym here) of a large food processing and packaging plant in Howick. His eyes glanced up to read my face and then dropped back down.

I suspected this workplace had something to do with his lack of enthusiasm. A job at Sunshine Foods would not have been on the list of career goals he had prepared in his job-readiness training program. In my first months in Mpophomeni, I met more people who had quit working at Sunshine Foods than any other job.[4] The factory was one of the largest employers in the Howick area with over three hundred employees. I spent four days conducting research at the company, talking with employees and managers, eating in the lunchroom and standing with workers as they loaded food containers into crates. Working in the warehouse was one of the easier jobs to get in the area. People got work there by taking a résumé to a labor contractor and waiting until a call came when a position opened—in some cases as quickly as the next day. Most entry-level positions were temporary, though. Thus a lot of people around the township had worked for Sunshine for some amount of time. One such ex-employee described his job there this way: "It's a job-because-you-need-a-job kind of a job."

Finding this job wasn't a matter of accomplishment for Sbu, it was a matter of consenting to the limited options available.

"And how is it?" I asked.

He looked at me, raised his eyes meaningfully, shrugged, and looked away again.

"What's your job there?"

"Packer." The food processing plant employed about seventy people in its packing department, plus fifteen on a night shift. Most were in their twenties or thirties. Packers loaded crates onto pallets and pushed carts stacked with pallets into refrigerated storage or onto trucks.

Sensing Sbu's ambivalence about his new job, I decided to be direct. "Do you think you'll stay?"

Again he shrugged, then said simply, "It pays."

As Sbu and I talked, Teeza appeared on the stage. He was organizing the hip hop event we were there to see. Teeza was in his element—dressed in a white sharp-shouldered blazer and brightly patterned skinny pants, a pair of sunglasses perched on his spiky dreadlocks. Teeza had not made it to his dream life either, but he radiated pride in his current hustle. The contrast was stark between the unemployed Teeza and the employed Sbu, who tomorrow morning would be out on an early morning bus ride to stack crates onto pallets. Sbu may have attended hours of training telling him that work could be a source of dignity and purpose, but a job at Sunshine was no source of street cred in this world.

## Reconciling the Dreams of Youth with the Realities of Adulthood

For trainers like Terry, it was a problem that black South Africans were not coming home proud to talk about their jobs. But her expectations were part of a middle-class view of work that did not fit with jobs like packing food at Sunshine. Sbu's reluctance to tell me about his job was not just shyness, it was a common narrative-shaping technique that distanced people's identities from their jobs.

Among middle-class, college-educated white people in South Africa as in much of the world, introductions often begin with a question about work. In these social groups, the question "What do you do?" is used as a way to gauge a person's identity. A person who fixes bicycles seems like a different kind of person than one who arranges flowers or conducts pharmaceutical research. Among groups who are less likely to have the opportunities afforded by whiteness, college education, and middle- or upper-class social status, linking identity to career can be a threatening or insulting prospect.

Terry and her coworker's comments that black South Africans did not readily talk about their jobs at home matched what I had found. Several times when adults mentioned their parents' employment, I had asked more about those jobs and learned that the son or daughter had little idea what their parents' job duties entailed or even where they worked. This tendency to avoid talking about the details of work had not ended with apartheid. As I asked people about their work histories, I counted at least nineteen who talked about a job in a way that avoided naming the kind of company they worked for or what they did at the job. Instead, they often referred to jobs by the part of the city they worked in, the amount of time they worked there, or the name of a business owner or manager they worked for.

This way of talking about a job shapes the meaning of the job. It subtly communicates that the place and the relationships of a job matter more than the duties at the job. Nearly everyone was eager to tell details about how they were treated at work, but when they thought about work, their job title or duties were not the first thing they thought to share—like a teacher, doctor, nurse, or engineer might. This subtle pattern in how people introduced their work pointed to a strategy that many people in low-wage work in South Africa and elsewhere in the world use to cope with their working circumstances: they deal with the disappointment and purposelessness of their work by differentiating their work from what is valuable in their lives.

That's not to say that young people never had dreams, however. Once I visited a high school class in which the teacher went around the room asking each student to say what they wanted to be when they grew up. In the class of about forty high school students, there were about ten aspiring social workers, ten police officers, ten doctors and nurses, and the rest a mix of soccer players, engineers, and a couple of other stray professions. In the years that followed, I heard this exercise several other times in workshops and classrooms, and the mix was always about the same. One high school teacher told me after class that he was tired of hearing young people talk about being nurses and soccer players. Most of them, he said, would be lucky to find jobs driving tractors. In a study of high school students in Malawi, the anthropologist Margaret Frye also found that young people talked about highly optimistic aspirations.[5] She noticed that talking about optimistic career plans served a purpose, even for high schoolers who had little means of accomplishing their career goals. By naming a respectable career goal, a young person portrayed themselves as a certain kind of person, building a persona in the present as someone who was aspiring and goal driven. That persona could also bring benefits like getting teachers and other adults to invest in their education. High schoolers in South Africa who claimed they would be doctors and soccer stars might be similarly performing a certain valued persona.

But when they became adults and entered real-world jobs, those jobs bore little resemblance to the kinds of jobs that signaled goal-driven aspirations. When kids who grow up telling people they hope to be soccer players and social workers end up as tractor drivers or food packagers, what would they tell people about their career now?

# What Does a Laborer Do?

To understand why people would downplay their involvement in a job, it's use-ful to be clear about what the experience of being "just a laborer" often entails. A couple of young women I got to know in Mpophomeni once offered me a visual picture of what work means to many black South Africans. I was walking with one woman when we came upon Nobuhle, another mutual friend. Nobuhle had no formal employment but owned a handheld brush-cutter that provided her, like many people in the township, a small business opportunity to earn money cutting lawns. She had cut three lawns already that day, and her body showed it. Sweat dripped from beneath the cloth she had tied over her braided hair. Her clothing was green with grass clippings, and she held her brush cutter low like its weight threatened to pull her to the ground. She mustered a smile and turned off the trimmer when we waved to her, then offered to buy me a cold drink with the money in her pocket. The woman walking with me playfully chided Nobuhle's bedraggled and exhausted appearance. Ever thoughtful of ways to inform my research, she explained to me, "*That* is what *work* looks like."

For women like Nobuhle and her friend, work is likely to be physically demanding, mentally disengaging, geographically and symbolically distanced from the important places in a worker's life, and dehumanizing. Take the jobs at Sunshine Foods for example. One morning in their warehouse, I watched three women unload one-kilogram packs of yogurt from a conveyor belt. They lifted the yogurt tubs one or two at a time with both arms, setting them into crates of five. Then they lifted those crates onto a pallet. Some of the shorter women were lifting yogurt tubs as high as their faces and lifting the pallets well above their shoulders. Everyone except the drivers and employees nearing retirement age stood up as they worked in the warehouse. When a pallet was filled above the women's heads, a man would come and drive the pallet on a dolly into the refrig-erated warehouse. In one morning, three women moved 1,650 tubs of one kind of yogurt, 6,615 of another, and 2,056 of another. That's 10,301 kilograms for the three of them, or around 3,300 kilograms per person—3.5 metric tons—before their one o'clock break. When the women noticed me checking their packing list and calculating these totals, they raised their eyebrows and reminded me that this was not a long day. On a long day, they might double that.

My own least favorite participant observation at a job site was the misty, cold day I spent with a team planting tree saplings for a large forestry company. We walked up and down recently burned off hillsides for eight working hours with two breaks to sit on the blackened ground to eat and rest. The women used large scissorlike tools to open holes in the soil, then dropped in seedlings and packed down the dirt with their boots. The men followed, sloshing on a mix of water and an antifungal chemical they referred to simply with the English word "poison." The managers said that up until a few years ago, the work would have been worse: now the industry required tools so that workers would not have to bend over. The foreman said the weather was lucky, too—if it had been pouring rain or blazing hot, they would be out there packing saplings all the same. At the end of the day, the workers had walked over muddied hillsides for several kilometers including two hours in the rain. They had carried hundreds of liters of water and hauled tools to prepare more than a thousand holes. The managers had not allowed me to do anything more physically demanding than walk alongside the workers, but even so, my shoes and pants were caked in mud and soot, and I was aching and tired.

Such work is also tiring because, paradoxically, it is so mentally easy. I asked one woman in Mpophomeni what she did in a short-term job she'd had at Sunshine Foods. "Nothing much," she replied. "Put stickers on packages. Not hard. Easy." When I asked if she would have liked to continue the job, she responded vehemently, "No ways! I would not be happy." I asked what kind of work would make her happy. She spoke about engaging her mind. She wanted to take classes in accounting or commerce and to work in an office.

Women and men both worked in physically demanding jobs, but for women in particular, hard physical labor can carry the added emotional weight of being out of their socially constructed gendered roles in society. Social changes including declining marriage rates and culturally shifting obligations between partners have contributed to a dramatic increase in the number of women seeking work in recent decades.[6] The percentage of South African women seeking or finding work went from 38 percent to 47 percent in just the four years after apartheid ended, and today is at about 52 percent.[7] But these increases in women seeking work did not necessarily correspond to women finding desirable jobs. In 2018 only 32 percent of managers in South Africa were women.[8] Women remained more likely than men to give up job searching without finding work, or to enter low-paid, insecure, informal, or even unpaid work.[9] By far the most common jobs women told me they aspired to have were nursing and social work, both jobs still done mainly by women. Four women told me that the good life for them meant having a spouse who worked so they could stay home, and one woman insisted that "every woman" wants that, but they can't get it. Instead, they and their female neighbors might be operating machinery in a water bottling company, sorting electrical parts, or running chain saws.

The same woman who had worked at Sunshine talked about the strain of going days at a time without seeing her preschooler daughter fully awake. In the darkness of early morning, she would sweep and mop her home, cook food for her family, make beds, kiss her sleeping daughter goodbye, and walk three kilometers to catch a bus that left at 7:30 a.m. In the busy season with overtime hours, she would return home at 10 p.m. Commuting in the dark brought the threat of crime. I knew multiple women who quit or turned down job offers because the commute involved long walks or waits on roads that were not safe.

In South Africa, *work* goes hand in hand with *commute*. The Group Areas Act of 1950 formally established a relationship between work spaces and living spaces for nonwhites by demarcating most areas with employment opportunities as whites-only. Black workers came to work by train, taxi, or on foot. They stayed for the day or for weeks at a time in staff housing. If they were fortunate, they found complete houses like the one Thami shared at the chicken farm; others lived in bunkhouses, crowded together according to the whims of their employers. People back at home, predominantly women and elders, subsidized lower than living-wage earnings by providing child care and other unpaid labor like growing food and building homes.[10] Logistically and symbolically, this meant that work happened in spaces cut off from all the familiarity, safety, tradition, and welcome associated with home. Those divisions have proven resilient long beyond the repeal of the laws that most blatantly enforced them. People like Thami had separate words for the "home" they lived in at the chicken farm versus the "home-home" or "the big home" where their families lived. The latter was a place that ancestors, living and dead, continued to inhabit, a place that established identity, and a place toward which their resources flowed in the form of gifts, ceremonies, and shared wages.

In addition to the geographic distance workers encountered between their homes and their work, they experienced a symbolic distance from many of the products they made. As I stood with women packing tubs of Greek style yogurt onto crates, one woman asked if I liked Greek style yogurt. She said she assumed that white people must like it, but black people don't, much as white people don't drink *maas*, a soured milk product many black South Africans ate. This separation from the product was reinforced by strong warnings never to taste the yogurt or steal from the company.

Current and former employees of Sunshine Foods had plenty of complaints—they disliked the unpredictable hours, the late and early shifts, the danger of commuting in the dark, the physical demands, and the boring repetition. On the whole, though, people did not consider Sunshine Foods to be an especially bad workplace. When people talked about jobs they disliked most they described situations that compromised their physical existence and their humanity.

I spoke at length with Mbeki, a man who worked at a company near my home. No buses came down our road when his shift ended, so I often gave rides to employees in his company. In one previous job, he was hired to sit outside in a forest as a security guard, keeping watch on a construction crane. "I had no *anything* to protect myself," he said. "The only thing the company gave me was a torch [a flashlight]." "I don't know what for. No phone signal even." Mbeki laughed at the absurdity of how little he could do if someone were to attempt to steal the equipment. He quit the job, he said, not just because of the danger but because he realized one night as he sat in that forest that the company valued the machine more than his life.

There were many ways a company could communicate that a human life does not matter. One woman described a job where people unloaded and sorted electrical supplies, work she called "difficult, heavy, and dangerous." One day a coworker fell several meters from a ladder and ended up "scraped up, maybe paralyzed." The company offered neither compensation nor apology. In Mbeki's current job, people who finished a shift at night were left to sleep on a cement floor until the morning when they could hitchhike home. The management forbade bringing in mattresses. Another man quit a job as soon as he realized he'd been hired as a scab the day after a dozen employees quit in protest over bad management. He feared that striking employees might retaliate by harming him. In one story I heard from a white neighbor, an employer supposedly kept a large snake in an aquarium to threaten his employees, knowing that Zulu people fear snakes for both their bite and their ties to spiritual evil. In these stories, managers treated workers in ways that demonstrated that the workers' own lives did not matter. People quit these jobs not because their pay was too low or their job duties too tiring, but because they placed a higher value on their lives than the employer did.

The methods used to hire people for generations in South Africa further reinforced the idea that workers are little more than undifferentiated bodies, endlessly replaceable by other bodies when one no longer functions. I saw this most clearly on a day I spent with people hoping to get chosen for day labor. Every morning in Howick, as on certain roadsides in nearly any city in South Africa, a crowd of people gathered along the main road waiting for day-labor positions. On the weekday morning I joined them, there were about thirty to fifty people, around 80 percent of them men. Many were migrants to the area from elsewhere in South Africa or other African countries. My English and Zulu were often translated into Sotho or other languages from person to person. Some carried shovels, gloves, or other tools. When I pulled up in my car to ask to talk about research, dozens of people flooded around me, eagerly asking how many I would hire. When I had explained my interest in interviewing rather than hiring, most of the group wandered off, soon to surround the next truck to arrive. A lucky three or four were asked to hop into the back of the truck. I could decipher little reason for who went and who got left behind. People told me that sometimes the employers just looked at people and chose, other times they asked for people with certain skills, but it was to your advantage to always say you had any skills requested. Particularly in jobs requiring physical labor, employers might meet laborers in the morning and give minimal instructions. Often white employers instructed employees through a translator or in fanakalo, a grammatically simplified broken isiZulu that some Zulu people complained about. Such a hiring system operated on the presumption that anyone with a fit body would have the few skills necessary for the job, or could learn those skills from simple instructions. Bosses and laborers hardly needed to speak to each other except in regard to the task at hand; laborers would go home with money when the boss said the job was done.

Yet many black South Africans in the township insisted that some jobs *should* be filled by randomized methods.[11] A Mpophomeni resident described a common practice in the township. Sometimes employers would "come with a loud speaker, saying like 'Tomorrow you must come, make it to the hall, and there will be job opportunities, you must bring your ID.' Sometimes they put the IDs in a big box, and they pick one, like then you got the job." The Mpophomeni residents I spoke with about this practice considered it a fair way to choose workers for low-skilled jobs, and in fact protests broke out in the township when evidence surfaced that hiring for a government-funded building project had not been handled strictly by this method. I stopped along the road to mingle among the fifty-plus people, most of them in their twenties and thirties, who were piling rocks in the road and burning tires to blockade the main entrance to the township in protest. The protestors accused township ward leaders of handpicking the employees, probably out of those leaders' own families and friends, rather than allowing luck to make the choice. They knew very well that any human who could lift a shovel could do these jobs, and pretending that qualifications mattered would only lead to unfair cronyism.

There is a fine line, though, between treating a laborer as an undifferentiated human body and treating a laborer as something less than human. As I mentioned in chapter 3, I witnessed or heard stories of employees being referred to as dogs, baboons, pigs, and machines. While I sat at a café once, a manager shouted curses out the door at an employee who was cutting grass close by and presumably disturbing customers, calling him "you monkey." Such slurs carry all the force of derogatory racial hatred plus a dehumanizing message. It was in these kinds of work experiences—dehumanizing, belittling, exhausting, and distanced from self-identity—in which people referred to themselves as "just a laborer."

## "I treat myself that I'm just the laborer"

Much recent research has found that believing in the purpose of a job contributes much to workplace satisfaction.[12] The behavioral economist Dan Ariely and his colleagues conducted experiments in which people performed repetitive tasks like assembling Lego pieces. In some conditions, their completed products were received by a person and set carefully aside. In other conditions, their work was immediately disassembled before their own eyes. Not surprisingly, people in the unrecognized and purposeless conditions required more pay to keep going at their assembly task.[13] Some research suggests that workers are able to change the ways they think about their work to make even mundane tasks more fulfilling. Amy Wrzensniewski and Jane Dutton, in a study of hospital custodians who thought of their work as a way to serve patients rather than a task of getting floors swept, called this infusion of purpose into one's own work "job crafting."[14]

Why, then, would South African low-wage workers call themselves just laborers? When job-readiness trainers advised people to recognize the purpose and dignity in their work, they were essentially telling people to job craft, because they believed it would make people happier and more likely to be promoted. And quite possibly it would—for some people. Barry Schwartz, another psychologist of work, raises an important warning: job crafting has limits. Schwartz writes, "There is no doubt that the attitudes people bring to their work are important, but I think there are limits to what an individual can do psychologically to interpret a soulless job as a meaningful one."[15] Unless managers value workers and their contributions, workers cannot invent themselves as valuable from scratch.

I doubt if many of the tree planters who led me over hillsides in the rain could make their job enjoyable by mustering up thoughts of meaningful uses of trees. Planting saplings is a job-because-you-need-a-job kind of job, not a job that brings dignity or significance. The employers even admitted as much. When I asked one forestry manager why he thought people came to work with his company, he paused for a moment and said in a regretful tone, "Because there's no other job. I honestly believe that if people could choose a job, let's say there are a list of ten jobs, this would be a nine or a ten." When I talked with another forestry manager, I asked what made a good employee. He listed three words, "strong, fit, healthy." Then he paused for some time, unable to think of any other characteristics. This is a job where bodies move tools and dirt and then go home with pay. Like Sbu, who settled for food packing as his best option in the present, and Thami who dreamed of becoming a nurse but took the job available, visionary career planning and identity fulfillment at work often prove to be unfeasible. Unless structural changes make it possible for black low-wage laborers to expect to be valued at work and capable of achieving their vision of a good life through work, it is incomplete and potentially harmful advice to tell people that they just need to *think* about their job as bringing dignity and as a stepping-stone to better work. People who think of themselves as just laborers were being realistic about the significance, dignity, and future prospects of their work.

They were also being strategic in protecting the limited energy and dignity they had. For people in disappointing jobs, calling themselves just laborers communicated that their jobs were just a way to earn money; it was not a determinant of their identity, their status, their dignity, or the good life. In some sense, they strategically estranged themselves from work. Karl Marx famously used words translated as "estrangement" and "alienation" to describe the ways that workers under capitalism become disconnected from their customers, the meaning of their production, and ultimately from their very identity. Social scientists have pointed out that there is a spectrum of degrees of estrangement from work—some forms of market transactions are more "embedded" in social relations, meaning they are surrounded by meaningful social ties, whereas other transactions—like workers making Greek yogurt, which they find distasteful, for customers they'll never meet—are less embedded. Usually, social scientists focus on the negative effects of alienation that are built into capitalist structures. Since Marx's time, social philosophers and economic anthropologists such as Karl Polanyi, Fred Block, and Katherine Browne have complicated the idea of alienation by pointing out that not all market societies and situations are the same.[16] They describe a spectrum of relational arrangements that can occur in market societies, ranging from those with high "marketness" in which market prices dictate behavior, to those in which market decisions are deeply "embedded" in— that is, determined by—the traditions, values, and cultures of the society.[17] In the next chapter, I'll describe a workplace that many workers appreciated, largely because it reduced the negative aspects of alienation. But something very different was happening when people spoke of themselves as just laborers—they were embracing some degree of alienation. They intentionally separated their identity, purpose, and social ties from their acts of productive labor. They could define their identity by their communities and interactions at home, not by their working life.

Thinking of themselves as just laborers also offered protections around workers' limited emotional and physical energy. When a boss complained, a laborer had an emotional barrier against caring too deeply—work problems were the boss's problem, not theirs. When a laborer found out they would have to quit for personal reasons or that their contract had been terminated, that person could leave without sacrificing something of their own identity. A laborer did not have to care if they were not welcomed into white spaces—their identity resided in black spaces. If work required wearing unflattering clothes like hardhats that crushed a hairstyle, performing demeaning tasks like cleaning bathrooms, or being treated as if one was less intelligent for not speaking English, then a laborer could ignore these things when the work day ended. The only thing a laborer needed to take home from work was pay.

In a paradoxical sense, laborers were voluntarily giving up agency in their own self-interest. The anthropologist Hirokazu Miyazaki uses the phrase "abeyance of agency" to describe the ways people strategically communicate that they do not—and do not wish to—control some aspect of life.[18] Like Thami, who was satisfied not to know how to operate certain machines, abeyance of agency could protect people from overtime, anxiety, risk, and blame. This, however, was not what employers wanted.

## The Battle of Narratives: Laborers versus Team Members

From the perspective of an employer, abeyance of agency from "just laborers" was bad for business. Employers wanted commitment at minimal cost. In various subtle refusals to give their all at work, workers who embraced the just-a-laborer narrative were declaring that they wouldn't give dedication without getting a better life—employers could not have one without the other.

Even as managers and middle managers reproduced a concept of work as little more than a monetary transaction in all the ways described above, they found that getting workers to care was in their best interest. Employers often complained that when problems arose, workers would all say *angazi*—I don't know what happened. They wanted workers who were loyal for as long as the company wanted them, with a sense of solidarity that would override their personal interest in stealing, working slowly, or quitting. But employers did not necessarily want to include low-wage workers in their decision-making about wages and company policies, to bear the cost of training workers who might use those skills elsewhere, or to allow black employees to be promoted over workers of other races.

The three largest companies I visited all had some kind of program in place to build loyalty and morale among employees. They posted slogans like "Win as a team" or "Sisonke" ("We are all together"). Two out of three companies admitted that this approach showed little success. They said the programs were stymied by various problems, including upper-level management not wanting to socialize with lower-level employees.

Often black middle managers were in the position of training people against the just-a-laborer narrative. One manager explained: "Some people they just come and work, and they work as much as they can, and at the end of the month, on the fortnight, they get money and then go home. So they don't care about the other things which are important. They don't have the idea, 'Why do we come and work? What are we doing on this farm?' You know? The only thing that's important to them is just get money, and then go home." He said he tried to explain to workers how their products would make customers happy, and how each job duty contributed something to a common goal of making people happy.

This black manager was not being forced to deliver that message to his coworkers—he believed what he said. He had been part of a program that trained and mentored dozens of black farm laborers to move into upper-level farm management. As a member of that program, the white owners of the farms where he worked gave him responsibilities and treated him in ways that showed they expected him to succeed. He had spent time in Australia managing a farm, and there he had been immersed in a different racialized social system where he was taken seriously as a prospective leader. He had encountered a life where he could be more than a laborer, and he wanted others to experience it too. Like this young man, many employees *did* want to be more than just laborers. They wanted to be part of a team that was producing something important; they wanted jobs that were worth committing to.

But for many people, such treatment at work was not available. So in many situations, employers and laborers mutually agreed, albeit begrudgingly, to treat their relationship as a minimally engaged crossing of paths to satisfy their mutual needs for financial gain. For Sbu and Thami, being just laborers was not the good life they sought. It was, however, a stable equilibrium, a kind of "good enough life" for now.[19]

# "I HAVE A GOOD STORY"
## Possibilities

Out of over one hundred people that I interviewed for this research, only five said they were currently living the good life. Together, these five make a thought-provoking picture of what works for achieving a good life. In each of the previous four chapters, we looked at various narratives of a good life that compete with the dominant laziness myth. In this chapter, rather than focus on one specific narrative, we will look at examples of how people weave together narratives to make lives that they consider good. This chapter includes the stories of some of those people: Muzi, an artist; Philani, an engineer; Nkosi, a shoe factory employee; and Duduzile, a recently unemployed female entrepreneur. Sarah, the fifth person who said they currently lived the good life, had connections to Nkosi's factory. I mention her briefly in Nkosi's story, but she moved to a new home midway through my research before I could learn enough to tell her tale at length.

Anthropologists have a tendency to think a lot about problems. In this book, I describe a number of them: joblessness, unfulfilling work, and a narrative that disguises the discrimination embedded in these, to name a few. Unless people recognize the social and historical factors surrounding such issues, they will tend to rely on hegemonic narratives that give incomplete or false explanations for them.

Understanding problems is not enough, though. We also need to identify alternatives to those dilemmas. This task requires both an eye for what people already experience as good and an imagination to project forward how that good might be expanded and multiplied. The anthropologist James Ferguson, who has spent decades studying both what works and what doesn't work on the African continent, encourages anthropologists to be involved in identifying new ways of thinking by studying people's real practices, what he calls "a process of conceptual and institutional innovation."[1] The economic anthropologist Edward Fischer, in his book *The Good Life*, similarly recommends what he calls a "positive anthropology," a way of "combining cultural critique with non-prescriptive, ethnographically informed positive alternatives that engage public policy debates."[2] He argues that "how we want the world to work is just as important as how it actually does work in understanding what drives us toward a particular future and what informs visions of the good life."[3] To that end, he gives examples from around the world of the kind of good life people want, even when their circumstances and actions are directed otherwise. The sociologist and black studies scholar George Lipsitz applies a similar strategy of recognizing both problems and alternative ways of thinking to "disassemble the fatal links that connect race, place, and power."[4] He calls for a "two-part strategy" including a "frontal attack on all the mechanisms that prevent people of color from equal opportunities to accumulate assets" as well as "a concomitant embrace of the Black spatial imaginary."[5] Likewise, my aim in this chapter is to generate innovation to disassemble racially discriminatory social systems by looking at ethnographic examples of people who have called their own lives "good."

Stories of black individuals living good lives have a complicated history in Africa and the diaspora.[6] A technique of selectively highlighting stories of exceptionally successful marginalized people has often been used throughout history to reinforce the laziness myth. Such narratives imply that by mustering enough grit and perseverance, these exemplary individuals set an example for all by overcoming whatever challenges racism may or may not present. Such a story reinforces the psychic and social stability of white people and others in power by denying the significance of antiblack structures that prevent millions of people from experiencing what occurred in these exceptional cases. Not only does reading these stories through that narrative reinforce a white-supremacist fallacy that racial inequalities result from the internal failings of individual black people; it ignores the ethnographic evidence. I worry that readers might skim this chapter and take away that same familiar trope: a few heroically entrepreneurial black individuals can show everyone else how to climb the path to career success, just like white people have done for centuries. This, however, is definitely not the narrative that any of these people used to describe their own lives. Listen closely and you will hear that their stories offer direct challenges to that pull-your-black-selves-up-by-your-bootstraps perspective. As you read, keep in mind the following questions: Did these people succeed as lone individuals through their own skills and determination, or because certain social factors succeeded in making their skills and determination possible and effective? By what standards did they define success, and how did these relate to work? And were their challenges and opportunities unique to their individual lives, or systematically widespread across certain groups?

My intention is not to prove that these people's lives are necessarily objectively better than the lives of other people. To say that someone *sees* their life as good differs from concluding that their life *is* definitely better by some universal standards. My aim instead is to record evidence of a set of possibilities for how people might *think* differently about a good life, as well as how people might change social structures to *act* differently toward creating good lives.

Nor can I claim that these five people were necessarily the most satisfied with their lives out of all of those I met. I did not ask everyone I interviewed whether they were currently living the good life. I typically did not ask employers and nonprofit leaders, nor people that had defined the good life in ways that clearly did not describe their current life circumstances. I also did not necessarily talk with people about whether they saw the good life as something they would have continuously or only temporarily. Interviewed on some other day, some of these people might have answered differently. Lives are complicated. Goodness is complicated. This handful of individuals I happened to meet are too few to draw statistically significant correlations from their commonalities alone.

Yet their lives do show certain patterns. Perhaps most notable is a certain absence of pattern: there is no consistent theme in what employment status they have. In fact, they display an almost perfect range of options. Philani told a rags-to-riches story of becoming a high-level engineer at his company; Nkosi was working in a low-wage factory job; Duduzile had recently become unemployed and was trying to start a new business; Muzi made his living selling artwork; and Sarah had been out of full-time work for over a year and was working only a few hours a month. If we want to know what work status has to do with achieving the good life, the evidence here points to the answer *very little*.

They also shared in common that they each defined the good life in a way that did not depend on work status. Even the engineer who made the most money of the five insisted that income did not correlate with the good life. "It will involve the things like love—something that you can't buy!" he said with a laugh as he summarized what he believed about the good life. Recall the Venn diagram introduced in the introduction showing the possible overlap between having work and having the good life. The diagram shows that, for some people, ideas of the good life have a lot of overlap with ideas about working—having a good job seems to them like the main determinant of whether they have a good life. Others see little overlap between work and the good life. They expect work to have little to do with the good life, or they expect that having work will make life worse. Of the people in this chapter, several talked about the importance of certain conditions of their job, but often those conditions could have been met in other jobs or in other ways outside of work. None conceptualized the status of being employed, unemployed, or self-employed as a key determinant of what made life good.

The stories that follow all mention elements of the narratives I've already described. All of them include talk about relationships or respect. Those with paid employment found themselves valued and humanized at work and went home proud of their work. None had to cope with disrespecting work situations by distancing themselves from work as "just laborers." Most experienced at least some period of hustling—taking whatever jobs they could get, building connections, or trying to find customers—and they tended to attribute their success more to chance or God than to their own perseverance or skill.

In this chapter, we move beyond looking at narratives as if they operate in isolation, to see how narratives intertwine with each other and with social structures to cocreate meanings and possibilities for the good life. In previous chapters, I've attempted to isolate sets of ideas that form narratives, but in reality, people do not simply choose a narrative and follow it. They weave together narrative elements that best make sense of their world. And narratives also interact with structures in two directions: explanatory and formative. Narratives help people explain the structures they find themselves in, so structures in some ways constitute narratives. But narratives also compel and guide actions that change societal structures, so narratives also constitute structures.

Looking across the examples in this chapter, then, I offer three points of reflection on the ways that narratives and structures cocreate possibilities for, and meanings of, the good life. First, people who saw their lives as good tended to have found a balance between agency and interdependency. They did not feel trapped by a lack of agency to shape their own lives, and yet they attributed many of their opportunities to circumstances beyond their control. Second, they had developed cultural habits and behaviors—or cultural capital—for interacting in situations where white people dominated, and yet they also experienced validation in black settings that recognized forms of cultural capital unique to black people. Third, they worked in settings that minimized the alienation or relational distance between themselves and their products or customers. I'll return to these three points at the end of the chapter. First, we'll look at the stories of the good life.

## Muzi: Crafting a Profession out of Purpose and Art

Muzi Ndlela (who asked me to use his real name) completed high school but failed the set of matric exams necessary to receive a high school diploma. High school students in South Africa choose subjects to focus on, much like a college major. He chose science and math. "I chose wrong," he told me, when I first interviewed him in his living room. "I had no clue. I hated it. If I could go back, I'd choose differently." He spoke quietly and cautiously, often smiling at me quizzically as if every question I asked surprised him anew at my interest in his life.

After he left high school, he stumbled upon a painting workshop offered at the art museum in Pietermaritzburg. Afterward, he scraped together money to continue painting on his own, and over the coming years attended as many art workshops as he could. At one workshop, he met a Zulu woman who was an art dealer. She encouraged him to think about art as his profession. "It opened my eyes," he said. "I saw this as a job." At her urging, he entered a national art competition, and, to his own surprise, he won third prize.

Muzi continued piecing together an education in painting techniques and business management through workshops and conversations with other artists. I first met him at a workshop offered by one of the many organizations pooling government and private funding to hold entrepreneurship trainings. A few months later, I spotted him in Howick sitting in a park near Howick Falls, a tourist destination. Spread out on the grass in front of him were a few acrylic paintings of township scenes.

I reintroduced myself, and Muzi invited me to talk more at his home in Mpophomeni. There he explained how hard it was to make a living in a job that his peers did not understand. "They look at you like you're lazy. They ask 'Why don't you do a real job?' They don't get why you charge R500 [$50] for a painting, not just R50 [$5]."

When I first asked Muzi what it meant to live the good life, his answer focused on connecting what he enjoyed with a "real job." "I would like to make a studio," he told me. "Then it would be like a real job. Like a normal person who's working. That is what I'd really like to do." He shared a two-bedroom house with his sister and her three children. His bedroom was his only space to paint in, and he worried about the paint fumes he was breathing in day and night.

Then he added, "I hate working for other people."

Not only did his peers in the township undervalue his art, he said, the tourists haggled for lower prices and seemed only interested in certain kinds of paintings. They wanted quaint scenes of quiet houses in townships. Only rarely did he find the time and money for materials to paint what he called "art for myself," like the painting inspired by the mine strikes showing a black man with piercing eyes holding a shovel. Muzi could relate to the exploited workers, and it inspired him to paint. In one of the few times he had been employed, he worked for a ceramics artist who was a white woman. For his full-time work as a potter in her studio, she paid him R500 ($50) per week. I had talked with other black artists who had worked in similar conditions—doing the creative and physical work of producing art while a white person put their name on the pieces and collected profits. "They're using us," he said. "It was like a factory. I am an artist. I hated that." If he could, he said, he would tell stories like that in paintings. "I want to show the darker side of our lives, too," he said.

He didn't use the word "hustling," but when I first met Muzi, his life was a hustle. He made a few hundred rand of profit here and there when he sold a painting, and he reinvested the profits he could spare into his next paintings. "I like oil paints," he told me, "but acrylic is cheaper so I use those." As he would tell me later, he also spent a lot of his earnings on alcohol with friends.

Months after our first meeting, I came to visit him with a list of follow-up questions that I hoped would explore some new topics. I asked, "Can you describe a time in your life when you have gone through a big change?"

He paused for a bit, as he often did, then responded. "Well, in November I became a born-again Christian." He had never talked about religion, and he seemed unsure whether I would want to hear about it.

"How did that come about?" I asked.

"I was just tired of the way I lived my life," he said. "I was drinking and smoking too much, and always in a financial crisis. I was in debt. Alcohol was taking a lot of money from me, and I was just thinking of something that would take that away." He paused. "I was thinking of rehab, but it's not easy to find those things. So the option was the church. And I think God has helped."

Most Zulu South Africans I knew attended church at least occasionally, and few would say they were anything other than Christian. There was a great diversity in how much Christianity affected people's lives, though. For Muzi, his conversion turned out to be a significant shift. He stopped drinking and smoking, which he said completely changed his financial situation, allowing him to buy more art supplies and contribute more to caring for his sister and her three children. As he explained it, before becoming a Christian he knew what he should do and was making good plans, but "my lifestyle was disturbing all my plans."

Not only did joining the church provide what he originally came for—a free alternative to alcohol rehab; it brought him into a different community. In the months and years that followed, he would tell me that his one regret was that many of his friends left him after he started going to church. "My friends just run away. When you are a Christian, they think you will try to change them. They think now your life is boring. But actually," he added with a sigh, "sometimes it is a relief because they can try to influence you." His words reminded me of Bullet and others who told me how hard it was to get ahead without being pulled down by people who were jealous or who saw others' success as a threat. People told stories revealing jealousies among church members, too, but for Muzi, the church offered a place where he found a new community and could escape what Bullet called the pressure to be "bad boys."

In June 2015, six months after he became a Christian, Muzi was working on a painting to give an older leader in the church. It was common for church members to give gifts to their mentors and leaders. Muzi's gift to his mentor, like the other ways in which he had begun building social ties in his church, could have long-term economic consequences. "People in the church don't know I'm a painter yet," he said when he told me about the gift. "But they're gonna see the painting and then they'll know, and then maybe I'm gonna get a lot of people ordering portraits."

Two years later, he had not sold many paintings to fellow church members, but the connections there had helped in other ways. A nearby neighbor from the church offered to rent Muzi a room as a studio. Just under a year from the time we met, Muzi achieved what he originally told me he wanted as the good life—a studio where he would not have to inhale paint fumes in his bedroom and where his painting could be "a real job." Around the time he opened his studio, I asked him one day as I gave him a ride to Howick whether he thought he was living the good life now. He said yes, but he did not bring up the studio or his previous definition of the good life as having a real job. Instead, he talked about having a right relationship with God. "Everything that has happened to me these days," he said, "is because I chose Jesus."

In the same conversation, I asked Muzi what he thought of people who predicted that South Africa would only get worse. He disagreed, saying he had learned to be optimistic about himself and about South Africa. "If you have disorder inside," he explained, "you see everything as disorder, and you're gonna see South Africa as just going to war. But if you have order inside, you see everything like that." He rehashed some of the many improvements he'd seen in his life recently—stopping drinking, paying off debts, finding a studio, selling more paintings. He said when you're right inside, all these things are possible.

Two years later, Muzi was invited to paint and sell art in a gallery at the Mandela Capture Site, a major tourist attraction near Mpophomeni. I visited his spacious new studio just days after he set up shop. When I walked in, he was standing at an easel sketching a large colored-pencil drawing of Mandela's face. The walls of the gallery were covered with paintings, and a dozen or so more lay in a stack on the floor—far more than he had ever been able to afford to accumulate when we first met. His recent paintings and charcoal drawings were rich with symbolism about the challenges in his own life and among black South Africans. Often he used images of goats to symbolize the connections between African culture and Christian beliefs, and many of his pieces dealt with the difficulty of finding hope in the township. In one painting, dozens of outstretched hands reached up from a sea of churning water toward a gray sky. "There's no hope there," he said simply when I asked him to explain. In another piece, a man walked bent forward carrying a heavy sack over his shoulder while a lone goat stood watching. This one, he said, has more hope. "When you struggle, there is always someone watching." Another painting showed a black man's face with the eyes smudged out and replaced with the scrawled words, "Who is he?"

Newspaper clippings on the gallery walls told about Muzi's recent solo exhibition at the Tathum Art Gallery, the largest art museum in the province and one of the most significant art centers in the country. The exhibition was titled "Belief or Identity?" A clipping by an unnamed newspaper editor said of Muzi's work, "His message is one of *ubuntu*, or humanity, where we all respect one another regardless of our different cultures and beliefs." In the years since I had met him, he had gone from selling art that appealed to a white imaginary of black township life, to creating and selling art that fueled a conversation about black experiences and identity. Much like Bullet, Teeza, Sma, and other hip hop artists, poets, and fashion designers in Mpophomeni, he was engaging a strategy of black empowerment that has been called moving from "community-based art making" to "art-based community making."[7]

Muzi also showed me a letter he had just received, announcing that he had been accepted into a one-year postgraduate program to study art with a full scholarship and a significant stipend. Even with Muzi's quiet demeanor, his excitement showed. Most applicants would have had three years of university study, whereas Muzi had never even passed his high school matric exam. With these successes, he said, he was beginning to set higher goals: to "catch the eye of the collectors" and to build an international reputation.

Muzi was one of those whose "hustle" paid off. Like many South Africans, though, he attributed his path to a good life not to his own ambitious hard work, but to right relationships with others like church leaders and a higher power—in his case, the Christian God. He had experienced failures and exploitation, and much like the many township hip hop artists, these hardships powered his drive to use art to tell others about his life and his community's struggles. He knew he was rare among artists to be able to live off his earnings from art, and he used his influence to mentor other artists and petition government leaders to create more professional avenues for artists. By 2019 he had started an after-school art center in Mpophomeni for children and young artists. On the wall, several paintings portrayed dark streets crossed with electric lines that Muzi said represented "hope coming in." Another showed a person carrying a burden through a rainstorm, with a goat nearby that Muzi said represented the help that is always at hand. In these paintings and the interactions that happened in that room, he communicated what mattered to him, which included both "the dark side" of township life and the hope that came through good relationships.

## Philani: From Rags to Relationships, Not Riches

My first meeting with Philani was the first time I recall witnessing a white administrative assistant serving tea to a Zulu supervisor. As an Afrikaner woman carried a tea tray into the boardroom where we met, Philani glanced at me with a faint smile, seeming to confirm that I noticed how unusual this was. I did notice—both the reversal of the apartheid hierarchy and how comfortable they seemed. He thanked her genuinely. She made eye contact with each of us and asked if there was anything else we needed. Their words were nothing unusual, but something in their mannerisms radiated respect for each other and an easy acceptance of their positions. For the next two hours as Philani talked, I felt I had walked into a kind of transformed South Africa, one very different from the lived experiences of most South Africans in the Howick-Mpophomeni area.

I had requested the interview based on a tip from one of Philani's coworkers, a white man. Philani grew up in a different township from Mpophomeni and worked in Pietermaritzburg, so he didn't fit neatly in my research plans, but I had not yet found any Zulu people who supervised white employees in Mpophomeni or Howick. So far the only upper-level Zulu employees I had been able to interview included three middle-level managers who supervised black workers in a factory and one business owner who turned out to be closely supervised by a group of white people who had provided his company's start-up money. Later in the year, I would meet another Zulu person who worked in Durban as an upper-level manager of a grocery store, and a Zulu person would be promoted to direct a nonprofit with white volunteers in Mpophomeni. I heard stories of relatives who got professional degrees and moved to higher-level positions in Durban or Johannesburg, and I met some of them when they were back visiting family in Mpophomeni. But when I met Philani, he was the only one of the black people I could find near the Howick area who supervised white employees.

Philani grew up in a large township between Pietermaritzburg and Mpophomeni and was raised by a single mother and his grandmother. His mother worked during the day but couldn't find an affordable preschool for him, so she enrolled him in elementary school a year early. In grade eight he moved from an all-black primary school to one of the formerly all-white public schools that, by then, was open to students of all racial backgrounds. "It was difficult," he said. "For white kids there, it was their first time they met a black person. The only relationship that they had with a black person was either with a maid or a gardener, and suddenly they had to be equal in class." In addition to adjusting to using English, he took classes in Afrikaans, a language many of his classmates spoke fluently. Even physical education class meant learning new sports. Playing soccer was looked down on as a black kids' sport, while cricket, rugby, and swimming brought social standing in the multiracial school.

"Luckily enough, though," Philani went on, "there was this guy who happened to be the father of one of my friends at school, a white guy, who took me under his wing." The friend's father started tutoring Philani in English, math, and public speaking. He encouraged Philani to apply for scholarships and helped him explore career possibilities, including taking him to meet with several engineers. Philani graduated from high school with high marks at the young age of sixteen and started university with a full scholarship from an engineering company that also gave him a job during school breaks. For the second of at least seven times in our conversation, Philani used the word "lucky" to explain this opportunity. He did not describe the mentor as some white savior without whose help he would have been lost, just acknowledged that he was fortunate to have met someone with resources and powerful networks, while so many of his neighbors had not. He described finding his way into engineering:

> At that time, you have to keep in mind that we were the first generation of black people to do engineering. No one before was ever given an opportunity to do that. So there were no black people that you could ask in terms of guidance. It was mainly white males. Obviously some of them—a lot of them—had preconceptions about the other races in terms of doing science and engineering. You walk in there and they still think that you're not good enough. You find that you have to do much more than the average white person in terms of getting up in the organization. Which is sad, but it was reality. I guess it's still a reality.

Philani finished university when he was just nineteen, and the engineering company that provided his scholarship offered him a position which would require him to move to Botswana. Like many other South Africans I met who turned down or quit jobs that conflicted with their vision of the good life, he refused, even though it meant more job searching. He found a job in a smaller company, possibly with less pay than the Botswana job offer. Over the next several years, Philani gained experience at that company, then moved to the company where we met.

The coworker who originally introduced us said he had never experienced anything like this work environment. People of different national, ethnic, racial, and religious backgrounds genuinely worked together as equals. He gave Philani the credit for creating that environment, saying that Philani thought deeply about what he wanted in life and made it happen.

Philani had originally scheduled our meeting for thirty minutes, but when he learned that I wanted to hear his thoughts on what makes work and life good, our conversation rolled on for over two hours. "I am a professional engineer but it's not me," he said. "Whereas most engineers focus on the detail, I'd rather be outside looking at the bigger picture, at the impact of what the engineers are doing." He learned this about himself when he completed a civil engineering project that brought water to twenty thousand people in the Durban area. The project won a national award, and more importantly, it opened his eyes to what he was capable of doing with his life.

"I started to realize the impact of an engineer was not just doing calculations and all that. It had a huge impact on how people lived. I mean, we prevent diseases as engineers. It will prevent things like cholera. We had to hire local labor, so people got employed." He listed off other ways his firm gave back to communities: talking about engineering in high schools, and starting school libraries with help from an NGO. "This is much bigger than me," he said. "At the end of the day, you're not here to do a design, you're here to serve." For Philani, the purpose of his work was improving people's lives.

Much of Philani's thinking about the good life developed a few years after university when he began reading the newspaper and asking broader questions about politics, economics, and philosophy. He stumbled upon a poster advertising a philosophy discussion group and kept coming back to the meetings. There members discussed what the good life meant and how to overcome racial divisions. He applied both lessons in his job as he moved into higher managerial roles. "I learned about humans, I mean how you inspire people, how you talk to their soul. It helped me understand the impact that we can have as humans, regardless of what you do, whether you play violin, or you're a nurse, or a doctor. It's where I learned about serving people—that each of us serve each other. . . . People are the same, regardless of where they are or where they come from. As a result, you find that for me it's much easier to talk to someone 'up' like a CEO and also talk to someone who's working like a maid making tea." He said discussing philosophy in a multiracial group was especially transformative because "coming from my background, we were very confined in our thinking. People tell you, 'As a black person, this is how you're supposed to think.' We're trying to break out of those chains, and I think philosophy let me go."

For five years, Philani had been supervising teams now totaling about one hundred people. I asked about his priorities as a supervisor. "The main thing for me is to trust people. And they trust me. That's it." Most often when people had brought up trust in my interviews, they talked about trust being broken or lost. I pressed further on the topic. "How do you rebuild trust where it is broken?" Philani sighed deeply and paused, lowering his forehead into his palms. "To actually gain trust, you have to do much more than to lose it. It's not a science. It's a very difficult thing." Talking a lot about vision and values helps, he said, "so everyone understands why you are here." He also had tried to "create an environment where people are free to think. No one owns ideas. And everyone must have a say."

He said trust requires going out of your way to learn from others. "If you speak someone's language, it takes a shorter time for someone to trust." He gave the example of a coworker, a white man from Europe who spent five years learning to speak Zulu fluently enough to manage projects in the language. "Imagine, you have a white person speaking Zulu!" He raised his eyebrows and paused for effect. Until this point we had been speaking in English, so I told him I had also learned Zulu. He thanked me heartily. "It makes a huge difference," he said. "A huge difference." I recalled also that when he first greeted me, Philani had shaken my hand in the European/American style rather than the handshake Zulu people usually exchanged, clasping the left hand under the right forearm and rotating the handgrip twice. That conscious choice to operate in what he anticipated would be my style of communication fit with what he told me about how to make cross-cultural relationships work.

"The glue that binds everyone in the team that is diverse is respect," he said. "In whatever way, respect should be at the center in a team that is diverse. So you respect someone, you respect their ideas, you respect who they are." In two sentences, he had used the word respect five times. Respect makes diversity work, he said, and diversity is the key to a successful company. "I've got people from Uganda, Zimbabwe, New Zealand, Swaziland, Nigeria, Congo, South Africa, Lesotho." He made a point of hiring at least one new graduate every year, both as a way to train young people and because the team needed the perspectives of both new and experienced employees. "Look, there's good in everyone. Youngsters want things now. Older guys, they don't want to let go. But they need each other. That's the rule. Each one teach each other. . . . When there's a problem on the table, someone from Congo will look at it differently from someone from England, from someone from South Africa. . . . So when you take that solution to a client, it's a well-rounded solution, rather than coming from a certain point of view."

Building a diverse team founded on respect was not just a means to make his company successful, it was at the core of his conception of the good life. When I asked what the good life meant to him, he replied, "Without relationships I don't think you'll have a good life. And I'm not even talking about money.

I mean relationships, you can't buy relationships. It's priceless. If you have good relationships around you, whether it's your parents, your kids, your colleagues, you'll be living a very rich life. And in order for you to have those relationships, you've got to forget about yourself. You've got to be interested in people around you. You got to be genuine also. Because people see through you. You got to be a person that people can trust. You got to have relationships." I followed this with the question, "Are you able to live that kind of life now?" He replied simply, "I have good relationships." Then he broke into a wide smile.

## Nkosi: Someone Made That Shoe

Nkosi was threading laces into a finished pair of shoes when I wandered into his corner of the factory and struck up a conversation. He was eager to show me his role in the shoe production process. He took out the wooden lasts that the shoes are formed on, burned off threads left from sewing, polished each shoe, threaded in laces, wrapped them gently in sheets of tissue paper, and set them in shoeboxes labeled Groundcover Leather Company.[8] He finished polishing one shoe and set it on a shelf next to its match, then stood back to admire the work. "You see that shoe in the shop, and you've got to respect that shoe. You see it on the shelf, and you know that someone made it."

The shop Nkosi referred to was not just any shop, but a place that sold shoes right across the driveway from his factory. The company could keep wages high without compromising profits mainly because they sold most of their products directly at their own shop rather than at wholesale prices to other stores. The company's founders had worked with other business owners in the area to develop and promote a chain of shops, restaurants, bed-and-breakfasts, and other attractions called the Midlands Meander that drew visitors off an interstate and through their rural area, even along dirt back roads. This arrangement also gave employees like Nkosi the frequent satisfaction of meeting customers who strolled across the parking lot to meet the people making their shoes. Theirs was a capitalist production system that minimized the alienation between workers, products, consumers, and employers. For Nkosi, seeing those customers face to face was one of many subtle choices the company made that told him he was "someone." Being treated as "someone" was central to what he said made his life as a low-wage shoe factory employee good.

When I asked Nkosi to describe what the good life meant to him, he said, "To share with other people. Talk nicely. Respect other people because he's a child of God. Don't treat him like an animal. If you treat me like a dog, what you expect? He'll act like a dog. Come right. Don't be selfish." I asked, "Do you have that good life now?" He answered enthusiastically, "Yeah! Just what I have now, I'm happy for that."

As I talked with Nkosi and got to know the Groundcover Leather Company, it was clear he had the pieces that fit in his definition of a good life. Coworkers told me that Nkosi was well-respected in his neighborhood as an active church member and someone who was willing to share with others. He had built a home for his parents, his wife also worked in a job she liked, he had children, and he owned a car—many of the milestones often cited as integral to the good life.

He was not the only person I met at Groundcover who spoke highly of their lives. One afternoon near the end of the workday, I stood talking with a man who made belts. He suddenly paused from his work, stared into the distance with a deep smile on his face, and said, "I have a good story to tell about this place. I think I could write a whole book about how this place is helping people." He paused again, and when he looked back at me, there were tears in his eyes. "I get emotional thinking about it. These people, they took me places. I think they saw something in me."

Several coworkers had worked elsewhere, and as one employee put it, they knew that "the grass wasn't greener anywhere else." Nkosi had begun working at a much larger shoe factory when he was just a teenager to earn money for his family. "I wanted to be a teacher, but there was no money in the family for school," he said. He came to Groundcover about a decade later when the other shoe factory downsized. He said he still loved teaching, but he could experience that at home by teaching his own children. Now he did not want to work anywhere else. He said he liked showing his pride in his work by wearing nicely polished shoes and a shirt from his company as a way of advertising the shoes in his township. "When you come home and they ask how was work," he said, "I say it was good."

Other Groundcover employees spoke similarly of their pride in wearing shirts with the Groundcover logo around their neighborhoods. One young man explained, "Everybody says, 'Eh, you working there!' Not because we earn a lot of money. People look at you like you are different. I think that comes with the management doing their job nicely to all the staff, treating them right."

His remark summarizes something that by this point should sound familiar: people who loved their work often loved it for the relationships.[9] When people talked about what they liked about Groundcover, they usually did not talk about what "Groundcover does"; they talked about Amanda or Justin, the white couple who had founded the company. Justin had passed away suddenly in a bike accident a few years earlier. Amanda continued running the company from her home, which was located on the property just a few paces from the door of the factory. More than any other company I visited, the relationships between the company's white managers and black staff were intertwined with a striking level of trust. When Amanda and I met to talk at the dining room table in her home, staff members were ducking in and out the open door to ask questions, boil water for tea, or use the bathroom when the staff bathroom was in use. The open door to her home mirrored her own openness to being involved in employees' lives.

At about four o'clock in the afternoon, the Groundcover van pulled into the driveway and a dozen children climbed out and ran into the factory to greet their relatives in the company. Some children settled at tables to do homework, sometimes asking for help from adults nearby. Others went outside to bounce on a trampoline or pet Amanda's big bushy dog. As employees explained, Amanda paid half of the school fees for employees' children for whichever school they chose. The money came out of company funds, but their emphasis that "*Amanda paid*" reflected the reality that there were real people behind the structures affecting employees. Most Groundcover families chose the multiracial English-speaking school in Howick with the highest public school fees in the area. The employees explained that they much preferred having Groundcover pay school fees rather than put the money into their paycheck because it reduced the pressure they faced from relatives requesting money for other needs. Amanda knew all the children by name, and as they graduated from high school she worked closely with them to apply for colleges, scholarships, and better jobs elsewhere. Children whose parents had hardly had the chance to learn to read had gone on to travel to Europe and find scholarships to top universities.

About half the employees came from families that had lived for generations on the rural property of the shoe factory. I visited several of their homes. There I met a young woman who introduced herself by an English name, Sarah. I first arrived while she was collecting vegetables in a small garden that she and her mom planted. Sarah worked a couple of weekends a month in the Groundcover shop, and she hoped to start nursing school in the coming year. Since graduating from Howick High School, she had also worked for a few months as an office assistant at another business. She quit the job because the hours did not line up well with the few taxis to her rural home. Sarah and her family decided it was not safe for her to walk such long distances along country roads in the dark.

When I asked Sarah what the good life meant, she began by describing her present life: "I love where I live. It's quiet, peaceful." Beyond that, she wanted to get married, have children, and stay close to her family. Later that year, she married and became pregnant, and when I called her to check how life was going, she mentioned casually that she was "living the good life." She was the fifth person, then, who had told me they were currently living the good life, but when she moved in with her husband we lost touch and I heard little more from her beyond positive updates from her mom. Being able to cover all the expenses that come with a wedding was no small feat for her factory-employed family, and she hinted that Amanda had helped. She and her new husband were active in their church, and like Muzi, she stressed that God was the source of everything good in her life, including finding a husband who did not drink or smoke. "It's a blessing plus a bonus on top," she said cheerfully when she talked about how being a Christian affected her life. When I asked what she thought of Groundcover, she said, "It's one of a kind. They're like second parents to me." Amanda had gone with her to look for jobs, paid her school fees, even scolded her when she made poor life decisions. "Like family," she said with a playful smile.

"Like family" was a phrase I heard from at least five other employees, but it never came across as just a phrase they'd been taught to say in a company training as it seemed in some other companies. People often spoke about the unique level of trust and camaraderie at Groundcover. They gave examples that varied from little things like people never stealing each other's lunches, to bigger things like Amanda giving no-interest loans to help someone buy a car or get out of debt to a loan shark.

This family-like environment had not happened by accident. Amanda and Justin had started the company after working for several years with a development organization in Lesotho. "We lived in a village, and it was for us to kind of get a better understanding of how communities work before we came back to South Africa." But their experience with development organizations showed them that "training falls flat in many development programs because there's no realistic element to it." They decided that rather than tell people how to start jobs in an economy that had no good jobs, they should start a company offering good jobs. They prioritized building a trusting community, so they chose a home and business location amid the rural community where several Zulu families— including Sarah's—had lived for years. Amanda did not describe herself or Justin as white saviors or benefactors, but as people doing the obvious right thing for business and society. She said their commitment to people was what made their business thrive. "Our whole Western way of running businesses doesn't work," she told me. "That's why businesses last three years and they go under. Because our whole concept of how to set up a business and how to maintain it—I think it's flawed. It's all about profit and the bottom line and whatever. It's not about building a solid base, a solid base of people. Our business is people. That's it. It's not machines, designs, whatever—it's people. Without the people we don't have a business."

Amanda and other staff members were also clear that the company was not perfect. Aside from one or two employees being trained to take on more managerial responsibilities, there were few opportunities for promotion within the company. As I interviewed employees, I learned that many were getting around this lack of promotions by starting side businesses like home day care centers, installing solar water heaters, renting out vehicles, or raising chickens.[10] People also spoke directly or indirectly about the division between longer-term local employees and a group who had been hired from another company. Nkosi talked about learning to work past those divisions. "The first thing is, I just respect the people here, the style of the workers, the managers. Talk nicely to each other. Don't listen to those other people who are talking about others. I'm not here for that." And even with all the years of trust-building Amanda had put into relationships, there were still incidents when people fell back into habits of distrust across racial and employer-employee lines. The company had recently had to rewrite their contracts, and a few employees refused to sign until after a long conversation together as a company. As Nkosi explained it, some people still assumed that owners kept as much profit as they wanted. "When I see that they sell some shoes for R700 and I see what I get paid, I must not judge. I must talk to the manager. I must not just leave." The company also had roughly the same racial stratification as most companies: white people in upper management, a few Indian people in mid-level jobs, and black people mostly in the lower-paid jobs. As Don, the white manager of factory production, put it, "Some things you will change and some you won't all at once."

Don explained that the industry also faced international competition challenges much like the chicken industry described in chapter 2. He had worked as a manager at a larger company for over a decade before coming to Groundcover. Under apartheid, international boycotts protected the shoe industry from international competition, and the industry thrived selling to local buyers. After apartheid, trade opened up, and in the face of international competition, the majority of shoe factories shut down or moved their production to Asia. Demand also fell for the kinds of affordable high-quality leather shoes that Groundcover specialized in. When he started in the industry, Don said, Africans wanted high-quality leather shoes like Groundcover's because they walked long distances. More cars and bus routes made life easier, but also shifted the demand toward cheaper shoes and newer fashions.

Other companies handled these changes by paying employees per production unit for home-based assembly tasks. That system reduced company overhead but also made work less secure for employees. Another common option was to reduce staff to three-day weeks and pay less in benefits. Amanda fought hard to keep wages high, jobs consistent, and shoes affordable. They had raised shoe prices only slightly in the past years, and wages were higher than the national standards. Employees had tried paying into a national union for a while, but when the representatives showed up in their Mercedes cars and offered no improvements over what Groundcover already provided, employees dropped out of the union. They knew if they needed something, they could knock on Amanda's door or chat with her during a tea break. Every week Amanda led a company management meeting, and every employee took turns rotating as representatives in those meetings. In the two meetings I attended, discussions included how to display shoes in the shop, what to do about an older man who was no longer able to work, who would clean the men's bathroom, news about an employee whose baby was due soon, and what to do about some mismatched leather they had bought. Every person in the meeting chimed in freely.

Groundcover used the word "ubuntu" in their company branding, and it was more than lip service. Nkosi and other employees said that ubuntu actually happened there, even in this low-skilled, low-wage factory. Groundcover had systems in place that prioritized ubuntu. They rotated representatives to meetings, paid school fees, and attracted tourist customers to the shop through the local association of businesses that Amanda had helped found. They also had relationships rooted in deep trust that allowed them to override or adapt institutional systems in ways that communicated that each person mattered. I heard about times when Amanda loaned the company vehicle to transport people to a funeral, mediated in family disputes, and used her personal connections to find jobs elsewhere for employees' relatives. As Nkosi put it, "Every person must be seen for their importance. Managers, workers . . . you need each other."

## Duduzile: Not the High Class, Expensive Life

When I was visiting Duduzile, I often found myself not wanting to leave. Her quiet voice, her penchant for hospitality, and the enticing smells from her kitchen lulled me into procrastination. In earlier chapters, I recounted some of those conversations—her explanation of the phrase "just a laborer," and our difficult conversation about her idea that white people were "clever," but also obligated to share. One day I stopped at her house to eat my packed lunch and we sat in lawn chairs talking for three hours. The conversation ranged from her story of meeting a girl who called herself a Satanist, to her advice for my own academic job search. During one lull in the conversation, she looked into the distance and said sweetly, "I like talking to you." "I like talking to you, too," I said, and I meant it.

It occurred to me at the time that this was not something that grad school had trained me to expect. Interviewing people was a task I had somehow learned to tuck into a mental box I might label as either "work" or "dissertation." For graduate students and professors, fieldwork can be a stepping-stone to other accomplishments—graduation, publishing credits, jobs, and promotions. Sitting here with Duduzile, I was not just hearing someone tell me about respectful relationships in the context of work, I was experiencing one.

Duduzile related to me more like an aunt, a friend, or a counselor than a research informant. One afternoon I told her about several job openings I was considering. "Money won't make you happy," she advised me. "Don't ever take a job you won't want to go to when you wake up in the morning." Another day she shifted the conversation suddenly to say, "You should never think that you can do things on your own. You need God's help—he knows the past, the present, and the future, and who are you to say you can do things better than God?"

As I drove home that day, I thought how strikingly her words contrasted with the laziness narrative. In a way, she was telling me not to try too hard on my own, words that could be twisted to seem like advice to be lazy. I could imagine all too well someone criticizing her: *That kind of attitude is the reason she's not in a better job.* Just the night before I'd heard someone say nearly those words. A European volunteer who had been in South Africa for a decade was describing a woman who had not taken her sister to the hospital, when he said, "It's the attitude around here. They're used to having everything done for them." I did not know the woman he was describing, but I cringed. The woman lived in Shiyabazali, a squatter settlement where people built their own homes from scavenged metal and boards, wired their own electricity, and dug their own plumbing pipes because the local government did not recognize them as legal inhabitants. I had once given a ride to two women in Shiyabazali because I noticed that one was pushing the other uphill in a wheelbarrow, a makeshift wheelchair for this woman who was clearly very sick. The very name of the settlement, Shiyabazali, meant "We Leave Our Parents Behind," a sharply contrasting story to the narrative that people were "used to having everything done for them."

For Duduzile, relying on God meant doing more for herself, not less. She, too, was an expert at survivalist improvisation, having left a job because the stress of work relationships seemed to hurt her health and well-being. Through a nonprofit organization, she had been trained and certified to use her two-bedroom home as a bed-and-breakfast. She hosted a few visitors each month, mainly those coming for church conferences or as international volunteers. Besides that income, she and her mother subsisted mainly on her mother's social security pension of about $160 per month. Even in this precarious financial position, she assured me that she was not concerned because "the church can help out if we need groceries." Duduzile would know, because often she had helped with others' needs. As her bed-and-breakfast income grew, I learned that she paid for a neighbor child's school fees and provided child care for a working neighbor. Though she did not call herself an employer or manager, she paid neighbors for errands such as carrying water, because the government only provided water to her street periodically, most often in the middle of the night. She was openly HIV positive and met with others who were sick in her community to encourage, educate, and care for people. She was doing what she loved to do, and she was good at it. Her relationships were *lungile*—right.

"I just want to live the normal life," she told me in one of our first conversations about the good life, back when she was newly unemployed. "Not the expensive life. I like to have peace, and accept myself as I am." Over time I would come to think of her as one of the happiest and most relaxed people I knew. "I'm happy with the life that I live, and I enjoy in whatever circumstances I'm facing," she told me. "I'm trying by all means to take care of myself and have peace of mind. I don't want to look for things that I can't afford to have. But I accept the normal life. Even if I can have lots of money, I don't want that high-class, expensive life."

## Agency, Structure, and Chance

None of these people believed that their own choices and hard work alone produced their good life. None of them grew up in settings where personal agency strongly correlates to positive life outcomes. They needed narratives that could explain who makes it and who doesn't in ways that did not depend merely on hard work.

Their narratives tended to give credit to forces beyond themselves, including the forces of a generous person's help (such as Philani's friend's father), God's intervention (especially for Muzi, Sarah, and Duduzile), social structures (such as Groundcover's company systems), or luck (as Philani often mentioned). Muzi and Philani both spoke openly about times when they were among the very few who escaped prejudiced social structures that entrapped others no different from themselves. Philani could not explain why he had a mom who could send him to a multiracial high school while others didn't, or why he found companies that gave him scholarships and promotions that others didn't get. "I do what I do in the present, and then people recognize what I'm doing and say, 'Let's elevate him to another level,'" he said. "But how I've developed is sort of a mystery." He said at another point, "I find that most of the things that have happened in my life are not things that I have planned." Muzi said he made the choice to go to church because he wanted help with alcoholism, but he credited the power of God for the changes in his life. Duduzile insisted that it was even morally wrong to believe that you could succeed without the help of God.

Rather than sending them into despondency or fatalism, these narratives of luck and God's intervention seemed to help people make sense of their successes amid widespread poverty, and may have motivated them to take risks that others would not take, like Duduzile quitting her job. They used a technique of abeyance of agency, not to dismiss responsibilities as in the "just a laborer" narrative, but as a way to face their limitations amid social odds stacked against them. They interpreted their lives as a balance between making agential choices and interacting with forces and structures beyond their own control. In their communities, people who are seen as successful often experience stress over jealous friends, requests for help, and accusations that they think they are now above others. Abeyance of agency, claiming that success came from luck or God, may have helped them make decisions about how to handle these pressures.

Their narratives interpreted the reality that friends, relatives, and neighbors worked just as hard but did not have the successes they had. They took a realistic look at the ways structures help some people and hinder others. Such an awareness is useful more broadly, not just for imagining ways to achieve the good life, but for understanding why everyone does not.

## Valuing Black Cultural Capital

The French philosopher Pierre Bourdieu has argued that socioeconomic classes do not depend on financial resources alone.[11] A person's place in the class structure of a society also depends on what Bourdieu called cultural capital, the codes of knowledge and habits developed through a lifetime that enable people to fit into various class settings. In one famous example, he described how children raised in upper-class families learn how to behave in distinguished art museums. This knowledge is nothing more than familiarity with an arbitrary code of tastes, but because upper-class people treat such tastes as significant, they become significant in effect. Upper-class people come to believe that anyone who disagrees with such tastes is either poorly educated, poorly bred, or simply not suited to belong in a higher class, ignoring the ways that exclusionary systems produce the very tastes and habits used to distinguish classes.

People in South Africa are no exception to this tendency to rank social classes according unacknowledged categories of tastes and habits. The racial and ethnic divisions that have persisted long after apartheid make cultural capital differences especially rigid. Black Zulu South Africans find themselves excluded from a high social class not only through lack of opportunities and resources, but through subtle differences in behavior and taste learned over a lifetime. Consciously or unconsciously, promotion decisions take into account cultural capital like English fluency and mannerisms that white people learn from birth, like smiling, asking questions of leaders, and making eye contact with superiors.

For black people, displaying the kind of cultural capital that gets rewarded in white circles often means sacrificing cultural capital in black circles. Throughout the history of colonization and enslavement, Africans and their descendants have wrestled with this dilemma. To move up in a white-dominated social hierarchy, one must often behave like white people in ways that reject a portion of a black racial and cultural identity. Meanwhile, the dominant society ignores cultural capital learned in black spaces—everything from posture, to music, to creative linguistic expressions fused from multiple languages. Recall from the introduction how Bullet ultimately rejected a law school path steeped in white cultural capital (and likely financial capital) even though it meant years of unemployment.

The sociologist George Lipsitz offers an in-depth analysis of how racial segregation over time produces different sets of values and ideas in black and white spaces, and why the underrecognized values of black communities are essential for society. He writes that, "while it has been created by terrible and inexcusable injustices, the Black spatial imaginary has vitally important creative and constructive things to offer to this society."[12] Whereas white spaces show an inward-focused self-protectiveness of resources, black spaces have valued "the public good over private interests," prioritizing "efficient transportation, affordable housing, public education, and universal medical care as common responsibilities to be shared rather than as onerous burdens to be palmed off onto the least able and most vulnerable."[13] Spaces distanced from white presence in which black people can congregate and reinforce cultural norms, values, and artistry, what he calls "cultural safe houses," also offer essential "places for preserving, honing, and refining the resources of the street free from white surveillance and control."[14]

In the four stories of this chapter, the good life often involved forging some competency in white cultural capital, but more importantly finding "cultural safe houses" where their own black cultural capital was valued for producing the good life. For Duduzile, hosting international visitors required certain white cultural capital gained through workshops and her former job experiences. By hosting visitors, though, she also got to introduce outsiders to black cultural capital. Philani credited his white mentor with helping him learn a public-speaking style and workplace norms that differed from his home community, but over time he had taken an increasingly active role in educating coworkers about the need for black and foreign contributions to the company. Philani described meetings with government leaders, who were primarily black, in which white colleagues acknowledged the advantages of Philani's black cultural capital. Muzi learned the artistic codes of marketable art, but over time he shifted toward topics and symbols emerging from his cultural identity. Like Bullet and other "conscious rappers," he used art to reproduce a black social imaginary and community.

In the Howick area, settings that valued black cultural capital were sharply divided from those that valued white cultural capital, and the latter dominated the business world. These examples point to the crucial need for spaces legitimizing black cultural capital, including businesses and organizations formerly dominated by white cultural capital.

## Capitalism with Less Alienation

A final point that stands out in these stories is that people operated within capitalistic markets, but with a degree of personal interaction between customers, employers, and employees that is rare in capitalist societies. The Groundcover factory's location was perhaps the clearest visual representation of that connectivity. Inside the factory, workers walked freely into the company owner's office and made decisions through a leadership structure that rotated to include every worker. The home of Amanda, the company owner, was only a few meters from the factory, with the door unlocked and usually wide open. Customers parked next to the factory, then walked into the shop selling the shoes or into the factory for tours. A half kilometer down the driveway, many workers lived on land near where their ancestors were buried.

Groundcover created a market setting that intentionally dismantled alienation and embedded company decisions in black cultural and social priorities. Nkosi enjoyed meeting customers coming through the factory, and he wore clothes with the Groundcover label proudly. He and other employees described themselves as members of one family that included both workers and company management. Theirs was a capitalist production system that minimized the alienation between workers, products, and employers.

Likewise, in 2017 Muzi was selling art in a gallery where he interacted with customers even as he painted. Duduzile hosted visitors in her own home, and Philani saw his work as directly connected to improving communities like his own. Structures that minimize alienation closely correspond to the Zulu idea of respect outlined in chapter 3. Respect was not some second-rate alternative to socioeconomic reform or a surrender to whatever form capitalism may take. It was a moral order toward which people could direct their social reforms. In a country and a world where inequalities continue widening, respect does not require an overthrow of capitalism or a change in government, though it often requires an overhaul of the inner workings of both. These stories show glimpses of respect that was attainable, even in a highly stratified capitalist society.

Creating work settings with greater respect and less alienation depends largely on choices made by employers and policymakers. Groundcover had gone the furthest to design the structure of their company from its inception to foster respectful relationships between staff, management, and customers, but I found other companies that were also making decisions that improved the lives of their employees. Several were farms mentored by Judy Stuart, a South African dairy farm owner from Howick who founded a mentoring program to connect youth from disadvantaged backgrounds to farmers who would train them for management. Like Amanda at Groundcover, several had come to see that their company would thrive because of—not in spite of—structures designed to benefit employees.

This chapter has demonstrated how asking the question "What is the good life?" leads to different knowledge than questions like "How can we generate employment?" or "How can we achieve economic growth?" The stories in this chapter offer evidence that the good life does not necessarily depend on employment status. Instead, the good life comes about through complex interactions of social and individual factors as well as the ways that people learn to make meaning out of their circumstances. Muzi, Nkosi, Philani, and Duduzile shaped concepts of the good life that made sense of their experiences within an antiblack and segregated society. They found themselves in socially embedded economic structures, and spaces where black cultural capital was validated. The fact that they often attributed these circumstances to good fortune should not prevent us from imagining and implementing ways to replicate such structures.

# "DESPITE THE CONTRADICTIONS"

Howard Thurman, a leader of the US civil rights movement who served as a spiritual advisor to Martin Luther King Jr., offers a metaphor for the lives of people seeking the good life amid difficult circumstances. Thurman describes trees growing above the timber line on a high mountain. Such trees live amid "barrenness, sheer rocks, snow patches and strong untrammeled winds," but they still manage to somehow "survive despite the severe pressures." The shape of these trees adapts to their surroundings. Like "tufts of evergreen bushes," they hug the ground, "following the shape of the terrain," more shrubs than trees. Thurman identified something in those trees that he had seen in people facing oppression: a fierce vitality. He writes as if in the voice of the weather-beaten tree:

> I am destined to reach for the skies and embrace in my arms the wind, the rain, the snow and the sun, singing my song of joy to all the heavens. But this I cannot do. I have taken root beyond the timber line, and yet I do not want to die; I must not die. I shall make a careful survey of my situation and work out a method, a way of life, that will yield growth and development for me despite the contradictions under which I must eke out my days. In the end I may not look like the other trees, I may not be what all that is within me cries out to be. But I will not give up. I will use to the full every resource in me and about me to answer life with life.[1]

In this book we've explored the ways people make a careful survey of their situation and work out a method to yield growth despite life's contradictions and pressures. Like Bullet, they insist, "Dog, don't just lie down and play dead!"

If their lives look at times like wind-torn shrubs, that does not mean that they are poorly adapted or lethargic. Instead, it offers evidence of the hard work it takes to thrive in a world where the good life is hard to find.

Along with other scholars of antiblackness and marginalization, I seek to describe such lives in ways that resist both hegemonic narratives and trite optimism. I see my task as documenting what the anthropologist Marco Di Nunzio saw among street hustlers in Ethiopia: "a politics of open-endedness." That is, people struggle to "be something other than [their] constraints while remaining firmly embedded within experiences of subjugation and exclusion."[2] Saidiya Hartman, describing the "upheaval and transformation" of black women in the United States between 1890 and 1935, likewise sought to describe the very real results of "economic exclusion, material deprivation, racial enclosure, and social dispassion," and also show her subjects as "radical thinkers who tirelessly imagined other ways to live and never failed to consider how the world might be otherwise."[3] This book joins theirs in recounting the ways people contest oppression and imagine otherwise, even when the present evidence of improvements from those methods is faint to negligible.

"Every day you fight," Mtoko told me. There are many causes people fight for, and many ways to fight. Mtoko fought "every day just to wake up" to another hustle of survivalist improvisation. This book also fights for the good life. It does so by engaging in a confrontation of narratives. As I have shown, a dominant myth blaming inequality on laziness has guided, upheld, and justified racial inequalities in South Africa and the world since the earliest mercantile and colonial encounters between Europeans and Africans. That narrative was never eradicated, despite antislavery, civil rights, and anti-apartheid movements that achieved important legal and structural changes. The struggle to change this social narrative is an unglorified resistance with no clear ending point, but it is essential to the pursuit of the good life.

Since I began this research, there has been a surge of popular and academic interest in understanding well-being, happiness, and the good life. Some theorists—often those who have focused on measuring happiness—aim to find criteria that make life good for all humans, regardless of culture. On the other end of the spectrum are more culturally relativist theorists who expect to find people defining and achieving the good life in wholly distinct ways depending on their cultural context. While both of these kinds of research can offer valuable contributions to understanding well-being, one point I hope to make clear is that in studies of the good life, setting and culture do matter. Any attempt to find universal criteria for the good life must also acknowledge distinctions in how people think about, experience, and access the good life, and how those differences are influenced by privilege.

Clearly, creating more jobs and greater access to higher-wage jobs in South Africa could improve the lives of millions of South Africans. By the summer of 2019, the narrowly defined unemployment rate (those counted as actively seeking work) in South Africa topped 29 percent, the highest in over sixteen years. Over 6.6 million South Africans could not find work. However, not all efforts to create jobs or raise wages will have the same effects. Nor will those effects be interpreted in the same way by everyone. In policy decisions, the first goal must be to ask what the good life means to people, and the question of how to deal with an unemployment crisis must follow from that goal. Policies like keeping wages low or protecting short-term contracts, for example, might produce more jobs, but can simultaneously get in the way of many employees' ideas of a better life. By starting with the bigger question in mind—What is the good life?—we can evaluate approaches to job creation in that context.

In this book we have also seen evidence that in order to generate employment while aiming for the higher goal of seeking good, South Africa must address the history of antiblack disrespect that perpetuates dysfunctional employment structures. Dismantling such structures will include some actions that cannot easily be mandated by legal policies. In order to establish trust between white employers and black employees, employers need to voluntarily increase benefits to employees and eradicate discrimination in hiring and promotions. Rather than begrudge these changes or only minimally comply with legal requirements, employers need to communicate genuine respect. Innumerable small shifts in relationships can demonstrate the human dignity of employees and demonstrate to them that engaging as more than "just a laborer" will be worthwhile for them, not just for their employers. Lower worker turnover benefits both employees and employers, and higher wages and job security for employees have knock-on benefits throughout society as people share with family and friends to cover education and job-seeking expenses.

Employment, as we have seen, does not itself guarantee the good life. The conditions people experience at work matter. Many of my findings about job satisfaction echo what has been found elsewhere in the world. The psychologist Barry Schwartz offers similar conclusions about the need to respect employees as complex and capable human beings, based on research mainly in the United States. He and other researchers have found that people are most satisfied in their work when they have the discretion to think for themselves, opportunities for meaningful training, levels of pay and long-term job security that communicate their value, and personal connections to the overall purpose of their organization.[4] Schwartz points out that greater job satisfaction is not something that an employee can drum up entirely of their own volition. Managers need to take the lead in improving workplaces. And there is more to making work good than getting managers to tweak some habits of interactions with employees. Widespread improvements in workplace satisfaction also require shifting society's deeply rooted ideas about work. Schwartz writes that "ideology bears a large measure of the responsibility for the nature of our work." Ideologies of work can become self-fulfilling prophecies. When people think of work as mundane tasks endured only for money, they create jobs that make work that way, and workers conform to what they are expected to be. Likewise, as I have shown on a macro-level, when people believe that black, Zulu, or other groups of people are inherently lazy, they organize society in ways that leave a self-fulfilling legacy of long-term damage. South Africa's history could be seen as a grand experiment testing whether withholding high-status jobs from a group of people while accusing them of laziness could motivate people to work hard. Certainly that experiment has proved disastrous.

But there were other dimensions to the experiment of South Africa as well. Under apartheid, international boycotts forced many supply chains to operate entirely locally. Business sizes remained fairly small and protected from international conglomeration. Meanwhile, many white employees saw it as their Christian duty to serve as benefactors to their black employees. In many cases they housed employees on their property, took workers to doctor visits, threw birthday parties for them, drove them on shopping trips, and referred to them as family, even while excluding them from white spaces and activities in ways that clearly denied their kinship. These acts were often paternalistic distractions from confronting racialized social structures, like the fact that wages were too low for workers to own cars, public transportation was impractical, and public health clinics were underfunded. Since 1994, such paternalistic work arrangements in South Africa have been shifting, but the social structures perpetuating poverty remain unmoved in many cases. With the postapartheid reopening of trade, globalization has brought competition, conglomeration, and corporatization. The new postapartheid constitution also opened avenues for black South Africans to legally contest land rights and human resource decisions. These legal changes have made important advances toward land security and workers' rights for black South Africans, but they have also fueled distrust between black and white neighbors and reduced the number of employers offering on-site housing and other benefits for employees. Studies of farm workers and domestic laborers have found that, at least in some cases, workers who received legally enforced minimum-wage increases were less satisfied with their jobs afterward because their employers responded by reducing personalized interactions and in-kind benefits like food parcels, school tuition, or rides to doctor's appointments. Because antiblack social structures still leave huge gaps between the haves and the have-nots, such uncontracted benefits are still crucial for many black South

Africans. Meanwhile, the country is facing the potential extinction of something hard to measure—the amorphous but socially essential element called trust.[5] As Amanda at Groundcover pointed out, trusting relationships between workers and employers produce economic gains in the long run. This book offers a picture of why trust matters, and a warning that economic policy decisions must take into account the implications for social trust: "Once lost, trust is hard to recover."[6]

I hope to leave readers with an appreciation for complexity. Outliers and contradictions are inevitable in qualitative ethnographic research that takes into account all the variables of real humans in real situations. When we are willing to ask important questions, we find significant and complex answers. Humans cannot be reduced to numbers. Even if there are trends, there are individuals both confirming and defying those trends. When I spoke with Sma the fashion designer in 2017, I explained what I had been writing. She had employees herself in her sewing business now, and she was finding it challenging to be a manager. "There are two sides to everything," she said. My aim is to show two sides, or better yet more than two, not so that readers choose a side, but so that solutions may be found that take into account more sides.

Since the first year I spent researching this topic from 2014 to 2015, I have returned to South Africa every two years. Each time I have found that real-life narratives are complex and unpredictable. Take for example Mr. Khumalo, the middle-aged man described in chapter 4 who in 2015 was putting the finishing touches on his new restaurant on the main street of Mpophomeni. In 2017 when I turned onto that street, I was confused. In the place where I remembered the restaurant was a charred remnant of a building. I stopped and studied the evidence, realizing this was indeed the restaurant. On the fence a sign was still posted saying "Now Open," as if the two years had utterly disappeared along with Mr. Khumalo's investment. I asked around. One person said the restaurant had lasted only one week, even though I had been there when the restaurant was open for more than a week. Another said she heard that the owner burned it down himself for the insurance money. Sma went silent when I told her that rumor. "Ask him," she said. "Don't trust gossip." She went on, "But what I know, I would never burn this place down. A business is your baby," she said. "You don't give up on it."

Among all the people I have been able to stay in touch with while changing cell phone numbers and addresses, none has given up, but the struggle is often plainly evident. When I tracked down one young man who had moved away from Mpophomeni, he gestured an imaginary knife slicing across his throat and said in a few suggestive words that he was running from a fight that ended in a death threat. Another acquaintance drank a liter of diesel fuel in a series of attempts at suicide. Sometimes I returned to find people's voices had grown slower or more slurred, their eyes yellowed and twitching with the effects of marijuana, wunga, or other drugs. When I asked Sma in 2017 if anything had changed in Mpophomeni, she said, "Nothing changes." Then she added, "Only there's more drugs."

With each return visit, I heard speculations over whether South Africa was spiraling downward toward poverty or even civil war. Over the years of my research, the South African top news stories covered xenophobic violence, electricity shortages, droughts, antiracism protests, the ousting of President Jacob Zuma, and billionaires controlling the government in what was termed "state capture." People speculated that a new exodus of white and upper-class South Africans was beginning, and I heard several people state resignedly that "the rainbow nation is dead." White people were losing their privileged sheltering from the effects of a broken economy. Fearmongering spread as white people attempted to hold together the pieces of a hegemonic laziness narrative that had never accurately portrayed the real experiences or intentions of South Africans.

I heard equally pessimistic national predictions from a few young black people, but with different reasons. Two young rappers spoke of their anger over the colonization and capitalism that stole African land and also replaced the "everybody's welcome" attitude of Africans with selfishness. They told about the futility of people basing their hopes on a system of "money that has no value," and they predicted social turmoil as eventually economic systems "will be crushed." One of the men rapped accounts of racism, brainwashed people, colonization, corporatization, and the "heavy artillery used to kill Africans, destruction of the human race, subjecting my people to poverty and starvation." His rap ended, "This is the book of Revelation like never heard before and this is how it ends." Theirs was a picture of coming doom, predicated on the injustice of capitalism, the unhealed wounds of colonialism, human greed, and exploitation.

Neither the fearful whites nor the black anticapitalists saw doom as the only possibility, though. When I asked the young rappers if they saw any way forward for black Africans, they spoke of restored relationships—to "be one like the ancient times," to have unity and "have that humanity." Many white people also recognized that fearmongering was keeping people from real changes that needed to happen. In a conversation about a particularly fearmongering article that was going viral on social media, one white man said, "The only way to overcome it is to drop our guards and dialogue and get to the bottom of some of this stuff. There's so many stereotypes, misconceptions, misunderstandings, and this is where the media is not really helping us. Because it doesn't sell. Who wants to read about guys who are making really good progress and working well together?"

The people described in this book refuse to conform to narratives of inevitable happy endings or easy hope, but neither do their stories end only in despair. Sma's fashion design business, Black Teardrop, continued to grow and thrive. When I saw her in 2019, she was working on a woman's blazer, ironing sections and sewing in shoulder pads and casually piecing together layers of fabric and lining as we spoke. Another younger woman I had not met before now worked on a sewing machine next to Sma. I asked Sma how her life was now, and she said she was still not where she wanted to be. "Another three years," she said with a playful smile. "Come back in three years and I'll be perfect."

Teeza found a variety of odd jobs through the years, but mainly continued to focus his energy on the concerts and musician gatherings he organized in Mpophomeni and the surrounding area. He was never more in his element than at these events.

Through international donations, Muzi opened a community art studio in Mpophomeni where he and another artist from the area shared studio space and taught children and adults to understand their community and identities through art. In 2019 Muzi was in the process of exchanging gifts with his new fiancé's family in the *ilobola* marriage process.

By 2019 Nomusa had left her abusive husband and moved with her children into their own home. He came and smashed the windows of her new home, so she moved again. She found a job that paid just R50 ($5) a day, less than half the legal minimum wage. "They're robbing us," she said, "but what are you gonna do?" Ever hustling, she soon quit that job and used what she had saved in earnings to buy supplies for baked goods she could sell on paydays.

International funding had dropped precipitously for some of the nonprofit organizations in Mpophomeni by 2019, and Duduzile's homestay business was hurting as international volunteers came less frequently. She and her mother earned some income by caring for four two-year-olds from the neighborhood while the children's mothers worked. The children were quietly snoozing under their blankets when I arrived at her home midmorning, then contentedly found their way to the living room to cuddle on her lap, get scooped up onto the older woman's back, or cradle bowls of porridge while we talked. "My life is good," she said. "I'm struggling financially, but . . ." She paused for a moment to formulate her thoughts, then continued, "this situation does not take away my happiness. At the end of the day I have food to eat." And she reiterated, "I trust God for the living. You might have all the money in the world, but without happiness and without peace, you are nothing.

I met up with Bullet in 2019 over lunch at a restaurant in Pietermaritzburg and he filled me in on the details of the last four years since we'd talked in person.

Around 2016, he ended up in a jail cell three times in just a few months, each time for a minor offense. Not long after, a close friend was stabbed and killed, and it shook him to the core. Meanwhile, his dad was recovering from a stroke and kept asking Bullet to drive him to church. In a comment much like Muzi's explanation of church, Bullet explained, "If we were paying money for it, we'd call it rehab, but at the church it's free." The church offered Bullet a place to stay overnight and enter a community of friends that got him away from what he called "bad influences." He said he felt "a feeling of peace" there that he had previously only experienced while making music. When his sister, a nurse, told him about an all-expenses-paid three-year training program for surgical technicians, he decided to apply. He got in.

Somewhat to his surprise, he found himself liking the work, and he was good at it. Now back in Pietermaritzburg, he was working forty-two hours a week as a surgical technician and investigating ways to work overseas for a while. That was complicated in part because he now had a ten-month-old son living in Mpophomeni and was exchanging *ilobola* gifts with the baby's mom. In a strange throwback to Bullet's earliest plans after high school, she was studying law in Johannesburg.

But Bullet's narrative doesn't have a happy ending simply because a protagonist named Bullet came out OK. At the level of structures and cultural narratives of antiblackness, not much had changed. Walking down a hallway at work surrounded by white employees one day, Bullet suddenly felt a woman grasp his shoulders. She held him steady as he walked. "Stop walking like that," the white woman said, referring to his rhythmic, hip hop–inspired gait. She demanded, "Why are you walking like that? Why are you swaying? You're not at home." He walked with the rhythmic confidence of a rapper from the township, and it was clear she associated that with blackness and all she feared, distrusted, or hated about it. Another time, a white instructor interrupted a conversation he was having with a black employee at lower pay grade. He pulled Bullet aside and scolded him, "You're here to learn. You have nothing to learn from *him*," gesturing toward the black low-waged employee. Out of the twelve trainees who began the program with Bullet, only two finished. He said it probably helped that he was away from home so he wasn't distracted from studying. Besides, he said, he had grown used to expecting racism. The culture of antiblackness and the structures of inequitable access to resources were still intact. If obtaining the good life is in any sense the product of hard work, then the work of changing those narratives and structures is the work that still needs doing.

In his music, Bullet could speak out against such narratives and structures that perpetuated injustices. Even through the busy years of his training, he never stopped writing music. From our lunch meeting, he was heading to the home of a friend to record a set of songs for the first album he'd recorded in five years. He said having a job gave him the stability to make music with less pressure and more professional assistance, and he'd been writing more music than ever. The day after our conversation, I realized I'd forgotten to ask Bullet one important question. I texted him, "Hey, can you text an answer to one question I try to ask everyone: Would you say you're living the good life right now?" He texted back, "In short, yes. I'm at peace with what I want and need and have."

# Notes

## INTRODUCTION

1. Scholars differ in their opinions about whether to capitalize the word "black" when referring to the racial group. Scholars emphasizing the shared racial and cultural identity as well as the dignity of this racial group have often capitalized "Black." While I share these aims, I chose to follow what seems to be the more common practice among Southern African scholars of not capitalizing, though I retain the original capitalization when quoting other scholars.

2. Rumors of mortuary owners harvesting bodies may stem also in part from the fact that black-owned mortuaries are lucrative. White people banned and excluded black people from running nearly every kind of businesses under apartheid, but the same prejudiced imaginary of blackness as disagreeable and unclean prevented whites from handling black bodies. Black mortuary owners make profits in the context of their own neighbors' suffering, making them targets for jealousies and the accusations of witchcraft that often go hand in hand with jealousy in South Africa. See Adam Ashforth, *Witchcraft, Violence, and Democracy in South Africa* (Chicago: University of Chicago Press, 2005); and Suzanne E. Smith, *To Serve the Living: Funeral Directors and the African American Way of Death* (Cambridge, MA: Belknap Press of Harvard University Press, 2010).

3. Christina Sharpe, *In the Wake: On Blackness and Being* (Durham, NC: Duke University Press, 2016), 7.

4. Wan He, Daniel Goodkind, and Paul Kowal, "An Aging World: 2015," US Census Bureau, International Population Reports, P95/16–1 (Washington, DC: US Government Publishing Office, 2016).

5. About apartheid, as with many other topics in this book, far more has and should be said than what will fit in these pages. I hope that readers will seek out some of that "far more." Citations and suggested readings in footnotes will offer some possible places to start. To read more on the history of apartheid, see Patrick Bond, *Elite Transition: From Apartheid to Neoliberalism in South Africa* (London: Pluto Press, 2000); and Nancy L. Clark and William H. Worger, *South Africa: The Rise and Fall of Apartheid* (London: Routledge, 2013).

6. Statistics South Africa, "National and Provincial Labour Market: Youth," June 29, 2015.

7. By 2018 this number had risen to 27.2 percent.

8. The "not economically active" category also counts adults in school and people caring for children at home.

9. James Ferguson, "Formalities of Poverty: Thinking about Social Assistance in Neoliberal South Africa," *African Studies Review* 50, no. 2 (September 2007): 71–86. See also Abhijit Banerjee et al., "Why Has Unemployment Risen in the New South Africa?," *Economics of Transition* 16, no. 4 (2008): 715–40; Jean Comaroff and John L. Comaroff, introduction to *Millennial Capitalism and the Culture of Neoliberalism* (Durham, NC: Duke University Press, 2001); and Duncan Hodge, "Growth, Employment, and Unemployment in South Africa," *South African Journal of Economics* 77, no. 4 (2009): 488–504.

10. Jeremy Seekings and Nicoli Nattrass, *Class, Race, and Inequality in South Africa* (New Haven, CT: Yale University Press, 2005).

11. Jean Comaroff and John Comaroff, "Alien-Nation: Zombies, Immigrants, and Millennial Capitalism," *The South Atlantic Quarterly* 101, no. 4 (2002): 798; Ferguson, "Formalities of Poverty," 82.

12. Many scholars have studied narratives of the good life to understand people's understandings of the world and their external circumstances. To offer a few examples, an edited volume by the anthropologist Cheryl Mattingly explores the importance of narratives in healing and healthcare. The psychologist Dan McAdams traces the ways narratives shape people's concerns for each other. Imani Perry explains the importance of narratives in social constructions of race, and recommends that "ethnographies of racial narratives in social life would be a wonderful research area." Jerome Bruner offers a foundational theoretical essay explaining how attention to narratives can contribute to understanding culture and the nature of reality. Cheryl Mattingly and Linda C. Garro, eds., *Narrative and the Cultural Construction of Illness and Healing* (Berkeley: University of California Press, 2000); Dan McAdams, *The Redemptive Self: Stories Americans Live By* (New York: Oxford University Press, 2005); Imani Perry, *More Beautiful and More Terrible: The Embrace and Transcendence of Racial Inequality in the United States* (New York: New York University Press, 2011), 48; Jerome Bruner, "The Narrative Construction of Reality," *Critical Inquiry* 18, no. 1 (1991): 1–21.

13. Linda C. Garro and Cheryl Mattingly, "Narrative as Construct and Construction," in *Narrative and the Cultural Construction of Illness and Healing* (Berkeley: University of California Press, 2000), 17.

14. McAdams, *Redemptive Self*, 3.

15. Arlene Kaplan Daniels, "Invisible Work," *Social Problems* 34, no. 5 (December 1, 1987): 403–15; J. K. Gibson-Graham, *A Postcapitalist Politics* (Minneapolis: University of Minnesota Press, 2006); Susan Himmelweit, "The Discovery of 'Unpaid Work': The Social Consequences of the Expansion of 'Work,'" *Feminist Economics* 1, no. 2 (July 1995): 1–19; Joan Smith and Immanuel Wallerstein, *Creating and Transforming Households: The Constraints of the World-Economy* (Thousand Oaks, CA: Cambridge University Press, 1992).

16. John Paul II, *Laborem Exercens: Encyclical Letter of the Supreme Pontiff John Paul II on Human Work* (London: Catholic Truth Society, 1981), 3.

17. Daniela Casale, Colette Muller, and Dorrit Posel, "'Two Million Net New Jobs': A Reconsideration of the Rise in Employment in South Africa, 1995–2003," *South African Journal of Economics* 72, no. 5 (2004): 978–1002; Imraan Valodia, "Informal Employment, Labour Markets and Social Protection: Some Considerations Based on South African Estimates," *IDS Bulletin* 39, no. 2 (2008): 57–62.

18. As George Lipsitz writes, the goal of dismantling racism entails "more than removing negative racist obstacles in the way of Black assimilation and upward mobility." In addition, the goal is to "change the entire society" by making visible what has been made invisible of black people—their ideas, moral systems, and situated knowledge that places high value on human connectivity, responsibility, and solidarity. George Lipsitz, *How Racism Takes Place* (Philadelphia, PA: Temple University Press, 2011), 124.

19. By the time the organization closed, research across the world was raising serious concerns about the replicability, poverty-reducing effectiveness, and possible net negative effects of microfinance. For example, see Julia Elyachar, *Markets of Dispossession: NGOs, Economic Development, and the State in Cairo* (Durham, NC: Duke University Press, 2005); and Anke Schwittay, "The Financial Inclusion Assemblage: Subjects, Technics, Rationalities," *Critique of Anthropology* 31, no. 4 (2011): 381–401.

20. Edward F. Fischer, *The Good Life: Aspiration, Dignity, and the Anthropology of Wellbeing* (Stanford, CA: Stanford University Press, 2014); Lawrence J. Jost and Roger A. Shiner, *Eudaimonia and Well-Being: Ancient and Modern Conceptions* (Kelowna, BC: Academic Printing and Publishing, 2003); Joel Robbins, "Beyond the Suffering Subject:

Toward an Anthropology of the Good," *Journal of the Royal Anthropological Institute* 19, no. 3 (2013): 447–62; Joel Robbins, "On Happiness, Values, and Time: The Long and the Short of It," *HAU: Journal of Ethnographic Theory* 5, no. 3 (December 23, 2015): 215–33.

21. Sherry B. Ortner, "On Key Symbols," *American Anthropologist* 75, no. 5 (1972): 1341.

22. In the interactions I counted as interviews (compared to the many casual conversations that occurred in various settings), I kept notes or recorded and transcribed according to people's preferences. Most interviewees preferred to speak English while using the occasional isiZulu word or phrase, and I followed their lead. I translated interviews in Zulu in consultation with bilingual friends for exact quotations.

23. My research is necessarily limited as a demographic representation of South Africa as a whole. Howick and the province of KwaZulu-Natal are made up of more English than Afrikaner people, as compared to the white population across the country. I chose to focus on interactions between white and black residents, but Indian and colored people also make up a small but not insignificant proportion of the Howick-area population.

24. Deborah Rosemary Bonnin, "Claiming Spaces, Changing Places: Political Violence and Women's Protests in KwaZulu-Natal," *Journal of Southern African Studies* 26, no. 2 (June 2000): 301–16.

25. Umngeni Municipal Council, "Umngeni Municipal Integrated Development Plan Review: People Centered Development—Intuthuko Kubantu," 2015, www.umngeni.gov.za.

26. Umngeni Municipal Council, "Umngeni Municipal Integrated Development Plan Review."

27. Hal Herzog, *Some We Love, Some We Hate, Some We Eat: Why It's So Hard to Think Straight about Animals* (New York: Harper Perennial, 2011), 12.

28. Achille Mbembe, *On the Postcolony* (Berkeley: University of California Press, 2001), 4.

29. The four subdisciplines of anthropology include cultural or sociocultural anthropology (this book), linguistics, physical anthropology (involving biological aspects of humans, thus at times bones or apes), and archaeology (involving cultures of the past up to the present, thus at times stone tools). Paleontologists study dinosaur bones.

30. One survey done in the United States found that 81 percent of people who graduated with a major in anthropology reported that "things were generally going well" with their career, and they ranked their job satisfaction higher than majors including computer engineering, fine arts, kinesiology, and neuroscience. Students review, "Job Satisfaction by Major," accessed July 5, 2019, https://www.studentsreview.com/satisfaction_by_major.php3?sort=Satisfied.

31. Ruth Gomberg-Muñoz, "Willing to Work: Agency and Vulnerability in an Undocumented Immigrant Network," *American Anthropologist* 112, no. 2 (2015): 295–307.

32. Michael J. Dumas and kihana miraya ross, "'Be Real Black for Me': Imagining BlackCrit in Education," *Urban Education* 51, no. 4 (April 1, 2016): 415–42; Lewis Gordon, *Existentia Africana* (New York: Farrar, Straus and Giroux, 2007); Frank B. Wilderson III, *Red, White, and Black: Cinema and the Structure of US Antagonisms* (Durham, NC: Duke University Press, 2010).

33. Kimberlé Crenshaw, "Demarginalizing the Intersection of Race and Sex: A Black Feminist Critique of Antidiscrimination Doctrine, Feminist Theory and Antiracist Politics," *University of Chicago Legal Forum* 1989 (1989): 139–67.

34. Clifford Geertz, *The Interpretation of Cultures: Selected Essays* (New York: Basic Books, 1973).

35. Barbara Ehrenreich, *Nickel and Dimed: On (Not) Getting By in America* (New York: Metropolitan Books, 2001), 220.

36. Data from the General Social Survey conducted by the National Opinion Research Center, available at http://gss.norc.org, cited by Raj Patel and Jason W. Moore in *A History of the World in Seven Cheap Things* (Berkeley: University of California Press, 2017), 41.

37. Douglas S. Massey, *Categorically Unequal: The American Stratification System* (New York: Russell Sage Foundation, 2008), 66. See also Lipsitz, *How Racism Takes Place*, 28, 250; and David M. P. Freund, *Colored Property: State Policy and White Racial Politics in Suburban America* (Chicago: University of Chicago Press, 2010).

38. Jason E. Shelton and Michael Emerson, *Blacks and Whites in Christian America: How Racial Discrimination Shapes Religious Convictions* (New York: New York University Press, 2012). For more on the ways racism affects unemployment and the narratives people use to explain it, see also David Karjanen, "The Limits to Quantitative Thinking: Engaging Economics on the Unemployed," in *Anthropologies of Unemployment: New Perspectives on Work and Its Absence*, ed. Jong Bum Kwon and Carrie M. Lane (Ithaca, NY: Cornell University Press, 2016); Devah Pager, *Marked: Race, Crime, and Finding Work in an Era of Mass Incarceration* (Chicago: University of Chicago Press, 2007); Perry, *More Beautiful and More Terrible*; and Glenn E. Singleton, *Courageous Conversations about Race: A Field Guide for Achieving Equity in Schools—Catalog—UW-Madison Libraries* (Thousand Oaks, CA: Corwin Press, 2006).

39. Perry, *More Beautiful and More Terrible*, 49.

40. Perry, *More Beautiful and More Terrible*, 45.

41. Katherine S. Newman, *No Shame in My Game: The Working Poor in the Inner City* (New York: Vintage Books, 2000), 93.

42. David Harvey, *The Condition of Postmodernity: An Enquiry into the Origins of Cultural Change* (Cambridge, MA: Blackwell, 1990), 230. See also James Ferguson, *Give a Man a Fish: Reflections on the New Politics of Distribution* (Durham, NC: Duke University Press, 2015).

43. Arne L. Kalleberg, *Good Jobs, Bad Jobs: The Rise of Polarized and Precarious Employment Systems in the United States, 1970s–2000s* (New York: Russell Sage Foundation, 2011).

44. United States Department of Labor, "Unemployment Rate 2.5 Percent for College Grads, 7.7 Percent for High School Dropouts, January 2017," Economics Daily: US Bureau of Labor Statistics, February 7, 2017, https://www.bls.gov/opub/ted/2017/unem ployment-rate-2-point-5-percent-for-college-grads-7-point-7-percent-for-high-school-dropouts-january-2017.htm.

45. Robert Wuthnow, *The Left Behind: Decline and Rage in Rural America* (Princeton, NJ: Princeton University Press, 2018), 70.

46. Jaison R. Abel, Richard Deitz, and Yaqin Su, "Are Recent College Graduates Finding Good Jobs?," *Current Issues in Economics and Finance* 20, no. 1 (2014): 1–8.

47. Katherine J. Cramer, *The Politics of Resentment: Rural Consciousness in Wisconsin and the Rise of Scott Walker* (Chicago: University of Chicago Press, 2016); Wuthnow, *Left Behind*.

48. Daniela Casale and Dorrit Posel, "The Continued Feminisation of the Labour Force in South Africa," *South African Journal of Economics* 70 (2002): 156–84. On the shifts in marital and parenting patterns, migrations, and social status of various kinds of work that often accompany feminization of the workforce in South Africa and elsewhere, see also Mark Hunter, *Love in the Time of AIDS: Inequality, Gender, and Rights in South Africa* (Bloomington: Indiana University Press, 2010); Sarah Mosoetsa, *Eating from One Pot: The Dynamics of Survival in Poor South African Households* (Johannesburg: Wits University Press, 2011); Hanna Rosin, *The End of Men: And the Rise of Women* (New York: Riverhead Books, 2012); and Melissa W. Wright, "The Dialectics of Still Life: Murder, Women, and Maquiladoras," in Comaroff and Comaroff, *Millennial Capitalism and the Culture of Neoliberalism*, 125–46.

49. Comaroff and Comaroff, introduction to *Millennial Capitalism and the Culture of Neoliberalism*, 2.

50. Jonah Lehrer, *Imagine: How Creativity Works* (New York: Houghton Mifflin Harcourt, 2012); William Maddux and Adam Galinsky, "Cultural Borders and Mental Barriers:

The Relationship between Living Abroad and Creativity," *Journal of Personality and Social Psychology* 96 (2009): 1047–61; Cyrus Rolbin and Bruno Della Chiesa, "'We Share the Same Biology . . .': Cultivating Cross-Cultural Empathy and Global Ethics through Multilingualism," *Mind, Brain, and Education* 4, no. 4 (December 1, 2010): 196–207.

51. Aimé Césaire, *Discourse on Colonialism*, trans. Joan Pinkham (New York: Monthly Review Press, 2000); Robin DiAngelo, "White Fragility," *International Journal of Critical Pedagogy* 3, no. 3 (2011): 54–70.

52. Saidiya Hartman describes how white people have historically used both of these types of empathy as a means to further subjugate black people and black bodies. Such supposed empathy "fails to expand the space of the other but merely places the self in its stead" and "requires that the white body be positioned in the place of the black body in order to make this suffering visible and intelligible." Saidiya Hartman, *Scenes of Subjection: Terror, Slavery, and Self-Making in Nineteenth-Century America* (Oxford: Oxford University Press, 1997), 20, 19.

53. "A Call for 'Radical Empathy' at Middlebury," *Burlington Free Press*, May 27, 2018, https://www.burlingtonfreepress.com/story/news/local/2018/05/27/middlebury-college-commencement-isabel-wilkerson-calls-radical-empathy/35428649/.

54. Quoted by Krista Tippett in "Luis Alberto Urrea—What Borders Are Really about, and What We Do with Them," On Being, July 12, 2018, https://onbeing.org/programs/luis-alberto-urrea-what-borders-are-really-about-and-what-we-do-with-them-jul2018/.

55. Philippe Bourgois, *In Search of Respect: Selling Crack in El Barrio* (Cambridge, MA: Cambridge University Press, 2003), 143.

## 1. "THEY DON'T WANT TO WORK"

1. The term "taxi" refers locally to a minibus typically seating fifteen to sixteen people, charging a set rate, and running on a set route.

2. People often find this word challenging to pronounce when they first encounter it. Note that the noun form—hegemony—has the accent on the second or first syllable: hi-*jem*-uh-nee, or *hej*-uh-moh-nee. The adjectival form—hegemonic—has the accent on the third syllable: hej-uh-*mon*-ik.

3. Antonio Gramsci, *Gramsci's Prison Letters: Lettere dal carcere; A Selection Translated and Introduced by Hamish Henderson* (London: Zwan, in association with the *Edinburgh Review*, 1988), 12.

4. Pierre Bourdieu describes a similar concept to hegemony using the word "doxa." Doxa includes all that is taken for granted in a society, that which "goes without saying because it comes without saying." Included in these taken-for-granted ideas are assumptions about who deserves positions and resources in society. Pierre Bourdieu, *Outline of a Theory of Practice* (New York: Cambridge University Press, 1977), 169. Karl Marx also described the tendency of ideologies and culture to reinforce inequalities, but saw economic structures of the means of production as ultimately the driver behind the ideologies upheld in society. Karl Marx, "The Economic and Philosophic Manuscripts of 1844," in *The Marx-Engels Reader*, ed. Robert C. Tucker, 2nd ed. (New York: W. W. Norton, 1978), 66–125.

5. Marco Di Nunzio, *The Act of Living: Street Life, Marginality, and Development in Urban Ethiopia* (Ithaca, NY: Cornell University Press, 2019), 18. See also Michael Burawoy, "The Roots of Domination: Beyond Bourdieu and Gramsci," *Sociology* 46, no. 2 (April 1, 2012): 187–206.

6. Jean Comaroff and John L. Comaroff, *Of Revelation and Revolution*, vol. 1, *Christianity, Colonialism, and Consciousness in South Africa* (Chicago: University of Chicago Press, 1991), 25.

7. A corollary to the fact that power often operates by normalizing its ideas to the point of invisibility is the fact that power can also maintain itself by demanding that the ideas of oppressed people be made visible or known. Michel Foucault has argued that acquiring and hoarding knowledge of others is one technique of power. And as Édouard Glissant points out, one way people subvert domination is through exercising "the right to opacity," or being untranslatable and different on their own terms from those in power. Michel Foucault, *The History of Sexuality, An Introduction*, reissue ed. (New York: Vintage, 1990); Édouard Glissant, *Poetics of Relation*, trans. Betsy Wing (Ann Arbor: University of Michigan Press, 1997).

8. Comaroff and Comaroff, *Of Revelation and Revolution*, 1:29–30.

9. Comaroff and Comaroff, *Of Revelation and Revolution*, 1:29.

10. Later, I found other scholars who had written about the ideas that make up the laziness narrative. Among the most helpful were James Ferguson, who writes that there is a "persistent (if delusional) fantasy that able-bodied men would (and should) all be in gainful employment if only they were not 'lazy'" (*Give a Man a Fish*, 46), and Franco Barchiesi and Keletso Atkins, who trace the historical scope of discourse on laziness in South Africa. Franco Barchiesi, "Work in the Constitution of the Human: Twentieth-Century South African Entanglements of Welfare, Blackness, and Political Economy," *South Atlantic Quarterly* 115, no. 1 (January 2016): 149–74; Keletso E. Atkins, *The Moon Is Dead! Give Us Our Money! The Cultural Origins of an African Work Ethic, Natal, South Africa, 1843–1900* (Portsmouth, NH: Pearson Education, 1993).

11. I debated whether to use the word "laziness" so prominently, lest it be taken as further reinforcement that certain people are in fact lazy. Partial explanations and misread research have often proven to be dangerous when social science research enters popular discourse and public policy. (See, for example, Daniel Geary, *Beyond Civil Rights: The Moynihan Report and Its Legacy* [Philadelphia: University of Pennsylvania Press, 2015]). I saw this unfold once when I was interviewed by a South African radio station. After I had explained that I was researching why people *thought* unemployment was caused by laziness, the radio show host nodded and said, "Right, so why is it that South African people are so lazy?" This was the very opposite of the point I was trying to make. The nature of hegemony made it easier for the host to read into my words what he believed to be true rather than hear what I was proposing. Despite these risks, I decided to call this the laziness narrative because that was the emic word people used for it. Exposing that reality-versus-narrative conflict at the heart of a hegemony—what the Comaroffs called the "vitality that remains in the forms of life it thwarts"—required calling it by the words people used, making those words visible and contestable.

12. Bongani Hans, "King's Anti-Foreigner Remarks Cause Alarm," *Mercury* (Durban), March 23, 2015.

13. Glissant, *Poetics of Relation*.

14. See also James Ferguson, *Expectations of Modernity: Myths and Meanings of Urban Life on the Zambian Copperbelt* (Berkeley: University of California Press, 1999).

15. CEIC Data, "South Africa Real GDP Growth," accessed October 21, 2019, https://www.ceicdata.com/en/indicator/south-africa/real-gdp-growth.

16. Michael J. Dumas, "Against the Dark: Antiblackness in Education Policy and Discourse," *Theory into Practice*, no. 55 (2016): 15.

17. Jonathan Haidt, *The Righteous Mind: Why Good People Are Divided by Politics and Religion* (New York: Pantheon Books, 2012), 167–81. Haidt suggests that fairness is one of five foundations of morality that humans tend to recognize. He points out that, unlike other values, fairness tends to be revered by conservatives, liberals, people across education levels, and people of various cultures. However, conservatives are more likely to see fairness as "proportionality," that is, believe that people "who work hard should get to keep the fruits of their labor. People who are lazy and irresponsible should suffer the

consequences" (169). In contrast, liberals tend to stress the importance of a "care" foundation of morality, which leads to emphasizing equality of opportunity and concern for those who have less.

18. For example, Malcolm Gladwell claims that because the people in Southern China historically worked in rice fields where they received the benefits of their own long and determined labor, over generations Chinese people developed a diligence in work that continues to play out in math classrooms today. Malcolm Gladwell, *Outliers: The Story of Success* (New York: Little, Brown, 2008).

19. Gibson-Graham, *Postcapitalist Politics*.

20. Ferguson, *Give a Man a Fish*; Kathi Weeks, *The Problem with Work: Feminism, Marxism, Antiwork Politics, and Postwork Imaginaries* (Durham, NC: Duke University Press, 2011).

21. A large body of literature covers the problematic repercussions and contradictions of neoliberalism, including the question of whether individuals are truly free in a positive sense without interventions to advocate and enforce equity and fairness in societies. See David Harvey, *A Brief History of Neoliberalism* (Oxford: Oxford University Press, 2005); M. Peters, "Governmentality, Education and the End of Neoliberalism?," in *Neoliberalism and After?* (New York: Peter Lang, 2011); John Rapley, *Globalization and Inequality: Neoliberalism's Downward Spiral* (Boulder, CO: Lynne Rienner, 2004); and Manfred B. Steger and Ravi K. Roy, *Neoliberalism: A Very Short Introduction* (Oxford: Oxford University Press, 2010).

22. Carrie M. Lane, *A Company of One: Insecurity, Independence, and the New World of White-Collar Unemployment* (Ithaca, NY: Cornell University Press, 2011), 4.

23. Kathrin Horschelmann, "Transitions to Work and the Making of Neo-Liberal Selves: Growing Up in (Former) East Germany," in A. Smith, Stenning, and Willis, *Social Justice and Neoliberalism*; Ergul Ergun, "Bargaining with the Devil: Neoliberalism, Informal Work and Workers' Resistance in the Clothing Industry of Turkey," in A. Smith, Stenning, and Willis, *Social Justice and Neoliberalism*; Lane, *Company of One*; Richard Sennett, *The Culture of the New Capitalism* (New Haven, CT: Yale University Press, 2006).

24. Elyachar, *Markets of Dispossession*; Ngai Pun, *Made in China: Women Factory Workers in a Global Workplace* (Durham, NC: Duke University Press, 2005); Biao Xiang, *Global "Body Shopping": An Indian Labor System in the Information Technology Industry* (Princeton, NJ: Princeton University Press, 2007); Wright, "Dialectics of Still Life"; Herbert S. Lewis, *After the Eagles Landed: The Yemenites of Israel* (Boulder, CO: Westview Press, 1989).

25. This list is far from complete. Nearly every immigrant group that has arrived in waves caused by poverty in their home country has experienced these stereotypes. A recent reminder is President Trump's reference in a conversation on immigration policy to Haiti and African countries as "shithole countries." Marwa Eltagouri, "South African Government Wants to Know Why Trump Thinks Its People Are 'Undesirable' Immigrants," *Washington Post*, January 15, 2018, https://www.washingtonpost.com/news/post-nation/wp/2018/01/15/south-african-government-wants-to-know-why-trump-thinks-its-people-are-undesirable-immigrants. Sources for this list include Catherine Besteman, "Somali Bantus in a State of Refuge," *Bidhaan: An International Journal of Somali Studies* 12, no. 8 (2012): 11–33; Bourgois, *In Search of Respect*; Duane Champagne, "Tribal Capitalism and Native Capitalists: Multiple Pathways of Native Economy," in Hosmer and O'Neill, *Native Pathways*, 308–29; and James O. Gump, *The Dust Rose Like Smoke: The Subjugation of the Zulu and the Sioux* (Lincoln: University of Nebraska Press, 1996).

26. Alice Littlefield and Martha C. Knack, *Native Americans and Wage Labor: Ethnohistorical Perspectives* (Norman: University of Oklahoma Press, 1996). See also Colleen M. O'Neill, "Rethinking Modernity and the Discourse of Development in American Indian History, an Introduction," in Hosmer and O'Neill, *Native Pathways*, 1–26.

27. Gomberg-Muñoz, "Willing to Work."

28. Willie James Jennings, *The Christian Imagination* (New Haven, CT: Yale University Press, 2010); Patel and Moore, *History of the World in Seven Cheap Things.*

29. Andrew Zimmerman, *Alabama in Africa: Booker T. Washington, the German Empire, and the Globalization of the New South* (Princeton, NJ: Princeton University Press, 2010), 39.

30. William Burchell, *Travels in the Interior of Southern Africa*, vols. 1 and 2 (Cape Town: C. Struik, 1967), facsimile reprint, 557.

31. Barchiesi, "Work in the Constitution of the Human"; Bernard Dubbeld, "Breaking the Buffalo: The Transformation of Stevedoring Work in Durban between 1970 and 1990," *International Review of Social History* 48 (2003): 97–122; Norman Levy, *The Foundations of the South African Cheap Labour System* (London: Routledge and Kegan Paul, 1982).

32. Alan Cobley, "'Lacking in Respect for Whitemen': 'Tropical Africans' on the Witwatersrand Gold Mines, 1903–1904," *International Labor and Working-Class History* 86 (2014): 36–54.

33. Cobley, "'Lacking in Respect for Whitemen,'" 51.

34. Cobley, "'Lacking in Respect for Whitemen.'"

35. Cobley, "'Lacking in Respect for Whitemen,'" 50.

36. Atkins, *Moon Is Dead!*

37. African colonial subjects were not alone in being forcefully initiated into the concept of time that European capitalist employers took for granted. Raj Patel and Jason Moore trace the history of European-American timekeeping as it intertwines with the transition to capitalism: from town bells introduced to measure the passing of hours in Belgium in the early fourteenth century, to English parish mechanical clocks measuring minutes and seconds in the sixteenth century, to the assembly lines of Henry Ford measuring worker time to a precision of one-thousandth of a second. Capitalism has throughout history been accompanied by a concept of time's scarcity and monetary value, and an insistence that those who waste it are lazy thieves of their bosses' time and profits. Patel and Moore, *History of the World in Seven Cheap Things*, 98.

38. Atkins, *Moon Is Dead!*, 17.

39. Atkins, *Moon Is Dead!*, 97.

40. Gump, *Dust Rose Like Smoke*, 90.

41. For example, the British author Aldous Huxley, witnessing "forced labour at the point of the bayonet" among Central Americans in the 1930s, wrote, "As slavery or some less brutal form, forced labour has everywhere been employed in the development of wild countries." Aldous Huxley, *Beyond the Mexique Bay* (London: Chatto and Windus, 1934), 145–46.

42. The effects of forced labor on South African society are too pervasive to enumerate. As a perfunctory list, scholars have described changes that include new ideas about who qualifies as an able-bodied versus an unfit laborer (Julie Livingston, *Debility and the Moral Imagination in Botswana* [Bloomington: Indiana University Press, 2005]); altered relationships and power dynamics between genders, generations, and the living and the ancestors (Giovanni Arrighi, "Labour Supplies in Historical Perspective: A Study of the Proletarianization of the African Peasantry in Rhodesia," in *Essays in the Political Economy of Africa*, ed. Giovanni Arrighi and J. Saul [New York: Monthly Review Press, 1973], 180–234; Peter Geschiere and Francis Nyamnjoh, "Capitalism and Autochthony: The Seesaw of Mobility and Belonging," in Comaroff and Comaroff, *Millennial Capitalism and the Culture of Neoliberalism*, 159–90); Livingston, *Debility and the Moral Imagination in Botswana*; Mosoetsa, *Eating from One Pot*; Zolani Ngwane, "'Real Men Reawaken Their Fathers' Homesteads, the Educated Leave Them in Ruins': The Politics of Domestic Reproduction in Post-Apartheid South Africa," in Weiss, *Producing African Futures*, 167–91; Hylton White, "Ritual Haunts: The Timing of Estrangement in a Post-Apartheid

Countryside," in Weiss, *Producing African Futures*, 141–66); introduction and intensification of disease (Steven Feierman, "Struggles for Control: The Social Roots of Health and Healing in Modern Africa," *African Studies Review* 28, nos. 2–3 [1985]: 73–147; David L. Schoenbrun, "Conjuring the Modern in Africa: Durability and Rupture in Histories of Public Healing between the Great Lakes of East Africa," *American Historical Review* 111, no. 5 [2006]: 1403–39); increased instances and accusations of rape (Isak Niehaus, "Witchcraft in the New South Africa," in Moore and Sanders, *Magical Interpretations*, 184–205); new forms and purposes of witchcraft (Henrietta L. Moore, introduction to Moore and Sanders, *Magical Interpretations*, 1–27); new flows and tastes in imports (Jeremy Prestholdt, *Domesticating the World: African Consumerism and the Genealogies of Globalization* [Berkeley: University of California Press, 2008]); and new patterns of accumulation and time orientation (Atkins, *Moon Is Dead!*).

43. Max Weber, *The Protestant Ethic and the Spirit of Capitalism and Other Writings*, ed. Peter Baehr and Gordon C. Wells (New York: Penguin Classics, 2002).

44. Charles Taylor, *A Secular Age* (Cambridge, MA: Belknap Press of Harvard University Press, 2007).

45. Max Gluckman, "Analysis of a Social Situation in Modern Zululand," *Bantu Studies* 14, no. 1 (1940): 1–30. See Jean Comaroff and John L. Comaroff, *Of Revelation and Revolution*, vol. 2, *The Dialectics of Modernity on a South African Frontier* (Chicago: University of Chicago Press, 1997), 30, 164.

46. Gluckman, "Analysis of a Social Situation in Modern Zululand."

47. Changes in agricultural practices due to migration and labor structures inadvertently fostered livestock disease in some instances, such as the cattle rinderpest plague in the 1890s that combined with war and land reduction to drastically reduce cattle herds in much of South Africa. Gump, *Dust Rose Like Smoke*; Seekings and Nattrass, *Class, Race, and Inequality in South Africa*.

48. Seekings and Nattrass, *Class, Race, and Inequality in South Africa*.

49. Levy, *Foundations of the South African Cheap Labour System*.

50. For more on taxes and poverty as an incentive for forced labor, see also Atkins, *Moon Is Dead!*; Gluckman, "Analysis of a Social Situation in Modern Zululand"; Levy, *Foundations of the South African Cheap Labour System*; and Livingston, *Debility and the Moral Imagination in Botswana*.

51. Dorrit Posel, James A. Fairburn, and Frances Lund, "Labour Migration and Households: A Reconsideration of the Effects of the Social Pension on Labour Supply in South Africa," *Economic Modelling* 23 (2006): 836–53.

52. Pierre Bourdieu, *Distinction: A Social Critique of the Judgement of Taste*, trans. Richard Nice (Cambridge, MA: Harvard University Press, 1984), 251.

53. One economic theory of company decisions explains that workers are worth only what they are worth within a system because one unreliable worker can slow down the productivity of an entire company. The risk of having even a few unreliable workers can cause wages in a region to decline as companies decide to move to regions where they anticipate having more reliable workers, even when that means paying higher wages. Thus, higher wages tend to congregate in certain groups, regions, and nations. Michael Kremer, "The O-Ring Theory of Economic Development," *Quarterly Journal of Economics* 108, no. 3 (August 1993): 551–75.

54. David Neves and Andries du Toit, "Money and Sociality in South Africa's Informal Economy," *Africa* 82 (2012): 131–49.

55. Wright, "Dialectics of Still Life."

56. Evidence that workers are both presumed to be unworthy of investment and deprived of opportunities to gain that supposed worthiness has been documented in various ways. The South African workforce has long been characterized by both oscillatory

migration between rural and urban areas and casual labor contracts. A study of South African farm laborers found that only a very small number of skilled workers secure long-term employment while the rest of the laborers fend for themselves in seasonal employment. A. Du Toit and F. Ally, *The Externalisation and Casualisation of Farm Labour in Western Cape Horticulture: A Survey of Patterns in the Agricultural Labour Market in Key Western Cape Districts, and Their Implications for Employment Justice* (Cape Town: Centre for Rural Legal Studies, 2003), 51. The income gap is expanding between high-skill and low-skill employees in South Africa. Banerjee et al., "Why Has Unemployment Risen in the New South Africa?" And provision of entitlements including pension, medical aid, and work-related training are also declining in both formal and informal private sector work. Miriam Altman and Imraan Valodia, "Introduction: Where to for the South African Labour Market? Some 'Big Issues,'" *Transformation: Critical Perspectives on Southern Africa* 60, no. 1 (2006): 1–5.

57. Lipsitz, *How Racism Takes Place*, 28.

58. The South African Labour Force Survey introduced in 2000 gives specific prompts to count even a single hour of work per week in gardening, fishing, or other informal income-generating activities as work (Valodia, "Informal Employment, Labour Markets and Social Protection"; Casale, Muller, and Posel, "'Two Million Net New Jobs'"). As a practical representation of how people understand their experience, however, such definitions of work raise concerns. The fact remains that most South African Zulu people do not see household activities in the same category as waged employment. On a few occasions I brought up the change in official definitions of work to include gardening or fishing, and people laughed at the absurdity of putting these activities in the same category as having work.

59. One study in the United States found that working-class minorities who are stereotyped as lazy in fact show a stronger drive to find work and make sacrifices than the population as a whole. They start work at younger ages, take less desirable jobs, admonish relatives to work hard for a better future, and overall overcome more challenges than people in the white middle-class who are more often associated with a work ethic.

60. For studies analyzing causes of unemployment, see also Altman and Valodia, introduction; Casale, Muller, and Posel, "'Two Million Net New Jobs'"; Gheeta Gandhi Kingdon and John Knight, "Unemployment in South Africa: The Nature of the Beast," *World Development* 32, no. 3 (2004): 391–408; and Sher Verick, "Unravelling the Impact of the Global Financial Crisis on the South African Labour Market," International Labor Organization Working Paper, 2010.

61. The government's affirmative action programs designed to incentivize businesses to overcome racial disparities in hiring and leadership (called broad-based black economic empowerment), implemented since the late 1990s, have sparked among some white people a sense that it is now more difficult for white people than black people to get hired. The rates for employment, especially in more highly skilled positions, demonstrate that white people are still far more likely to have higher-paying jobs. Altman and Valodia, introduction.

62. As Robin DiAngelo writes, white people are "taught to value the individual and to see themselves as individuals rather than as part of a racially socialized group," but not to extend this individualism to members of other racial groups. In addition to creating a mindset in which people of color are stereotyped and white people are not, this socializes white people to demand "the benefit of the doubt" in all situations, including believing themselves to be unaffected by racial messages in the culture. DiAngelo, "White Fragility," 59.

63. Arlie Russell Hochschild, *The Managed Heart: Commercialization of Human Feeling*, 3rd ed. (Berkeley: University of California Press, 2012).

64. Barchiesi, "Work in the Constitution of the Human."

65. James C. Scott, *Weapons of the Weak: Everyday Forms of Peasant Resistance* (New Haven, CT: Yale University Press, 1985). The term "weapons of the weak" was originally coined by Harriet Ann Jacobs in *Incidents in the Life of a Slave Girl: Written by Herself* (Cambridge, MA: Harvard University Press, 1987).

66. For similar accounts of people who operate outside formal employment for reasons including respect from their communities, see Bourgois, *In Search of Respect*; and Mitchell Duneier, Hakim Hasan, and Ovie Carter, *Sidewalk* (New York: Farrar, Straus and Giroux, 2000).

## 2. "YOU CAN'T UNDERSTAND IT"

1. Maxim Bolt's book, *Zimbabwe's Migrants and South Africa's Border Farms*, is one model I look to as an ethnography that sensitively describes black employees (both South African and Zimbabwean) as well as white employers in ways that acknowledge the humanity and complexity of each. Bolt theorizes white farmers' decisions with attention to their own perspectives, international market forces, and also ways that class, race, and ethnicity are each imagined by employers. Maxim Bolt, *Zimbabwe's Migrants and South Africa's Border Farms: The Roots of Impermanence* (Cambridge, MA: Cambridge University Press, 2015).

2. Sherry B. Ortner, *Anthropology and Social Theory: Culture, Power, and the Acting Subject* (Durham, NC: Duke University Press, 2006).

3. Jan Kemp Nel, *Win at the CCMA: A Practical and Informative Toolkit with Forms, Policies and Procedures* (Haltom City, TX: Knowres, 2014); Pieter A. Grobler, *Human Resource Management in South Africa*, 3rd ed. (London: Thompson Learning, 2005).

4. Shellee Colen, "'With Respect and Feelings': Voices of West Indian Child Care Workers in New York City," in *All American Women: Lines That Divide, Ties That Bind*, ed. Johnnetta B. Cole (New York: Free Press, 1986), 46–70; Faye D. Ginsburg and Rayna R. Reiter, *Conceiving the New World Order: The Global Politics of Reproduction* (Berkeley: University of California Press, 1995).

5. Nicolas Peterson, "Myth of the 'Walkabout': Movement in the Aboriginal Domain," in *Population Mobility and Indigenous Peoples in Australia and North America*, ed. John Taylor and Martin Bell (London: Routledge, 2003).

6. In George Lipsitz's words, this is a "two-part strategy that entails a frontal attack on all the mechanisms that prevent people of color from equal opportunities to accumulate assets that appreciate in value and can be passed down across generations, as well as a concomitant embrace of the Black spatial imaginary based on privileging use value over exchange value, sociality over selfishness, and inclusion over exclusion." Lipsitz, *How Racism Takes Place*, 61; Bourgois, *In Search of Respect*; Di Nunzio, *Act of Living*; William Julius Wilson, *More Than Just Race: Being Black and Poor in the Inner City* (New York: W. W. Norton, 2009).

7. This predicament in which suppliers far outnumber buyers is helpful for understanding the predicament of job-seekers in a high-unemployment economy as well. Job-seekers who don't like the labor conditions offered by one employer can't easily take their labor elsewhere.

8. Daniel Finnan, "South Africa Loses Game of Chicken in Renewal of US Trade Agreement," *RFI*, June 7, 2015, http://www.english.rfi.fr/africa/20150607-south-africa-loses-game-chicken-renewal-us-trade-agreement-agoa-poultry.

9. Paul Shapiro, "The Chicken Industry Loves Federal Handouts," *Huffington Post*, September 18, 2013, http://www.huffingtonpost.com/paul-shapiro/the-chicken-industry_b_3947857.html.

10. Mervyn Naidoo, "Rainbow Chicken on a Knife Edge," *IOL News*, January 8, 2017, https://www.iol.co.za/news/south-africa/kwazulu-natal/rainbow-chicken-on-a-knife-edge-7354387.

11. Myriam Velia and Glen Robbins, "Constraints to Growth and Employment in Medium and Large Manufacturing in EThekwini—Some Reflections," University of KwaZulu-Natal School of Built Environment and Development Studies, May 5, 2015.

12. Aleks Jablonska, Roche van Wyk, and Paul Sturrock, *Community Analysis of Howick, Mooi River, Mpophomeni and KwaHaza in KZN, South Africa: Compiled for Ethembeni* (Cape Town: Learn to Earn Association, 2014).

13. Robert D. Putnam, "Bowling Alone: America's Declining Social Capital," *Journal of Democracy* 6, no. 1 (January 1, 1995): 65–78; Robert B. Reich, *The Common Good* (New York: Knopf, 2018).

14. Lisa Steyn, "The Downward Spiral of SA Unions," *Mail and Guardian*, November 14, 2014, https://mg.co.za/article/2014-11-13-the-downward-spiral-of-sa-unions/; South African Institute of Race Relations, Johannesburg, press release, "Trade Unions Lose Control of the Workshop Floor," February 9, 2015.

15. Statistics South Africa, "Quarterly Labour Force Survey: Quarter 3 2015" (Pretoria: Statistics South Africa, October 27, 2015), http://www.statssa.gov.za/publications/P0211/P02113rdQuarter2015.pdf.

16. Unions in South Africa today, and in Howick in particular, occupy a complicated place in social imaginaries. South African academics I interacted with were generally more optimistic about the power of collective action than were Howick and Mpophomeni residents. I heard several black people as well as white people express their disillusionment about unions, saying union leaders were exploitative, strikes were ineffective, or decisions to join unions created divisions among black employees that made their work experiences worse. I also heard union members express their opinion that unions, while imperfect, were better than the alternative of leaving workers without organizational structures for collective bargaining at all. The negative sentiments regarding unions may be seasoned in part by Howick's history of violent strikebreaks, and without comparative evidence from elsewhere, I do not wish to represent a skewed picture of collective bargaining across South Africa today.

17. Bond, *Elite Transition*; Comaroff and Comaroff, introduction; Du Toit and Ally, *Externalisation and Casualisation of Farm Labour*; Harvey, *Brief History of Neoliberalism*; Sennett, *Culture of the New Capitalism*.

18. Du Toit and Ally, *Externalisation and Casualisation of Farm Labour*.

19. John B. Thompson, *Studies in the Theory of Ideology* (Berkeley: University of California Press, 1984), 6.

20. Weber, *Protestant Ethic and the Spirit of Capitalism* (trans. Kalberg). Later theorists who drew on Weber's culture-based approach to understanding human behavior included interpretive anthropologists such as Clifford Geertz, as well as structuralists like Claude Lévi-Strauss.

21. Max Weber, *Protestant Ethic and the "Spirit" of Capitalism and Other Writings*, trans. and ed. Peter Baehr and Gordon C. Wells (New York: Penguin Classics, 2002), 24.

22. Weber, *Protestant Ethic and the Spirit of Capitalism* (trans. Kalberg), 37.

23. Marx, "Economic and Philosophic Manuscripts of 1844."

24. Sherry Ortner has a particularly helpful analysis of how a number of theorists, including herself and Anthony Giddens, Pierre Bourdieu, Paul Willis, James C. Scott, and others, developed ways of seeing human behavior as a product of both culture and socioeconomic structures. See Bourdieu, *Outline of a Theory of Practice*; Anthony Giddens, *The Constitution of Society: Outline of the Theory of Structuration* (Cambridge: Polity Press, 1984); Ortner, *Anthropology and Social Theory*; Scott, *Weapons of the Weak*; and Paul E.

Willis, *Learning to Labour: How Working Class Kids Get Working Class Jobs* (Farnborough: Saxon House, 1977).

25. Lipsitz, *How Racism Takes Place*, 37.

## 3. "I NEED TO RESPECT THAT PERSON AND THAT PERSON NEEDS TO RESPECT ME"

1. For more on how shopkeepers manage relationships and debts, see Isabelle Guérin, "Women and Money: Lessons from Senegal," *Development and Change* 37, no. 3 (May 2006): 549–70.

2. Frederick Engels and Karl Marx saw the power dynamics of marital relationships as a precursor and microcosm of the power inequalities inherent in capitalism. Friedrich Engels, "The Origin of the Family, Private Property, and the State," in *The Marx-Engels Reader*, ed. Robert C. Tucker, 2nd ed. (New York: W. W. Norton, 1978), 734–59.

3. United States Central Intelligence Agency, "Country Comparison: Distribution of Family Income—Gini Index," *The World Factbook*, accessed September 28, 2018, https://www.cia.gov/library/publications/the-world-factbook/rankorder/2172rank.html.

4. Anna Orthofer, "Wealth Inequality in South Africa: Insights from Survey and Tax Data," *Redi3x3* Working Paper 15 (June 2015): 50.

5. Actually, it has been widely held that the global wealth distribution—with a Gini coefficient of over .91—is more unequal than any single country, but a study by Anna Orthofer found that South Africa actually approaches or surpasses that level of inequality. James B. Davies, Rodrigo Lluberas, and Anthony F. Shorrocks, "Estimating the Level and Distribution of Global Wealth, 2000–2014," *Review of Income and Wealth* 63, no. 4 (December 2017): 731–59; Orthofer, "Wealth Inequality in South Africa."

6. Imani Perry, *Prophets of the Hood: Politics and Poetics in Hip Hop* (Durham, NC: Duke University Press, 2004); Jeff Friesen and Steve Heinrichs, eds., *Quest for Respect: The Church and Indigenous Spirituality* (Winnipeg: Mennonite Church Canada, 2017), https://www.commonword.ca/ResourceView/16/19134; Sennett, *Culture of the New Capitalism*; Richard Sennett, *Respect: In a World of Inequality* (New York: W. W. Norton, 2003).

7. Clayborne Carson and Kris Shepard, eds., *A Call to Conscience: The Landmark Speeches of Dr. Martin Luther King, Jr.* (New York: Warner Books, 2001), 60; NPR Staff, "'Respect' Wasn't a Feminist Anthem until Aretha Franklin Made It One," NPR, *All Things Considered*, February 14, 2017, https://www.npr.org/2017/02/14/515183747/respect-wasnt-a-feminist-anthem-until-aretha-franklin-made-it-one.

8. In one account of an incident in which a man stole a woman's purse then shot her, the man said later that he'd shot her "because of the way she was looking at him. He shot her because he didn't think she was taking him seriously, and wasn't giving him any respect." Malcolm Gladwell, *David and Goliath: Underdogs, Misfits, and the Art of Battling Giants* (New York: Little, Brown, 2013), 242. The very title of Philippe Bourgois's ethnography of crack dealers in New York City summarizes the reason many people turn to crime: in search of respect. Bourgois, *In Search of Respect*.

9. Guy Raz and Christian Picciolini, "Why We Hate," NPR, *TED Radio Hour*, accessed July 23, 2018, https://www.npr.org/programs/ted-radio-hour/628546919/why-we-hate.

10. Richard G. Wilkinson and Kate Pickett, *The Spirit Level: Why Greater Equality Makes Societies Stronger* (New York: Bloomsbury Press, 2010).

11. Society for Applied Anthropology (SfAA) website, accessed July 19, 2019, https://www.sfaa.net/.

12. James Ferguson, "Declarations of Dependence: Labour, Personhood, and Welfare in Southern Africa," *Journal of the Royal Anthropological Institute* 19, no. 2 (2013): 223–42; Naomi Haynes, "Desirable Dependence, or What We Learn from Pentecostalism," *Journal*

*of the Royal Anthropological Institute* 19, no. 2 (2013): 250–51; Andrew Sayer, "Dignity at Work: Broadening the Agenda," *Organization* 14, no. 4 (2007): 565–81; Sennett, *Respect*.

13. See John L. Comaroff and Jean Comaroff, "Goodly Beasts, Beastly Goods: Cattle and Commodities in a South African Context," *American Ethnologist* 17, no. 2 (May 1, 1990): 195–216; James Ferguson, "The Bovine Mystique: Power, Property and Livestock in Rural Lesotho," *Man* 20, no. 4 (December 1985): 647–74; and Paul K. Bjerk, "They Poured Themselves into the Milk: Zulu Political Philosophy under Shaka," *Journal of African History* 47, no. 1 (2006): 1–20.

14. Christine Jeske, "Are Cars the New Cows? Changing Wealth Goods and Moral Economies in South Africa," *American Anthropologist* 118, no. 3 (September 2016): 483–94.

15. Franco Barchiesi, *Precarious Liberation: Workers, the State, and Contested Social Citizenship in Postapartheid South Africa* (Scottsville, South Africa: University of KwaZulu-Natal Press, 2011); Andrea Muehlebach, "On Precariousness and the Ethical Imagination: The Year 2012 in Sociocultural Anthropology," *American Anthropologist* 115, no. 2 (2013): 297–311; Sennett, *Culture of the New Capitalism*; Anna Lowenhaupt Tsing, *The Mushroom at the End of the World: On the Possibility of Life in Capitalist Ruins* (Princeton, NJ: Princeton University Press, 2015).

16. Carol B. Stack, *All Our Kin: Strategies for Survival in a Black Community* (New York: Basic Books, 1983).

17. Steven Feierman, "Reflections on African Medical History and the History of Science" (presentation at the University of Wisconsin, Madison, WI, 2012).

18. Karl Polanyi, *The Great Transformation* (Boston, MA: Beacon Press, 1957), 48.

19. Bronislaw Malinowski, "Tribal Economics in the Trobriands," in *Tribal and Peasant Economies: Readings in Economic Anthropology*, ed. George Dalton (Garden City, NY: Natural History Press, 1967), 185–223; Marcel Mauss, *The Gift: The Form and Reason for Exchange in Archaic Societies*, trans. W. D. Halls (New York: W. W. Norton, 1990).

20. Bourdieu, *Distinction*.

21. Marshall David Sahlins, *Stone Age Economics* (Chicago: Aldine, 1972).

22. David Graeber, "On the Moral Grounds of Economic Relations: A Maussian Approach," *Journal of Classical Sociology* 14, no. 1 (2014): 65–77.

23. Bourdieu, *Outline of a Theory of Practice*.

24. Luke 12:48 (New Revised Standard Version).

25. Other scholars have found similar moral systems in Africa obligating those with more to support those with less. Ferguson, "Bovine Mystique"; Jane I. Guyer, *Marginal Gains: Monetary Transactions in Atlantic Africa* (Chicago: University of Chicago Press, 2004); Naomi Haynes, *Moving by the Spirit: Pentecostal Social Life on the Zambian Copperbelt* (Berkeley: University of California Press, 2017); Hylton White, "A Post-Fordist Ethnicity: Insecurity, Authority, and Identity in South Africa," *Anthropological Quarterly* 85, no. 2 (2012): 397–428.

26. Sennett, *Respect*, 214, 262, 263.

27. See also Christine Jeske, "Why Work? Do We Understand What Motivates Work-Related Decisions in South Africa?," *Journal of Southern African Studies* 44, no. 1 (2018): 27–42.

28. Lipsitz, *How Racism Takes Place*, 56.

29. Statistics South Africa, "Quarterly Labour Force Survey: Quarter 2 2018" (Pretoria: Statistics South Africa, July 31, 2018), http://www.statssa.gov.za/publications/P0211/P02112rndQuarter2018.pdf.

30. Deborah James, *Money from Nothing: Indebtedness and Aspiration in South Africa* (Stanford, CA: Stanford University Press, 2014).

31. Nattavudh Powdthavee, "Are There Geographical Variations in the Psychological Cost of Unemployment in South Africa?," *Social Indicators Research* 80, no. 3 (April 2012): 629–52.

32. Dorrit Posel and Michael Rogan, "Measured as Poor versus Feeling Poor: Comparing Objective and Subjective Poverty Rates in South Africa" (WIDER Working Paper Series 133, United Nations University-World Institute for Development Economic Research, Helsinki, 2014).

33. One reason for people's increased dissatisfaction when wages increased was that their relationships with their employers shifted, leaving employers less likely to offer personal favors. Another cause had to do with changed relationships with dependents. Farm workers in one case study had previously been paid in part with sacks of corn, which limited the money they were expected to share with dependents, whereas a salary entirely in cash was more fungible and presented logistical challenges for shopping and resisting requests. Shireen A. Ally, *From Servants to Workers: South African Domestic Workers and the Democratic State* (Ithaca, NY: Cornell University Press, 2009); Astrid Boehm and Stefan Schirmer, "Development by Decree: The Impact of Minimum Wage Legislation on a Farming Area in North West Province," in *Development Dilemmas*, ed. Bill Freund and Harald Witt (Scottsville, South Africa: University of KwaZulu-Natal Press, 2010), 248–74.

34. See also Hylton White, *What Shapes Young People's Job Preferences? A View from Rural KwaZulu-Natal*, Coping with Unemployment (Johannesburg: Centre for Development and Enterprise, 2012).

35. See also Christine Jeske, "Are Cars the New Cows? Changing Wealth Goods and Moral Economies in South Africa" *American Anthropologist* 118, no. 3 (September 2016): 483–94.

36. In many Zulu communities, people experience intense social pressure to have children. Women who have had children are often referred to not by their own names, but as "the mother of" with their children's names. In church services, people are often separated into groups of "children," "fathers," and "mothers," leaving no category for an adult who is not a parent.

## 4. "HUSTLING IS WHEN YOU TRY TO MAKE A GOOD LIFE"

1. Teeza (a nickname he went by in addition to his given name, Thembelani) and Sma (short for Simangelo) requested to use their own names and the actual name of their company, Black Teardrop.

2. Small Enterprise Development Agency, "Annual Review 2013/2014: Seda Technology Programme," 2014; South African Government News Agency, "SA News," 2014, http://www.sanews.gov.za/.

3. The model of the Grameen Bank is more complicated than simply dispersing loans. Small groups of friends, usually women, take out loans as individuals but meet frequently to make small loan payments and to reinforce other habits of healthy and productive living, such as tree-planting, responding to domestic abuse, and improving nutrition for children. In lieu of the collateral that prevents many people in poverty from accessing formal loans, group members guarantee each other's loans. See Muhammad Yunus, *Banker to the Poor: The Autobiography of Muhammad Yunus, Founder of Grameen Bank* (London: Aurum Press, 1999).

4. One extreme version of ostentatious spending that sometimes came up in township discussions—usually with a mix of criticism and sympathetic understanding—was a practice called *i'khotane*, literally short for "licking the snake." Groups of youth called i'khotane in larger cities publicly burned or destroyed expensive goods and cash. The scholars Simon Howell and Louise Vincent write about i'khotane: "The participants, in their daily lives, are economically and politically marginalized, facing an uncertain future. . . . They have found new arenas, new paths, and new traditions upon which to build their identities. While clothing and battles are the vehicle, it is ultimately respect

that it desired." Simon Howell and Louise Vincent, "'Licking the Snake'—the i'khothane and Contemporary Township Youth Identities in South Africa," *South African Review of Sociology* 45, no. 2 (2014): 72.

5. The category of "youth" in South Africa often includes adults up to the age of 35. Statistics South Africa uses the range of 15–35, the National Youth Commission uses 14–35, and other groups choose alternative ranges, such as 21–35 or 14–28. Sources of data on youth unemployment include International Labour Organization, "Unemployment, Youth Total (% of Total Labor Force Ages 15–24)," World Bank Data, 2014, http://data.worldbank.org/indicator/SL.UEM.1524.ZS; National Youth Commission, South Africa, "National Youth Policy: 2009–2014," 2009; and Statistics South Africa, "Quarterly Labour Force Survey: Quarter 3 2015."

6. For more about generational conflicts and fears associated with African youth, see Comaroff and Comaroff, introduction, 18; Ngwane, "'Real Men Reawaken Their Fathers' Homesteads'"; and Robert Serpell, *The Significance of Schooling: Life-Journeys in an African Society* (Cambridge: Cambridge University Press, 1993).

7. Frank B. Wilderson III, "Afro-Pessimism and the End of Redemption," *Humanities Futures: Franklin Humanities Institute* (blog), 2016, https://humanitiesfutures.org/papers/afro-pessimism-end-redemption/.

8. Wilderson, "Afro-Pessimism and the End of Redemption"; Hortense Spillers, *Black, White, and in Color: Essays on American Literature and Culture* (Chicago: University of Chicago Press, 2003).

9. Derrick Bell, *Faces at the Bottom of the Well: The Permanence of Racism* (New York: Basic Books, 1992), 12.

10. Bell, *Faces at the Bottom of the Well*, 198.

11. Tatiana Adeline Thieme pointed out that in Kenya and across the globe the term "hustling" "normalizes and affirms experiences of uncertainty"—that is, when uncertainty and struggle are unavoidable, hustling names and legitimizes that mode of existence. Hustling shows up in studies around the world, among people ranging from church leaders in Botswana, to medical trial participants in the United States. Tatiana Adeline Thieme, "The Hustle Economy: Informality, Uncertainty and the Geographies of Getting By," *Progress in Human Geography* 42, no. 4 (August 2018): 531; Torin Monahan and Jill A. Fisher, "'I'm Still a Hustler': Entrepreneurial Responses to Precarity by Participants in Phase I Clinical Trials," *Economy and Society* 44, no. 4 (October 2, 2015): 545–66; Richard P. Werbner, *Holy Hustlers, Schism, and Prophecy: Apostolic Reformation in Botswana* (Berkeley: University of California Press, 2011).

12. Michael Morris and Leyland Pitt, "Informal Sector Activity as Entrepreneurship: Insights from a South African Township," *Journal of Small Business Management* 33, no. 1 (January 1995): 78–86; Ernest North, "A Decade of Entrepreneurship Education in South Africa," *South African Journal of Education* 22, no. 1 (2002): 24–27.

13. Keith Hart, "Bureaucratic Form and the Informal Economy," in *Linking the Formal and Informal Economy: Concepts and Policies*, ed. Basudeb Guha-Khasnobis, Ravi Kanbur, and Elinor Ostrom (New York: Oxford University Press, 2007); Neves and du Toit, "Money and Sociality in South Africa's Informal Economy."

14. My observations suggested that the percentage of businesses operated by Zulu South Africans was higher at the end of the month, when the arrival of paychecks and grant payments fed money into the local economy, making small businesses more lucrative.

15. For more in-depth explanations of the social factors affecting entrepreneurship among immigrants to South Africa, see Bolt, *Zimbabwe's Migrants and South Africa's Border Farms*; and Jason Hickel, "'Xenophobia' in South Africa: Order, Chaos, and the Moral Economy of Witchcraft," *Cultural Anthropology* 29, no. 1 (2014): 103–27.

16. Frederick Fourie and Caroline Skinner, eds., *The South African Informal Sector: Creating Jobs, Reducing Poverty* (Johannesburg: HSRC Press, 2018).

17. Andrew Charman and Leif Petersen, "Informal Micro Enterprises in a Township Context: A Spatial Analysis of Business Dynamics in Five Cape Town Localities," in Fourie and Skinner, *South African Informal Sector*, 253–84.

18. Newman, *No Shame in My Game*, 93.

19. Newman, *No Shame in My Game*, 215.

20. Newman, *No Shame in My Game*, 217.

21. In another take on hustling in the United States, Torin Monahan and Jill Fisher found that individuals who volunteer for intensive residential pharmaceutical testing often see the practice as a form of entrepreneurship and also associate hustling with their identity. Torin Monahan and Jill A. Fisher, "'I'm Still a Hustler': Entrepreneurial Responses to Precarity by Participants in Phase I Clinical Trials," *Economy and Society* 44, no. 4 (October 2, 2015): 545–66.

22. Daniel Mains, "Youth Unemployment, Progress, and Shame in Urban Ethiopia," in *Anthropologies of Unemployment: New Perspectives on Work and Its Absence*, ed. Jong Bum Kwon and Carrie M. Lane (Ithaca, NY: Cornell University Press, 2016), 138.

23. A recent study found that success in informal entrepreneurship in South Africa is correlated with having previous employment experience. This lines up with the pattern I saw of people expecting to run a business after they had years of employment experience. Neil Lloyd, "Informal Enterprise Ownership: The Importance of Previous Employment Experience," *Econ 3X3* (blog), June 2018, http://www.econ3x3.org/article/informal-enterprise-ownership-importance-previous-employment-experience.

24. For a comparison between the ways South Africans stored up wealth in cattle versus cars and other vehicles, see Jeske, "Are Cars the New Cows?"

25. South Africa's constitution implements a tender system for virtually all government purchases and services, from purchasing pencils to constructing roads. Newspapers and other media advertise "tenders," or plans for government purchases, and companies bid for the opportunity to provide the products and services, presumably with the lowest price and highest quality winning. While the system was designed to avoid nepotism and foster a neoliberal-style privatized efficiency in the new South African government, the system has been widely criticized for generating the exact opposite. James, *Money from Nothing*.

26. Ferguson, *Give a Man a Fish*.

27. Trevor Noah, *Born a Crime: Stories from a South African Childhood* (New York: Spiegel and Grau, 2016), 212–13.

28. Bhekizizwe Peterson, "Kwaito, 'Dawgs' and the Antimonies of Hustling," *African Identities* 1, no. 2 (2003): 208.

29. B. Peterson, "Kwaito, 'Dawgs' and the Antimonies of Hustling," 198.

30. B. Peterson, "Kwaito, 'Dawgs' and the Antimonies of Hustling," 208.

31. Di Nunzio, *Act of Living*, 16, 17.

32. See two influential texts on consumption as performance in postcolonial Africa: Ferguson, *Expectations of Modernity*; and Sasha Newell, *The Modernity Bluff: Crime, Consumption, and Citizenship in Côte d'Ivoire* (Chicago: University of Chicago Press, 2012).

33. For more on the intertwining of hope and performance, see Hirokazu Miyazaki, *The Method of Hope: Anthropology, Philosophy, and Fijian Knowledge* (Stanford, CA: Stanford University Press, 2004).

34. Philippe Bourdieu describes this process of performing class in French society. He points out the gamelike elements of the process, as people unconsciously agree to follow the rules of the game that surrounds them by acquiring distinction through purchases, behaviors, and knowledge to demonstrate belonging in a higher class. Members of every class group experience pressure to play the game and "seek to distinguish themselves from the group immediately below (or believed to be so), which they use as a foil, and to identify themselves with the group immediately above (or believed to be so), which they thus recognize as the possessor of the legitimate life-style." Bourdieu, *Distinction*, 246.

35. Newell, *Modernity Bluff*, 15.

36. Thorstein Veblen, *The Theory of the Leisure Class* (New York: Dover, 1994).

37. While the young man did not mention Tupac by name, he and others knew and highly respected Tupac. The lyrics are worth mentioning: "Did you hear about the rose that grew from a crack in the concrete? / Provin' nature's laws wrong / It learned to walk without having feet / Funny it seems but by keeping its dreams / it learned to breathe fresh air / Long live the rose that grew from concrete / when no one else, even cared."

38. Again, I recommend Philippe Bourgois's excellent explanation of this situation of structure, agency, and destruction quoted in part in the introduction. "[They have] not passively accepted their structural victimization. On the contrary, by embroiling themselves in the underground economy and proudly embracing street culture, they are seeking an alternative to their social marginalization. In the process, on a daily level, they become the actual agents administering their own destruction and their community's suffering." Bourgois, *In Search of Respect*, 143.

39. Much like the powers anthropologists have described as associated with witchcraft, hustlers had ambiguous powers that could be both prosocial and antisocial, depending on one's interpretation. Henrietta L. Moore and Todd Sanders, eds., *Magical Interpretations, Material Realities: Modernity, Witchcraft, and the Occult in Postcolonial Africa* (London: Routledge, 2001).

40. See also Christine Jeske, "Contesting Moral Well-Being: Two Narratives among Zulu South Africans," *Science, Religion, and Culture* 6, no. 1 (2019): 59–66.

41. David J. Grelotti et al., "Whoonga: Potential Recreational Use of HIV Antiretroviral Medication in South Africa," *AIDS and Behavior* 18, no. 3 (August 17, 2013): 511–18; F. Larkan, B. Van Wyk, and J. Saris, "Of Remedies and Poisons: Recreational Use of Antiretroviral Drugs in the Social Imagination of South African Carers," *African Sociological Review / Revue Africaine de Sociologie* 14, no. 2 (2010): 62–73.

## 5. "I'M JUST A LABORER"

1. Significant portions of this chapter draw from the Christine Jeske article, "People Refusing to Be Wealth: What Happens When South African Workers Are Denied Access to 'Belonging In,'" *Economic Anthropology* (March 4, 2020), doi.org/10.1002/sea2.12175.

2. The anthropologists Jean and John Comaroff found that South Africans speaking the Tshidi language had separate words and separate concepts corresponding roughly to "labor" and "work." "Labor" meant waged employment and "work" meant tasks around homesteads. No such linguistic division exists in isiZulu, where *ukusebenza* is the verb for work whether in the household or for wages. That may have something to do with people inserting the English word "laborer" into Zulu conversations. Using English perhaps also holds the concept of "labor" at a linguistic distance in a way that reinforces an emotional distance. John L. Comaroff and Jean Comaroff, "The Madman and the Migrant: Work and Labor in the Historical Consciousness of a South African People," *American Ethnologist* 14, no. 2 (May 1, 1987): 191–209.

3. Chinguno Crispen, "Marikana Massacre and Strike Violence Post-Apartheid," *Global Labour Journal* 4, no. 2 (2013): 160–66.

4. While I met more people from Sunshine Foods who had left the job than from any other company, this did not necessarily mean Sunshine was any less desirable a workplace than elsewhere; it could be merely a factor of the size of their workforce. People ended all sorts of jobs with a frequency that surprised me. Out of thirty-three currently unemployed people whom I asked about work experience, only one, the nineteen-year-old woman quoted in the conversation with her mother, could not list any work experience. Two more said they had no work experience, but described ways they made money in the township. By their mid-twenties, most could list one to four jobs they had held.

5. Margaret Frye, "Bright Futures in Malawi's New Dawn: Educational Aspirations as Assertions of Identity," *American Journal of Sociology* 117, no. 6 (2012): 1565–1624.

6. Some analysts go so far as to suggest that the influx of women into the workplace is the most significant cause of high unemployment numbers in the country. Hodge, "Growth, Employment, and Unemployment in South Africa." For an in-depth study of social changes affecting love and gender roles, see Hunter, *Love in the Time of AIDS.*

7. Casale and Posel, "Continued Feminisation of the Labour Force in South Africa"; Statistics South Africa, "Quarterly Labour Force Survey: Quarter 2 2018."

8. Statistics South Africa, "How Do Women Fare in the South African Labour Market?," *Stats SA* (blog), August 1, 2018, www.statssa.gov.za/?p=11375.

9. Casale and Posel, "Continued Feminisation of the Labour Force in South Africa."

10. Comaroff and Comaroff, "Madman and the Migrant," 191–209; Levy, *Foundations of the South African Cheap Labour System*; Moore, introduction; Gay Seidman, "Is South Africa Different? Sociological Comparisons and Theoretical Contributions from the Land of Apartheid," *Annual Review of Sociology* 25 (1999): 419–40; Hylton White, "Outside the Dwelling of Culture: Estrangement and Difference in Postcolonial Zululand," *Anthropological Quarterly* 83, no. 3 (Summer 2010): 497–518; Harold Wolpe, "Capitalism and Cheap Labour—Power in South Africa: From Segregation to Apartheid," *Economic Sociology* 111 (1972): 425–56.

11. Black people have long found ways to use their invisibility and indistinguishability in the eyes of white people to their own advantage. Slaves escaping the American South sometimes worked alongside slaves on different plantations during the day, trusting that masters could not distinguish between the black bodies working in their own fields. Lipsitz, *How Racism Takes Place*, 53.

12. Dan Ariely, Emir Kamenica, and Dražen Prelec, "Man's Search for Meaning: The Case of Legos," *Journal of Economic Behavior and Organization* 67, no. 3 (September 1, 2008): 671–77; Jeffrey Pfeffer, *The Human Equation* (Cambridge, MA: Harvard Business Review Press, 1998); Barry Schwartz, *Why We Work* (New York: Simon and Schuster, 2015).

13. Ariely, Kamenica, and Prelec, "Man's Search for Meaning."

14. Amy Wrzensniewski and J. E. Dutton, "Crafting a Job: Revisioning Employees as Active Crafters of Their Work," *Academy of Management Review* 26 (2001): 179–201.

15. Schwartz, *Why We Work*, 26.

16. Fred Block, *Postindustrial Possibilities: A Critique of Economic Discourse* (Berkeley: University of California Press, 1990); Katherine Browne, "Economics and Morality: Introduction," in *Economics and Morality: Anthropological Approaches*, ed. Katherine Browne and Lynne Milgram (Lanham, MD: AltaMira Press, 2009), 1–40; Polanyi, *Great Transformation.*

17. Block, *Postindustrial Possibilities.*

18. Miyazaki, *Method of Hope*, 105.

19. Rachael Goodman, "Sociality, Survival, and Secrets: Making Life 'Good Enough' through NGO Projects in Kumaon, India" (PhD diss., University of Wisconsin–Madison, 2017).

## 6. "I HAVE A GOOD STORY"

1. Ferguson, *Give a Man a Fish*, 27.

2. Fischer, *Good Life*, 19.

3. Fischer, *Good Life*, 16.

4. Lipsitz, *How Racism Takes Place*, 61.

5. Lipsitz, *How Racism Takes Place*, 61.

6. Jared Sexton, *Amalgamation Schemes: Antiblackness and the Critique of Multiracialism* (Minneapolis: University of Minnesota Press, 2008).

7. Lipsitz, *How Racism Takes Place*, 138.

8. Most company names are pseudonyms, but with the owner's and staff members' permission, I used the real name of this company.

9. Christine Jeske, "Why Work? Do We Understand What Motivates Work-Related Decisions in South Africa?," *Journal of Southern African Studies* 44, no. 1 (2018): 27–42.

10. For more on the frequency of entrepreneurship among people who are employed, see Lloyd, "Informal Enterprise Ownership."

11. Bourdieu, *Distinction*; Bourdieu, *Outline of a Theory of Practice*.

12. Lipsitz, *How Racism Takes Place*, 69.

13. Lipsitz, *How Racism Takes Place*, 69.

14. Lipsitz, *How Racism Takes Place*, 136.


## CLOSING THOUGHTS

1. Howard Thurman, *Meditations of the Heart* (1953; repr., Boston: Beacon, 1981), 123–24. Note that marginalized people are not the only ones disfigured by racialization. Author Debby Irving uses a similar analogy to describe the distortion of white people because of their refusal to acknowledge their own privilege and misconceptions. She compares herself as a white person to a gourd that is wrapped in string as it grows. The fruit becomes misshapen and remains so even when the strings are removed, just as the effects of racism across all society take generations to undo. Debby Irving, *Waking Up White, and Finding Myself in the Story of Race* (Cambridge: Elephant Room Press, 2014).

2. Di Nunzio, *Act of Living*, 1.

3. Saidiya Hartman, *Wayward Lives, Beautiful Experiments: Intimate Histories of Social Upheaval* (New York: W. W. Norton, 2019), xv.

4. Pfeffer, *Human Equation*; Schwartz, *Why We Work*.

5. Francis Fukuyama, *Trust: The Social Virtues and the Creation of Prosperity* (New York: Free Press, 1995).

6. See also Schwartz, *Why We Work*, 56.

# Bibliography

Abel, Jaison R., Richard Deitz, and Yaqin Su. "Are Recent College Graduates Finding Good Jobs?" *Current Issues in Economics and Finance* 20, no. 1 (2014): 1–8.

Ally, Shireen A. *From Servants to Workers: South African Domestic Workers and the Democratic State.* Ithaca, NY: Cornell University Press, 2009.

Altman, Miriam, and Imraan Valodia. "Introduction: Where to for the South African Labour Market? Some 'Big Issues.'" *Transformation: Critical Perspectives on Southern Africa* 60, no. 1 (2006): 1–5.

Ariely, Dan, Emir Kamenica, and Dražen Prelec. "Man's Search for Meaning: The Case of Legos." *Journal of Economic Behavior and Organization* 67, no. 3 (September 1, 2008): 671–77.

Arrighi, Giovanni. "Labour Supplies in Historical Perspective: A Study of the Proletarianization of the African Peasantry in Rhodesia." In *Essays in the Political Economy of Africa*, edited by Giovanni Arrighi and J. Saul, 180–234. New York: Monthly Review Press, 1973.

Ashforth, Adam. *Witchcraft, Violence, and Democracy in South Africa.* Chicago: University of Chicago Press, 2005.

Atkins, Keletso E. *The Moon Is Dead! Give Us Our Money! The Cultural Origins of an African Work Ethic, Natal, South Africa, 1843–1900.* Portsmouth, NH: Pearson Education, 1993.

Banerjee, Abhijit, Sebastian Galiani, Jim Levinsohn, Zoe McLaren, and Ingrid Woolard. "Why Has Unemployment Risen in the New South Africa?" *Economics of Transition* 16, no. 4 (2008): 715–40.

Barchiesi, Franco. *Precarious Liberation: Workers, the State, and Contested Social Citizenship in Postapartheid South Africa.* Scottsville, South Africa: University of KwaZulu-Natal Press, 2011.

——. "Work in the Constitution of the Human: Twentieth-Century South African Entanglements of Welfare, Blackness, and Political Economy." *South Atlantic Quarterly* 115, no. 1 (January 2016): 149–74.

Bell, Derrick. *Faces at the Bottom of the Well: The Permanence of Racism.* New York: Basic Books, 1992.

Besteman, Catherine. "Somali Bantus in a State of Refuge." *Bidhaan: An International Journal of Somali Studies* 12, no. 8 (2012): 11–33.

Bjerk, Paul K. "They Poured Themselves into the Milk: Zulu Political Philosophy under Shaka." *Journal of African History* 47, no. 1 (2006): 1–20.

Block, Fred. *Postindustrial Possibilities: A Critique of Economic Discourse.* Berkeley: University of California Press, 1990.

Boehm, Astrid, and Stefan Schirmer. "Development by Decree: The Impact of Minimum Wage Legislation on a Farming Area in North West Province." In *Development Dilemmas*, edited by Bill Freund and Harald Witt, 248–74. Scottsville, South Africa: University of KwaZulu-Natal Press, 2010.

Bolt, Maxim. *Zimbabwe's Migrants and South Africa's Border Farms: The Roots of Impermanence.* Cambridge: Cambridge University Press, 2015.

Bond, Patrick. *Elite Transition: From Apartheid to Neoliberalism in South Africa.*
London: Pluto Press, 2000.
Bonnin, Deborah Rosemary. "Claiming Spaces, Changing Places: Political Violence
and Women's Protests in KwaZulu-Natal." *Journal of Southern African Studies*
26, no. 2 (June 2000): 301–16.
Bourdieu, Pierre. *Distinction: A Social Critique of the Judgement of Taste.* Translated by
Richard Nice. Cambridge, MA: Harvard University Press, 1984.
——. *Outline of a Theory of Practice.* Cambridge Studies in Social Anthropology 16.
Cambridge: Cambridge University Press, 1977.
Bourgois, Philippe. *In Search of Respect: Selling Crack in El Barrio.* Cambridge:
Cambridge University Press, 2003.
Browne, Katherine. "Economics and Morality: Introduction." In *Economics and
Morality: Anthropological Approaches*, edited by Katherine Browne and Lynne
Milgram, 1–40. Lanham, MD: AltaMira Press, 2009.
Bruner, Jerome. "The Narrative Construction of Reality." *Critical Inquiry* 18, no. 1
(1991): 1–21.
Burawoy, Michael. "The Roots of Domination: Beyond Bourdieu and Gramsci."
*Sociology* 46, no. 2 (April 1, 2012): 187–206.
Burchell, William. *Travels in the Interior of Southern Africa.* Vols. 1 and 2. Cape Town:
C. Struik, 1967. Facsimile reprint.
Carson, Clayborne, and Kris Shepard, eds. *A Call to Conscience: The Landmark
Speeches of Dr. Martin Luther King, Jr.* New York: Warner Books, 2001.
Casale, Daniela, Colette Muller, and Dorrit Posel. "'Two Million Net New Jobs':
A Reconsideration of the Rise in Employment in South Africa, 1995–2003."
*South African Journal of Economics* 72, no. 5 (2004): 978–1002.
Casale, Daniela, and Dorrit Posel. "The Continued Feminisation of the Labour Force
in South Africa." *South African Journal of Economics* 70 (2002): 156–84.
CEIC Data. "South Africa Real GDP Growth." Accessed October 21, 2019. https://www.
ceicdata.com/en/indicator/south-africa/real-gdp-growth.
Césaire, Aimé. *Discourse on Colonialism.* Translated by Joan Pinkham. New York:
Monthly Review Press, 2000.
Champagne, Duane. "Tribal Capitalism and Native Capitalists: Multiple Pathways of
Native Economy." In Hosmer and O'Neill, *Native Pathways*, 308–29.
Charman, Andrew, and Leif Petersen. "Informal Micro Enterprises in a Township
Context: A Spatial Analysis of Business Dynamics in Five Cape Town Localities."
In Fourie and Skinner, *South African Informal Sector*, 253–84.
Clark, Nancy L., and William H. Worger. *South Africa: The Rise and Fall of Apartheid.*
London: Routledge, 2013.
Cobley, Alan. "'Lacking in Respect for Whitemen': 'Tropical Africans' on the
Witwatersrand Gold Mines, 1903–1904." *International Labor and Working-Class
History* 86 (2014): 36–54.
Colen, Shellee. "'With Respect and Feelings': Voices of West Indian Child Care
Workers in New York City." In *All American Women: Lines That Divide, Ties
That Bind*, edited by Johnnetta B. Cole, 46–70. New York: Free Press, 1986.
Comaroff, Jean, and John L. Comaroff. Introduction to Comaroff and Comaroff,
*Millennial Capitalism and the Culture of Neoliberalism*, 1–56.
——, eds. *Millennial Capitalism and the Culture of Neoliberalism.* Durham, NC: Duke
University Press, 2001.
——. "Occult Economies and the Violence of Abstraction: Notes from the South
African Postcolony." *American Ethnologist* 26, no. 2 (May 1, 1999): 279–303.

——. *Of Revelation and Revolution*. Vol. 1, *Christianity, Colonialism, and Consciousness in South Africa*. Chicago: University of Chicago Press, 1991.

——. *Of Revelation and Revolution*. Vol. 2, *The Dialectics of Modernity on a South African Frontier*. Chicago: University of Chicago Press, 1997.

Comaroff, John L., and Jean Comaroff. "Goodly Beasts, Beastly Goods: Cattle and Commodities in a South African Context." *American Ethnologist* 17, no. 2 (May 1, 1990): 195–216.

——. "The Madman and the Migrant: Work and Labor in the Historical Consciousness of a South African People." *American Ethnologist* 14, no. 2 (May 1, 1987): 191–209.

Cramer, Katherine J. *The Politics of Resentment: Rural Consciousness in Wisconsin and the Rise of Scott Walker*. Chicago: University of Chicago Press, 2016.

Crenshaw, Kimberlé. "Demarginalizing the Intersection of Race and Sex: A Black Feminist Critique of Antidiscrimination Doctrine, Feminist Theory and Antiracist Politics." *University of Chicago Legal Forum* 1989 (1989): 139–67.

Crispen, Chinguno. "Marikana Massacre and Strike Violence Post-Apartheid." *Global Labour Journal* 4, no. 2 (2013): 160–66.

Daniels, Arlene Kaplan. "Invisible Work." *Social Problems* 34, no. 5 (December 1, 1987): 403–15.

Davies, James B., Rodrigo Lluberas, and Anthony F. Shorrocks. "Estimating the Level and Distribution of Global Wealth, 2000–2014." *Review of Income and Wealth* 63, no. 4 (December 2017): 731–59.

DiAngelo, Robin. "White Fragility." *International Journal of Critical Pedagogy* 3, no. 3 (2011): 54–70.

Di Nunzio, Marco. *The Act of Living: Street Life, Marginality, and Development in Urban Ethiopia*. Ithaca, NY: Cornell University Press, 2019.

Dubbeld, Bernard. "Breaking the Buffalo: The Transformation of Stevedoring Work in Durban between 1970 and 1990." *International Review of Social History* 48 (2003): 97–122.

Dumas, Michael J. "Against the Dark: Antiblackness in Education Policy and Discourse." *Theory into Practice*, no. 55 (2016): 11–19.

Dumas, Michael J., and kihana miraya ross. "'Be Real Black for Me': Imagining BlackCrit in Education." *Urban Education* 51, no. 4 (April 1, 2016): 415–42.

Duneier, Mitchell, Hakim Hasan, and Ovie Carter. *Sidewalk*. New York: Farrar, Straus and Giroux, 2000.

Du Toit, A., and F. Ally. *The Externalisation and Casualisation of Farm Labour in Western Cape Horticulture: A Survey of Patterns in the Agricultural Labour Market in Key Western Cape Districts, and Their Implications for Employment Justice*. Cape Town: Centre for Rural Legal Studies, 2003.

Ehrenreich, Barbara. *Nickel and Dimed: On (Not) Getting By in America*. New York: Metropolitan Books, 2001.

Elyachar, Julia. *Markets of Dispossession: NGOs, Economic Development, and the State in Cairo*. Politics, History, and Culture. Durham, NC: Duke University Press, 2005.

Engels, Friedrich. "The Origin of the Family, Private Property, and the State." In *The Marx-Engels Reader*, edited by Robert C. Tucker, 734–59. 2nd ed. New York: W. W. Norton, 1978.

Ergun, Ergul. "Bargaining with the Devil: Neoliberalism, Informal Work and Workers' Resistance in the Clothing Industry of Turkey." In A. Smith, Stenning, and Willis, *Social Justice and Neoliberalism*, 114–34.

Feierman, Steven. "Struggles for Control: The Social Roots of Health and Healing in Modern Africa." *African Studies Review* 28, nos. 2–3 (1985): 73–147.

———. "Reflections on African Medical History and the History of Science." Presentation at the University of Wisconsin, Madison, WI, 2012.

Ferguson, James. "The Bovine Mystique: Power, Property and Livestock in Rural Lesotho." *Man* 20, no. 4 (December 1985): 647–74.

———. "Declarations of Dependence: Labour, Personhood, and Welfare in Southern Africa." *Journal of the Royal Anthropological Institute* 19, no. 2 (2013): 223–42.

———. *Expectations of Modernity: Myths and Meanings of Urban Life on the Zambian Copperbelt.* Berkeley: University of California Press, 1999.

———. "Formalities of Poverty: Thinking about Social Assistance in Neoliberal South Africa." *African Studies Review* 50, no. 2 (September 2007): 71–86.

———. *Give a Man a Fish: Reflections on the New Politics of Distribution.* Durham, NC: Duke University Press, 2015.

Fischer, Edward F. *The Good Life: Aspiration, Dignity, and the Anthropology of Wellbeing.* Stanford, CA: Stanford University Press, 2014.

Foucault, Michel. *The History of Sexuality.* Vol. 1, *An Introduction.* Reissue ed. New York: Vintage, 1990.

Fourie, Frederick, and Caroline Skinner, eds. *The South African Informal Sector: Creating Jobs, Reducing Poverty.* Johannesburg: HSRC Press, 2018.

Freund, David M. P. *Colored Property: State Policy and White Racial Politics in Suburban America.* Chicago: University of Chicago Press, 2010.

Friesen, Jeff, and Steve Heinrichs, eds. *Quest for Respect: The Church and Indigenous Spirituality.* Winnipeg: Mennonite Church Canada, 2017. https://www.commonword.ca/ResourceView/16/19134.

Frye, Margaret. "Bright Futures in Malawi's New Dawn: Educational Aspirations as Assertions of Identity." *American Journal of Sociology* 117, no. 6 (2012): 1565–1624.

Fukuyama, Francis. *Trust: The Social Virtues and the Creation of Prosperity.* New York: Free Press, 1995.

Garro, Linda C., and Cheryl Mattingly. "Narrative as Construct and Construction." In *Narrative and the Cultural Construction of Illness and Healing,* 1–49. Berkeley: University of California Press, 2000.

Geary, Daniel. *Beyond Civil Rights: The Moynihan Report and Its Legacy.* Philadelphia: University of Pennsylvania Press, 2015.

Geertz, Clifford. *The Interpretation of Cultures: Selected Essays.* New York: Basic Books, 1973.

Geschiere, Peter, and Francis Nyamnjoh. "Capitalism and Autochthony: The Seesaw of Mobility and Belonging." In Comaroff and Comaroff, *Millennial Capitalism and the Culture of Neoliberalism,* 159–90.

Gibson-Graham, J. K. *A Postcapitalist Politics.* Minneapolis: University of Minnesota Press, 2006.

Giddens, Anthony. *The Constitution of Society: Outline of the Theory of Structuration.* Cambridge: Polity Press, 1984.

Ginsburg, Faye D., and Rayna R. Reiter. *Conceiving the New World Order: The Global Politics of Reproduction.* Berkeley: University of California Press, 1995.

Gladwell, Malcolm. *David and Goliath: Underdogs, Misfits, and the Art of Battling Giants.* New York: Little, Brown, 2013.

———. *Outliers: The Story of Success.* New York: Little, Brown, 2008.

Glissant, Édouard. *Poetics of Relation.* Translated by Betsy Wing. Ann Arbor: University of Michigan Press, 1997.

Gluckman, Max. "Analysis of a Social Situation in Modern Zululand." *Bantu Studies* 14, no. 1 (1940): 1–30.

Gomberg-Muñoz, Ruth. "Willing to Work: Agency and Vulnerability in an Undocumented Immigrant Network." *American Anthropologist* 112, no. 2 (2015): 295–307.

Goodman, Rachael. "Sociality, Survival, and Secrets: Making Life 'Good Enough' through NGO Projects in Kumaon, India." PhD diss., University of Wisconsin–Madison, 2017.

Gordon, Lewis. *Existentia Africana.* New York: Farrar, Straus and Giroux, 2007.

Graeber, David. "On the Moral Grounds of Economic Relations: A Maussian Approach." *Journal of Classical Sociology* 14, no. 1 (2014): 65–77.

Gramsci, Antonio. *Gramsci's Prison Letters: Lettere dal carcere; A Selection Translated and Introduced by Hamish Henderson.* London: Zwan, in association with the *Edinburgh Review*, 1988.

Grelotti, David J., Elizabeth F. Closson, Jennifer A. Smit, Zonke Mabude, Lynn T. Matthews, Steven A. Safren, David R. Bangsberg, and Matthew J. Mimiaga. "Whoonga: Potential Recreational Use of HIV Antiretroviral Medication in South Africa." *AIDS and Behavior* 18, no. 3 (August 17, 2013): 511–18.

Grobler, Pieter A. *Human Resource Management in South Africa.* 3rd ed. London: Thompson Learning, 2005.

Guérin, Isabelle. "Women and Money: Lessons from Senegal." *Development and Change* 37, no. 3 (May 2006): 549–70.

Gump, James O. *The Dust Rose Like Smoke: The Subjugation of the Zulu and the Sioux.* Bison Books. Lincoln: University of Nebraska Press, 1996.

Guyer, Jane I. *Marginal Gains: Monetary Transactions in Atlantic Africa.* Chicago: University of Chicago Press, 2004.

Haidt, Jonathan. *The Righteous Mind: Why Good People Are Divided by Politics and Religion.* New York: Pantheon Books, 2012.

Hart, Keith. "Bureaucratic Form and the Informal Economy." In *Linking the Formal and Informal Economy: Concepts and Policies*, edited by Basudeb Guha-Khasnobis, Ravi Kanbur, and Elinor Ostrom. New York: Oxford University Press, 2007.

Hartman, Saidiya. *Scenes of Subjection: Terror, Slavery, and Self-Making in Nineteenth-Century America.* Oxford: Oxford University Press, 1997.

——. *Wayward Lives, Beautiful Experiments: Intimate Histories of Social Upheaval.* New York: W. W. Norton, 2019.

Harvey, David. *A Brief History of Neoliberalism.* Oxford: Oxford University Press, 2005.

——. *The Condition of Postmodernity: An Enquiry into the Origins of Cultural Change.* Cambridge, MA: Blackwell, 1990.

Haynes, Naomi. "Desirable Dependence, or What We Learn from Pentecostalism." *Journal of the Royal Anthropological Institute* 19, no. 2 (2013): 250–51.

——. *Moving by the Spirit: Pentecostal Social Life on the Zambian Copperbelt.* Berkeley: University of California Press, 2017.

He, Wan, Daniel Goodkind, and Paul Kowal. "An Aging World: 2015." US Census Bureau, International Population Reports, P95/16–1. Washington, DC: US Government Publishing Office, 2016.

Herzog, Hal. *Some We Love, Some We Hate, Some We Eat: Why It's So Hard to Think Straight about Animals.* New York: Harper Perennial, 2011.

Hickel, Jason. "'Xenophobia' in South Africa: Order, Chaos, and the Moral Economy of Witchcraft." *Cultural Anthropology* 29, no. 1 (2014): 103–27.

Himmelweit, Susan. "The Discovery of 'Unpaid Work': The Social Consequences of the Expansion of 'Work.'" *Feminist Economics* 1, no. 2 (July 1995): 1–19.

Hochschild, Arlie Russell. *The Managed Heart: Commercialization of Human Feeling.* 3rd ed. Berkeley: University of California Press, 2012.

Hodge, Duncan. "Growth, Employment, and Unemployment in South Africa." *South African Journal of Economics* 77, no. 4 (2009): 488–504.

Horschelmann, Kathrin. "Transitions to Work and the Making of Neo-Liberal Selves: Growing Up in (Former) East Germany." In A. Smith, Stenning, and Willis, *Social Justice and Neoliberalism,* 135–63.

Hosmer, Brian, and Colleen O'Neill, eds. *Native Pathways: American Indian Culture and Economic Development in the Twentieth Century.* Boulder: University Press of Colorado, 2004.

Howell, Simon, and Louise Vincent. "'Licking the Snake'—the i'khothane and Contemporary Township Youth Identities in South Africa." *South African Review of Sociology* 45, no. 2 (2014): 60–77.

Hunter, Mark. *Love in the Time of AIDS: Inequality, Gender, and Rights in South Africa.* Bloomington: Indiana University Press, 2010.

Huxley, Aldous. *Beyond the Mexique Bay.* London: Chatto and Windus, 1934.

International Labour Organization. "Unemployment, Youth Total (% of Total Labor Force Ages 15–24)." World Bank Data, 2014. http://data.worldbank.org/indicator/SL.UEM.1524.ZS.

Irving, Debby. *Waking Up White, and Finding Myself in the Story of Race.* Cambridge: Elephant Room Press, 2014.

Jablonska, Aleks, Roche van Wyk, and Paul Sturrock. *Community Analysis of Howick, Mooi River, Mpophomeni and KwaHaza in KZN, South Africa: Compiled for Ethembeni.* Cape Town: Learn to Earn Association, 2014.

Jacobs, Harriet A. *Incidents in the Life of a Slave Girl: Written by Herself.* Cambridge, MA: Harvard University Press, 1987.

James, Deborah. *Money from Nothing: Indebtedness and Aspiration in South Africa.* Stanford, CA: Stanford University Press, 2014.

Jennings, Willie James. *The Christian Imagination.* New Haven, CT: Yale University Press, 2010.

Jeske, Christine. "Are Cars the New Cows? Changing Wealth Goods and Moral Economies in South Africa." *American Anthropologist* 118, no. 3 (September 2016): 483–94.

——. "Contesting Moral Well-Being: Two Narratives among Zulu South Africans." *Science, Religion, and Culture* 6, no. 1 (2019): 59–66.

——. "People Refusing to Be Wealth: What Happens When South African Workers Are Denied Access to 'Belonging In,'" *Economic Anthropology* (2020), doi: 10.1002/sea2.12175.

——. "Why Work? Do We Understand What Motivates Work-Related Decisions in South Africa?" *Journal of Southern African Studies* 44, no. 1 (2018): 27–42.

John Paul II. *Laborem Exercens: Encyclical Letter of the Supreme Pontiff John Paul II on Human Work.* London: Catholic Truth Society, 1981.

Jost, Lawrence J., and Roger A. Shiner. *Eudaimonia and Well-Being: Ancient and Modern Conceptions.* Kelowna, BC: Academic Printing and Publishing, 2003.

Kalleberg, Arne L. *Good Jobs, Bad Jobs: The Rise of Polarized and Precarious Employment Systems in the United States, 1970s–2000s.* New York: Russell Sage Foundation, 2011.

Karjanen, David. "The Limits to Quantitative Thinking: Engaging Economics on the Unemployed." In *Anthropologies of Unemployment: New Perspectives on Work and Its Absence,* edited by Jong Bum Kwon and Carrie M. Lane, 34–52. Ithaca, NY: Cornell University Press, 2016.

Kingdon, Gheeta Gandhi, and John Knight. "Unemployment in South Africa: The Nature of the Beast." *World Development* 32, no. 3 (2004): 391–408.

Kremer, Michael. "The O-Ring Theory of Economic Development." *Quarterly Journal of Economics* 108, no. 3 (August 1993): 551–75.

Krista Tippett. "Luis Alberto Urrea—What Borders Are Really about, and What We Do with Them." On Being. Accessed July 12, 2018. https://onbeing.org/programs/luis-alberto-urrea-what-borders-are-really-about-and-what-we-do-with-them-jul2018/.

Lane, Carrie M. *A Company of One: Insecurity, Independence, and the New World of White-Collar Unemployment*. Ithaca, NY: Cornell University Press, 2011.

Larkan, F., B. Van Wyk, and J. Saris. "Of Remedies and Poisons: Recreational Use of Antiretroviral Drugs in the Social Imagination of South African Carers." *African Sociological Review / Revue Africaine de Sociologie* 14, no. 2 (2010): 62–73.

Lehrer, Jonah. *Imagine: How Creativity Works*. New York: Houghton Mifflin Harcourt, 2012.

Levy, Norman. *The Foundations of the South African Cheap Labour System*. International Library of Sociology. London: Routledge and Kegan Paul, 1982.

Lewis, Herbert S. *After the Eagles Landed: The Yemenites of Israel*. Boulder, CO: Westview Press, 1989.

Lipsitz, George. *How Racism Takes Place*. Philadelphia, PA: Temple University Press, 2011.

Littlefield, Alice, and Martha C. Knack. *Native Americans and Wage Labor: Ethnohistorical Perspectives*. Norman: University of Oklahoma Press, 1996.

Livingston, Julie. *Debility and the Moral Imagination in Botswana*. African Systems of Thought. Bloomington: Indiana University Press, 2005.

Maddux, William, and Adam Galinsky. "Cultural Borders and Mental Barriers: The Relationship between Living Abroad and Creativity." *Journal of Personality and Social Psychology* 96 (2009): 1047–61.

Mains, Daniel. "Youth Unemployment, Progress, and Shame in Urban Ethiopia." In *Anthropologies of Unemployment: New Perspectives on Work and Its Absence*, edited by Jong Bum Kwon and Carrie M. Lane, 135–54. Ithaca, NY: Cornell University Press, 2016.

Malinowski, Bronislaw. "Tribal Economics in the Trobriands." In *Tribal and Peasant Economies: Readings in Economic Anthropology*, edited by George Dalton, 185–223. Garden City, NY: Natural History Press, 1967.

Marx, Karl. "The Economic and Philosophic Manuscripts of 1844." In *The Marx-Engels Reader*, edited by Robert C. Tucker, 66–125. 2nd ed. New York: W. W. Norton, 1978.

Massey, Douglas S. *Categorically Unequal: The American Stratification System*. New York: Russell Sage Foundation, 2008.

Mattingly, Cheryl, and Linda C. Garro, eds. *Narrative and the Cultural Construction of Illness and Healing*. Berkeley: University of California Press, 2000.

Mauss, Marcel. *The Gift: The Form and Reason for Exchange in Archaic Societies*. Translated by W. D. Halls. New York: W. W. Norton, 1990.

Mbembe, Achille. *On the Postcolony*. Berkeley: University of California Press, 2001.

McAdams, Dan. *The Redemptive Self: Stories Americans Live By*. New York: Oxford University Press, 2005.

Miyazaki, Hirokazu. *The Method of Hope: Anthropology, Philosophy, and Fijian Knowledge*. Stanford, CA: Stanford University Press, 2004.

Monahan, Torin, and Jill A. Fisher. "'I'm Still a Hustler': Entrepreneurial Responses to Precarity by Participants in Phase I Clinical Trials." *Economy and Society* 44, no. 4 (October 2, 2015): 545–66.

Moore, Henrietta L. Introduction to Moore and Sanders, *Magical Interpretations*, 1–27.

Moore, Henrietta L., and Todd Sanders, eds. *Magical Interpretations, Material Realities: Modernity, Witchcraft, and the Occult in Postcolonial Africa*. London: Routledge, 2001.

Morris, Michael, and Leyland Pitt. "Informal Sector Activity as Entrepreneurship: Insights from a South African Township." *Journal of Small Business Management* 33, no. 1 (January 1995): 78–86.

Mosoetsa, Sarah. *Eating from One Pot: The Dynamics of Survival in Poor South African Households*. Johannesburg: Wits University Press, 2011.

Muehlebach, Andrea. "On Precariousness and the Ethical Imagination: The Year 2012 in Sociocultural Anthropology." *American Anthropologist* 115, no. 2 (2013): 297–311.

National Youth Commission, South Africa. "National Youth Policy: 2009–2014." 2009.

Nel, Jan Kemp. *Win at the CCMA: A Practical and Informative Toolkit with Forms, Policies and Procedures*. Haltom City, TX: Knowres, 2014.

Neves, David, and Andries du Toit. "Money and Sociality in South Africa's Informal Economy." *Africa* 82 (2012): 131–49.

Newell, Sasha. *The Modernity Bluff: Crime, Consumption, and Citizenship in Côte d'Ivoire*. Chicago: University of Chicago Press, 2012.

Newman, Katherine S. *No Shame in My Game: The Working Poor in the Inner City*. New York: Vintage Books, 2000.

Ngwane, Zolani. "'Real Men Reawaken Their Fathers' Homesteads, the Educated Leave Them in Ruins': The Politics of Domestic Reproduction in Post-Apartheid South Africa." In Weiss, *Producing African Futures*, 167–91.

Niehaus, Isak. "Witchcraft in the New South Africa." In Moore and Sanders, *Magical Interpretations*, 184–205.

Noah, Trevor. *Born a Crime: Stories from a South African Childhood*. New York: Spiegel and Grau, 2016.

North, Ernest. "A Decade of Entrepreneurship Education in South Africa." *South African Journal of Education* 22, no. 1 (2002): 24–27.

NPR Staff. "'Respect' Wasn't a Feminist Anthem until Aretha Franklin Made It One." NPR, *All Things Considered*, February 14, 2017. https://www.npr.org/2017/02/14/515183747/respect-wasnt-a-feminist-anthem-until-aretha-franklin-made-it-one.

O'Neill, Colleen M. "Rethinking Modernity and the Discourse of Development in American Indian History, an Introduction." In Hosmer and O'Neill, *Native Pathways*, 1–26.

Orthofer, Anna. "Wealth Inequality in South Africa: Insights from Survey and Tax Data." *Redi3x3* Working Paper 15 (June 2015): 50.

Ortner, Sherry B. *Anthropology and Social Theory: Culture, Power, and the Acting Subject*. Durham, NC: Duke University Press, 2006.

——. "On Key Symbols." *American Anthropologist* 75, no. 5 (1972): 1338–46.

Pager, Devah. *Marked: Race, Crime, and Finding Work in an Era of Mass Incarceration*. Chicago: University of Chicago Press, 2007.

Patel, Raj, and Jason W. Moore. *A History of the World in Seven Cheap Things*. Berkeley: University of California Press, 2017.

Perry, Imani. *More Beautiful and More Terrible: The Embrace and Transcendence of Racial Inequality in the United States*. New York: New York University Press, 2011.

——. *Prophets of the Hood: Politics and Poetics in Hip Hop*. Durham, NC: Duke University Press, 2004.

Peters, M. "Governmentality, Education and the End of Neoliberalism?" In *Neoliberalism and After?* New York: Peter Lang, 2011.

Peterson, Bhekizizwe. "Kwaito, 'Dawgs' and the Antimonies of Hustling." *African Identities* 1, no. 2 (2003): 197–213.

Peterson, Nicolas. "Myth of the 'Walkabout': Movement in the Aboriginal Domain." In *Population Mobility and Indigenous Peoples in Australia and North America*, edited by John Taylor and Martin Bell. London: Routledge, 2003.

Pfeffer, Jeffrey. *The Human Equation.* Cambridge, MA: Harvard Business Review Press, 1998.

Polanyi, Karl. *The Great Transformation.* Boston, MA: Beacon Press, 1957.

Posel, Dorrit, James A. Fairburn, and Frances Lund. "Labour Migration and Households: A Reconsideration of the Effects of the Social Pension on Labour Supply in South Africa." *Economic Modelling* 23 (2006): 836–53.

Posel, Dorrit and Michael Rogan. "Measured as Poor versus Feeling Poor: Comparing Objective and Subjective Poverty Rates in South Africa." WIDER Working Paper Series 133, United Nations University-World Institute for Development Economic Research, Helsinki, 2014.

Powdthavee, Nattavudh. "Are There Geographical Variations in the Psychological Cost of Unemployment in South Africa?" *Social Indicators Research* 80, no. 3 (April 2012): 629–52.

Prestholdt, Jeremy. *Domesticating the World: African Consumerism and the Genealogies of Globalization.* California World History Library 6. Berkeley: University of California Press, 2008.

Pun, Ngai. *Made in China: Women Factory Workers in a Global Workplace.* Durham, NC: Duke University Press, 2005.

Putnam, Robert D. "Bowling Alone: America's Declining Social Capital." *Journal of Democracy* 6, no. 1 (January 1, 1995): 65–78.

Rapley, John. *Globalization and Inequality: Neoliberalism's Downward Spiral.* Boulder, CO: Lynne Rienner, 2004.

Raz, Guy, and Christian Picciolini. "Why We Hate." NPR, *TED Radio Hour.* Accessed July 23, 2018. https://www.npr.org/programs/ted-radio-hour/628546919/why-we-hate.

Reich, Robert B. *The Common Good.* New York: Knopf, 2018.

Robbins, Joel. "Beyond the Suffering Subject: Toward an Anthropology of the Good." *Journal of the Royal Anthropological Institute* 19, no. 3 (2013): 447–62.

——. "On Happiness, Values, and Time: The Long and the Short of It." *HAU: Journal of Ethnographic Theory* 5, no. 3 (December 23, 2015): 215–33.

Rolbin, Cyrus, and Bruno Della Chiesa. "'We Share the Same Biology . . .': Cultivating Cross-Cultural Empathy and Global Ethics through Multilingualism." *Mind, Brain, and Education* 4, no. 4 (December 1, 2010): 196–207.

Rosin, Hanna. *The End of Men: And the Rise of Women.* New York: Riverhead Books, 2012.

Sahlins, Marshall David. *Stone Age Economics.* Chicago: Aldine Press, 1972.

Sayer, Andrew. "Dignity at Work: Broadening the Agenda." *Organization* 14, no. 4 (2007): 565–81.

Schoenbrun, David L. "Conjuring the Modern in Africa: Durability and Rupture in Histories of Public Healing between the Great Lakes of East Africa." *American Historical Review* 111, no. 5 (2006): 1403–39.

Schwartz, Barry. *Why We Work.* New York: Simon and Schuster, 2015.

Schwittay, Anke. "The Financial Inclusion Assemblage: Subjects, Technics, Rationalities." *Critique of Anthropology* 31, no. 4 (2011): 381–401.

Scott, James C. *Weapons of the Weak: Everyday Forms of Peasant Resistance*. New Haven, CT: Yale University Press, 1985.

Seekings, Jeremy, and Nicoli Nattrass. *Class, Race, and Inequality in South Africa*. New Haven, CT: Yale University Press, 2005.

Seidman, Gay. "Is South Africa Different? Sociological Comparisons and Theoretical Contributions from the Land of Apartheid." *Annual Review of Sociology* 25 (1999): 419–40.

Sennett, Richard. *Respect: In a World of Inequality*. New York: W. W. Norton, 2003.

———. *The Culture of the New Capitalism*. New Haven, CT: Yale University Press, 2006.

Serpell, Robert. *The Significance of Schooling: Life-Journeys in an African Society*. Cambridge: Cambridge University Press, 1993.

Sexton, Jared. *Amalgamation Schemes: Antiblackness and the Critique of Multiracialism*. Minneapolis: University of Minnesota Press, 2008.

Sharpe, Christina. *In the Wake: On Blackness and Being*. Durham, NC: Duke University Press, 2016.

Shelton, Jason E., and Michael Emerson. *Blacks and Whites in Christian America: How Racial Discrimination Shapes Religious Convictions*. New York: New York University Press, 2012.

Singleton, Glenn E. *Courageous Conversations about Race: A Field Guide for Achieving Equity in Schools—Catalog—UW-Madison Libraries*. Thousand Oaks, CA: Corwin Press, 2006.

Small Enterprise Development Agency. "Annual Review 2013/2014: Seda Technology Programme." 2014. http://www.sanews.gov.za/.

Smith, Adrian, Alison Stenning, and Katie Willis, eds. *Social Justice and Neoliberalism: Global Perspectives*. London: Zed Books, 2008.

Smith, Joan, and Immanuel Wallerstein. *Creating and Transforming Households: The Constraints of the World-Economy*. Thousand Oaks, CA: Cambridge University Press, 1992.

Smith, Suzanne E. *To Serve the Living: Funeral Directors and the African American Way of Death*. Cambridge, MA: Belknap Press of Harvard University Press, 2010.

Society for Applied Anthropology (SfAA). Accessed July 19, 2019. https://www.sfaa.net/.

Spillers, Hortense. *Black, White, and in Color: Essays on American Literature and Culture*. Chicago: University of Chicago Press, 2003.

Stack, Carol B. *All Our Kin: Strategies for Survival in a Black Community*. New York: Basic Books, 1983.

Statistics South Africa. "National and Provincial Labour Market: Youth," June 29, 2015.

———. "Quarterly Labour Force Survey: Quarter 2 2018." Pretoria: Statistics South Africa, July 31, 2018. http://www.statssa.gov.za/publications/P0211/P02112rnd Quarter2018.pdf.

———. "Quarterly Labour Force Survey: Quarter 3 2015." Pretoria: Statistics South Africa, October 27, 2015. http://www.statssa.gov.za/publications/P0211/P02113rd Quarter2015.pdf.

Steger, Manfred B., and Ravi K. Roy. *Neoliberalism: A Very Short Introduction*. Very Short Introductions 222. Oxford: Oxford University Press, 2010.

Students review. "Job Satisfaction by Major." Accessed July 5, 2019. https://www.studentsreview.com/satisfaction_by_major.php3?sort=Satisfied.

Taylor, Charles. *A Secular Age*. Cambridge, MA: Belknap Press of Harvard University Press, 2007.

Thieme, Tatiana Adeline. "The Hustle Economy: Informality, Uncertainty and the Geographies of Getting By." *Progress in Human Geography* 42, no. 4 (August 2018): 529–48.

Thompson, John B. *Studies in the Theory of Ideology*. Berkeley: University of California Press, 1984.

Thurman, Howard. *Meditations of the Heart*. Boston: Beacon Press, 1981. First published in 1953.

Tsing, Anna Lowenhaupt. *The Mushroom at the End of the World: On the Possibility of Life in Capitalist Ruins*. Princeton, NJ: Princeton University Press, 2015.

Umngeni Municipal Council. "Umngeni Municipal Integrated Development Plan Review: People Centered Development—Intuthuko Kubantu." 2015. www.umngeni.gov.za.

United States Central Intelligence Agency. "Country Comparison: Distribution of Family Income—Gini Index." *The World Factbook*. Accessed September 28, 2018. https://www.cia.gov/library/publications/the-world-factbook/rankorder/2172rank.html.

United States Department of Labor. "Unemployment Rate 2.5 Percent for College Grads, 7.7 Percent for High School Dropouts, January 2017." Economics Daily: US Bureau of Labor Statistics, February 7, 2017. https://www.bls.gov/opub/ted/2017/unemployment-rate-2-point-5-percent-for-college-grads-7-point-7-percent-for-high-school-dropouts-january-2017.htm.

Valodia, Imraan. "Informal Employment, Labour Markets and Social Protection: Some Considerations Based on South African Estimates." *IDS Bulletin* 39, no. 2 (2008): 57–62.

Veblen, Thorstein. *The Theory of the Leisure Class*. New York: Dover, 1994.

Velia, Myriam, and Glen Robbins. "Constraints to Growth and Employment in Medium and Large Manufacturing in EThekwini—Some Reflections." University of KwaZulu-Natal School of Built Environment and Development Studies, May 5, 2015.

Verick, Sher. "Unravelling the Impact of the Global Financial Crisis on the South African Labour Market." International Labor Organization Working Paper, 2010.

Weber, Max. *The Protestant Ethic and the Spirit of Capitalism*. Translated by Stephen Kalberg. Los Angeles: Roxbury, 2002. First published in 1905.

——. *The Protestant Ethic and the "Spirit" of Capitalism and Other Writings*. Translated and edited by Peter Baehr and Gordon C. Wells. New York: Penguin Classics, 2002.

Weeks, Kathi. *The Problem with Work: Feminism, Marxism, Antiwork Politics, and Postwork Imaginaries*. Durham, NC: Duke University Press, 2011.

Weiss, Brad, ed. *Producing African Futures: Ritual and Reproduction in a Neoliberal Age*. Leiden: Brill, 2004.

Werbner, Richard P. *Holy Hustlers, Schism, and Prophecy: Apostolic Reformation in Botswana*. Anthropology of Christianity 11. Berkeley: University of California Press, 2011.

White, Hylton. "Outside the Dwelling of Culture: Estrangement and Difference in Postcolonial Zululand." *Anthropological Quarterly* 83, no. 3 (Summer 2010): 497–518.

——. "A Post-Fordist Ethnicity: Insecurity, Authority, and Identity in South Africa." *Anthropological Quarterly* 85, no. 2 (2012): 397–428.

——. "Ritual Haunts: The Timing of Estrangement in a Post-Apartheid Countryside." In Weiss, *Producing African Futures*, 141–66.

——. *What Shapes Young People's Job Preferences? A View from Rural KwaZulu-Natal*. Coping with Unemployment. Johannesburg: Centre for Development and Enterprise, 2012.

Wilderson, Frank B., III. *Red, White, and Black: Cinema and the Structure of US Antagonisms*. Durham, NC: Duke University Press, 2010.

Wilkinson, Richard G., and Kate Pickett. *The Spirit Level: Why Greater Equality Makes Societies Stronger*. New York: Bloomsbury Press, 2010.

Willis, Paul E. *Learning to Labour: How Working Class Kids Get Working Class Jobs*. Farnborough: Saxon House, 1977.

Wilson, William Julius. *More Than Just Race: Being Black and Poor in the Inner City*. New York: W. W. Norton, 2009.

Wolpe, Harold. "Capitalism and Cheap Labour—Power in South Africa: From Segregation to Apartheid." *Economic Sociology* 111 (1972): 425–56.

Wright, Melissa W. "The Dialectics of Still Life: Murder, Women, and Maquiladoras." In Comaroff and Comaroff, *Millennial Capitalism and the Culture of Neoliberalism*, 125–46.

Wrzensniewski, Amy, and J. E. Dutton. "Crafting a Job: Revisioning Employees as Active Crafters of Their Work." *Academy of Management Review* 26 (2001): 179–201.

Wuthnow, Robert. *The Left Behind: Decline and Rage in Rural America*. Princeton, NJ: Princeton University Press, 2018.

Xiang, Biao. *Global "Body Shopping": An Indian Labor System in the Information Technology Industry*. In-Formation Series. Princeton, NJ: Princeton University Press, 2007.

Yunus, Muhammad. *Banker to the Poor: The Autobiography of Muhammad Yunus, Founder of Grameen Bank*. London: Aurum Press, 1999.

Zimmerman, Andrew. *Alabama in Africa: Booker T. Washington, the German Empire, and the Globalization of the New South*. America in the World. Princeton, NJ: Princeton University Press, 2010.

# Index

absenteeism, 57–60
abuse. *See* domestic violence
Afrikaners, 16, 34, 169, 197
agency, 56, 137, 142–43, 145
  abeyance of, 159, 180–81
  *See also* refusals and resistance
agriculture, 46, 184, 203n47
  poultry, 63–67, 139–43, 188
  *See also* gardening
AIDS and HIV, 3, 95, 107, 179
alcoholism, 85, 95, 166
alienation, 79, 154, 158, 173, 183–84
American Indians, 8, 40, 88
ANC (African National Congress), 16
  *See also* government
anthropology. *See* ethnographic methods
antiblack racism. *See* racism
apartheid, 1, 4, 52, 93
  dismantling of, 79, 104, 188
  legacy of, 15–16, 44, 48, 80, 90, 143
art, 164–68, 182

Bell, Derrick, 115
black critical theory (BlackCrit), 21
black excellence. *See* capital, cultural and social;
  music: black empowerment through
boredom, 5, 154
Born Free generation, 4, 143, 170
Bourdieu, Pierre, 48, 97–98, 181
Bourgois, Philippe, 24, 205n66, 207n8, 212n38
broad-based black economic empowerment,
  73, 120, 204n61
Bullet, 1–6, 18–19, 25, 92–93, 132–35, 191–93

capital, cultural, and social, 97–98, 181
capitalism
  assumptions regarding, 36, 56, 76
  critics of, 72, 78–79, 158, 190
  cultural mindsets accompanying, 77
  diverse forms of, 183–84
casualization of labor, 72, 75, 177, 203n56
CCMA (Commission for Conciliation,
  Mediation, and Arbitration), 58–59
  *See also* disciplinary hearings; labor laws
child care, 36, 47, 154

child grants. *See* welfare
Christians, 83, 99, 106, 166–67, 179, 180
  beliefs about work ethics, 77
  missionaries, 45
  prayer, 95–96
churches, 46, 96, 99, 106, 166–67, 179, 192
class, 78, 125–26, 131–32, 150, 181
colonization, 40–42, 45, 92, 186, 190
Comaroff, Jean and John, 29, 31
conspicuous consumption, 131–32, 209n4
  *See also* fashion
corporate social responsibility, 73, 120
cost of labor. *See* wages
crime, 137, 154
  perceptions of, 38, 44, 70, 73, 113
  social pressure into, 128–29, 134–35
  *See also* drugs: drug dealing
culture
  as blame for unemployment, 61–62
  versus social structure, 30, 61, 77–81, 157
  *See also* capital, cultural, and social

day labor, 32, 155–56
debt, 65–67, 84, 104, 128, 167
  of small business customers, 84, 96, 105
dependency, 104–5
  *See also* redistribution of resources
desirability of jobs, 53, 139, 165
  desirable jobs, 102, 106, 107, 139, 151
  undesirable jobs, 101, 123–25, 149, 154, 157
  *See also* good life: intersection with work
development organizations, 14, 45–46,
  111–12, 124, 176
  *See also* government: development strategies
  of; trainings for employment
Di Nunzio, Marco, 29, 130, 186
disciplinary hearings, 57–61, 68, 74
discouraged work seekers. *See* unemployment
  statistics: discouraged versus active
  job-seekers
discrimination, 1, 36
  in lending, 39
  in promotions, 13, 48, 101–2, 159, 170
  *See also* microaggression
displacement, 16, 41, 179, 188, 190

CPSIA information can be obtained
at www.ICGtesting.com
Printed in the USA
LVHW100534211222
735629LV00004B/402

9 781501 752513